CW00921141

ESSAYS IN
ANGLO-SAXON HISTORY

Silver brooch, diameter 3.5 cm., found with a large hoard of English silver coins in Rome, and likely evidence of an English visitor there early in the tenth century. The central roundel imitates a coin of Edward the Elder. *(British Museum)*

ESSAYS IN
ANGLO-SAXON HISTORY

JAMES CAMPBELL

THE HAMBLEDON PRESS
LONDON AND RONCEVERTE

Published by The Hambledon Press 1986

102 Gloucester Avenue, London NW1 8HX (U.K.)

309 Greenbrier Avenue, Ronceverte WV 24970 (U.S.A.)

ISBN 0 907628 32 X (Cased)
ISBN 0 907628 33 8 (Paper)

© James Campbell 1986

British Library Cataloguing in Publication Data

Campbell, James
   Essays in Anglo-Saxon history. – History series; 26)
   1. Civilization, Anglo-Saxon
   2. Great Britain – Civilization – to 1066
   I. Title   II. Series
   942.01   DA152.2

Library of Congress Cataloging-in-Publication Data

Campbell, James, 1935-
   Essays in Anglo-Saxon history: 400-1200

   Includes index.
   1. Great Britain – History – Anglo-Saxon period,
449-1066 – Addresses, essays, lectures.
   2. Great Britain – History – Medieval period, 1066-
1485 – Addresses, essays, lectures.
   I. Title.
DA152.C29   1986   942.01   85-30555

Printed by The Bath Press, Bath, Somerset

CONTENTS

LIST OF ILLUSTRATIONS

ACKNOWLEDGEMENTS

The articles reprinted here first appeared in the following places and are reprinted by the kind permission of the original publishers.

1   *Latin Historians*, edited by T.A. Dorey (Routledge and Kegan Paul, 1966), pp. 159-190.

2   *Bede. The Ecclesiastical History of the English People and other Selections*, translated by J. Campbell (Washington Square Press, Inc., New York, 1968), pp. vii-xxxii.

3   *Ampleforth Journal*, lxxvi (1971), pp. 12-29.

4   *Ampleforth Journal*, lxxviii (1973), pp. 12-26.

5   Jarrow Lecture (1979).

6   *Places, Names and Graves*, edited by P.H. Sawyer (Leeds, 1979), pp. 34-54.

7   *Studia Hibernica*, xv (1975), pp. 177-85.

8   *Sachsen und Angelsachsen* (the catalogue of an exhibition held at the Helms Museum, Hamburg, November 1978—February 1979), edited by C. Ahrens (Helms Museum, Hamburg, 1978), pp. 455-462. This appears in English for the first time here.

9   *The Church in Town and Countryside*, edited by Derek Baker; *Studies in Church History*, 16 (Blackwells, Oxford, 1979), pp. 119-35.

10   *Transactions of the Royal Historical Society*, 5th Series, xxv (1975), pp. 39-54.

11   *Histoire Comparée de l'Administration (IVe — XVIIIe Siècles)* (Actes du XIV Colloque Historique Franco-Allemand, Tours, 1977: Beihefte der Francia, IX: Munich 1980), edited by W. Paravicini and K.F. Werner, pp. 117-34.

12   *Ethelred the Unready. Papers from the Millenary Conference*, edited by David Hill (British Archaeological Reports, British Series 59, 1978), pp. 255-270.

13   *Peritia*, 3 (1984), pp. 131-50.

Introduction

These papers were written for varying audiences and at varying levels. They are reprinted as they were published (except that some blunders and slips have been corrected and that Chapter 8 is the English version of a paper published in German). Conventions, e.g. in the printing of diphthongs, have not been regularized. A note has been added to some of the papers indicating (though without attempting comprehensiveness) recent publications on the subjects concerned. In preparing this book for publication I have been assisted by Miss Elizabeth Danbury, Mr. Michael Leiserach and Dr. Hilary Turner; I thank them warmly. In composing the papers it contains, I have incurred obligations too numerous to list or even, I am sure, fully remember. So I will simply say that a large share of any merit they have is due to my teachers, colleagues, pupils and friends, and it is with gratitude and pleasure that I acknowledge it. I should, however, add that one of my benefactors ought not to be left nameless, Professor K. J. Leyser, who first interested me in medieval history, and has continued to do so since.

1

Bede I

Bede was not only, or even primarily, a historian. He finished the *Historia Ecclesiastica Gentis Anglorum* only three or four years before his death in 735. He may have known that it would be the last of his major works, for he ended it with an almost elegiac sketch of his own life and a list of his writings. These were numerous. Bede devoted a fairly long life – he was born in 672 or 673 – and formidable powers to become probably the most learned and certainly the most productive of the European scholars of his day. His works include treatises on grammar, metrics and chronology, lives of saints, homilies and, above all, commentaries on the Bible. Much that he wrote was unoriginal, in so far as it consisted of the views – often the words – of his predecessors pieced together with some rearrangement, clarification and amendment. He set out to master and pass on a large part of the learning of the Christian Church; and succeeded in this. Many of his works became standard and remained so through the Middle Ages and sometimes beyond. His historical works comprise, if hagiography is excluded, only the *Ecclesiastical History*, the *Lives* of the abbots of his abbey of Monkwearmouth-Jarrow and the chronicles – lists of the principal events in the history of the world – appended to *Liber de Temporibus* (703) and *De Temporum Ratione* (725). They are merely a part, though an important one, of what Bede wrote and what he was valued for through many centuries. His history has to be interpreted in relation to the rest of his work, that of a man whose dominant intention was to expound, spread and defend the Christian faith by all the means in his power.[1]

The *Ecclesiastical History* shows how great these means were. That

[1] The chronicles are best edited by T. Mommsen, *M. G. H. Scriptores Antiquissimi*, XIII (1898), 223–354, and the other historical works by C. Plummer, *Baedae Opera Historica* (2 vols., Oxford, 1896); references below are to Plummer's edition abbreviated as *H.E.*, unless otherwise stated. For editions of Bede's other works see M. L. W. Laistner and H. H. King, *Handlist of Bede Manuscripts* (Ithaca, N.Y., 1943) and M. T. A. Carroll, *The Venerable Bede: his Spiritual Teachings* (Catholic University of America, Studies in Mediaeval History, new ser., IX (Washington, 1946)). The poems, homilies and some of the commentaries have been re-edited in *Corpus Christianorum Series Latine*, CXIX and CXX, ed. D. Hurst, and CXXII, ed. D. Hurst and J. Fraipont (Turnhout, 1962, 1960 and 1955 respectively). For general accounts of Bede see *Bede, his Life, Times and Writings*, ed. A. Hamilton Thompson (Oxford, 1935), E. S. Duckett, *Anglo-Saxon Saints and Scholars* (New York, 1947), pp. 217–338, W. F. Bolton, 'A Bede Bibliography: 1935–60' *Traditio*, xviii (1962), 436–45.

which is first apparent to its readers is Bede's command of Latin. He writes grammatically and very clearly. Unlike some of his contemporaries, who wrote to impress by a florid style and an outré vocabulary, he intended to be understood by an audience the capacities of some of whom he did not value highly. He writes in his commentary on the Apocalypse, 'Anglorum gentis inertiae consulendum ratus . . . non solum dilucidare sensus verum sententias quoque stringere disposui'.[2] Bede knew very well how to be both simple and moving. The style in which he tells many of his stories recalls that of the gospels in its brevity, concentration on essentials, and use of direct speech. What he says is even more remarkable than the skill with which he says it. He sets out to give the history of the Church in his own land in about 85,000 words. Having begun with a short geographical and historical introduction, he gives some account of Christianity in Roman Britain, but devotes much of the first book and the whole of the remaining four to its progress in England from St Augustine's arrival in 597 until 731. The numerous sources which Bede collected and the skill with which he handled them make the *Ecclesiastical History* the masterpiece of Dark Age historiography. No history that can rival it appeared in Western Europe until the twelfth century.[3]

The *Ecclesiastical History* itself does much to explain how so remarkable a work could be undertaken. It shows the progress of Christianity in England to have been feeble and flickering until the generation following 635. But by 660 it was established in all the major kingdoms and began to flourish. Many monasteries were founded and many monks became learned. Theodore, archbishop of Canterbury 668–690, established a school at Canterbury where most subjects relevant to Christian learning, including Greek, could be studied. Benedict Biscop founded the twin monasteries of Monkwearmouth (674) and Jarrow (681–2) and collected abroad a library for them which must have been among the best in Europe. There were other important libraries and many monasteries owned books and contained more or less learned men, although only Aldhelm (?640–709) among Bede's English contemporaries approached him in eminence.[4] Although Bede lived on the edge of the civilised world he did not work in intellectual isolation. His reputation and his correspondence spread far beyond the borders of Northumbria. There were others in his own house who

[2] *Venerabilis Bedae Opera*, ed. J. A. Giles, XII (1844), 341.

[3] For Bede as a historian see e.g. W. Levison, 'Bede as Historian', in *Bede, his Life, Times and Writings, op. cit.*, pp. 111–51; C. W. Jones, *Saints' Lives and Chronicles in Early England* (Ithaca, N.Y., 1947) and 'Bede as Early Medieval Historian', *Medievalia et Humanistica*, fasc. IV (1946), 26–36; P. Hunter Blair, *Bede's Ecclesiastical History . . . and its Importance Today* (Jarrow Lecture 1959, Jarrow-on-Tyne, n.d.).

[4] For the history of the church see e.g. M. Deanesly, *The Pre-Conquest Church in England* (1961).

could write as well as him: perhaps the finest example of the Bedan style is the description of Bede's death by Cuthbert, his fellow-monk.[5] Bede's works were not only in great demand, but also occasionally criticized.[6] He was not alone in the production of hagiography and biography. We have biographical works by five of his English contemporaries and the fewness of the manuscripts of some of these makes it likely that there were other such works, now lost.[7] Bede would not have been able to accomplish what he did had he not been a member of a learned world with considerable intellectual resources. The achievements of his contemporaries hardly rivalled his, but we know them to have been considerable and may suspect them to have been more considerable than we know.

English learning was fed by that of other countries.[8] The chief debts were naturally to the sources of conversion, Italy and Ireland. Bede's scholarship depended largely on access to Italian manuscripts, the education of many of his contemporaries on access to Irish schools. Something was owed to Gaul, which gave England three bishops in the seventh century and with which some English ecclesiastics, especially Wilfrid, had close connections. The cosmopolitan nature of the Church and the willingness of clerics to move to countries other than their own brought influences from further afield and created multiple opportunities for the diffusion of ideas. Archbishop Theodore came from Cilicia; his companion Hadrian was an African. The Irish founded monasteries in Gaul, Germany and Italy besides England; Ireland had access to the learning of contemporary Spain and indirect

---

[5] Ed. Plummer, *Baedae Opera Historica* I, clx–clxiv.

[6] Carroll, *The Venerable Bede . . ., op. cit.*, pp. 43–6; M. L. Laistner, 'Bede as a Classical and Patristic Scholar', *Transactions of the Royal Historical Society*, 4th ser., XVI (1933), 83.

[7] The anonymous life of Ceolfrith and Eddius Stephanus's life of Wilfrid survive in only two manuscripts each, the Whitby life of Gregory the Great in only one (*Baedae Opera Historica*, ed. Plummer, I, cxl–cxli; *The Life of Bishop Wilfred by Eddius Stephanus*, ed. and trans. B. Colgrave (Cambridge, 1927), pp. xiii–xvi; B. Colgrave, 'The Earliest Life of Gregory the Great', in K. Jackson, N. K. Chadwick and others, *Celt and Saxon: Studies in the Early British Border* (Cambridge, 1963), pp. 119–21). So much damage seems to have been done by the Scandinavian invasions to English libraries that works which were not popular, and in particular not popular on the Continent, must have had only a limited chance of survival.

[8] For this paragraph, W. Levison, *England and the Continent in the Eighth Century* (Oxford, 1946); K. C. King, *The Earliest German Monasteries* (Nottingham, 1961); J. M. Wallace-Hadrill, 'Rome and the Early English Church', *Settimane di studio del centro italiano di studi sull'alto medioevo*, VII (Spoleto, 1960), 519–48; *Bede's Europe* (Jarrow Lecture 1962, Jarrow-on-Tyne, n.d.); K. Hughes, 'Irish Monks and Learning', *Los monjes y los estudios* (Abadia de Poblet, 1963), pp. 61–86, and H. Farmer, 'The Studies of Anglo-Saxon Monks A.D. 600–800', *ibid.*, pp. 87–103; J. N. Hillgarth, 'Visigothic Spain and Early Christian Ireland', *Proceedings of the Royal Irish Academy* LXII, C (1961–3), 167–94.

communication with the Near East. Between 690 and Bede's death Englishmen converted much of western Germany. Irish missionaries and perhaps a Spaniard were active there at the same time. One of Bede's English contemporaries went to Jerusalem and then settled at Monte Cassino. The Christian world stretched from Scotland and Ireland to Asia Minor and Spain. It was being reduced by the 'gravissima Sarracenorum lues', as Bede well knew, but it was still, if hardly united, much interconnected. The international connections of the Church were partly paralleled by those of the laity. The Anglo-Saxons had left kinsmen in Germany whom they recognised as such and sought to convert. Others had moved with the Lombards, to whom they were related, into Italy: this may have had something to do with the willingness of Englishmen to visit Italy and even to settle there.[9] Saxons had settled in Gaul as Franks may have settled in England. The coming and going of brides and exiles to and from Gaul accompanied and was connected with that of bishops and missionaries. The accumulation of instances may deceive. Many of the contacts between England and the Continent in the seventh century and the early eighth were episodic or tenuous. But there was enough communication to enable Bede to write as the heir to much of the learning of the Church and for an audience which was not entirely insular in its knowledge and interests.

In his historical works Bede was able to draw on many models and sources.[10] He made no use of the classical historians, though he could perhaps have done so – texts of some of their works which were available in Germany in the eighth century may have arrived there via England. His attitude towards most pagan authors was one of cautious reserve. The chief models and foundations for his work were, apart from the Bible, the works of Christian authors from the fourth century on. Perhaps the most important such author was Eusebius. His *Ecclesiastical History* set the standard for historians of the church.[11] It left secular affairs for the attention of the carnally minded. The wars it described were those against heresy and persecution; its heroes were the martyrs; the successions it recorded those not of emperors but of bishops. Distinguished from pagan historiography in technique as in content it included many documents and gave references to sources.

[9] Levison, *England and the Continent*, p. 40; C. E. Blunt, 'Four Italian Coins Imitating Anglo-Saxon Types', *British Numismatic Journal*, 3rd ser., V (1945–8), 285.

[10] M. L. W. Laistner, 'Bede as a Classical and Patristic Scholar', *op. cit.*; 'The Library of the Venerable Bede', *Bede, his Life, Times and Writings, op. cit.*, pp. 237–266; both articles are reprinted in *The Intellectual Heritage of the Early Middle Ages* (Ithaca, N.Y., 1957).

[11] A. Momigliano, 'Pagan and Christian Historiography in the Fourth Century A.D.', *The Conflict between Paganism and Christianity in the Fourth Century*, ed. A. Momigliano (Oxford, 1963), pp. 79–99.

Eusebius's *Chronicle* had a different function, to summarise universal history from a Christian point of view, correlating Biblical history with that of the rest of the world and showing the hand of God at work across millennia. Bede did not have either work in the original Greek; he used Rufinus's Latin translation and continuation of the *Ecclesiastical History* and Jerome's of the *Chronicle*. They provided models for his own work in either genre. He knew at least two other Christian histories, the *Adversus Paganos* of Orosius and Gregory of Tours's *Historia Francorum*. His view of history as the demonstration of the power of God, of orthodoxy and of sanctity, much resembles theirs and he owed a more direct debt to Orosius, whose geographical introduction he imitates and borrows from.[12] His aim seems to have been do do for the history of the Church in England what Eusebius had done for the whole and he follows him in choice of subject-matter and in technique. Nevertheless there are important differences between Bede's *Ecclesiastical History* and its predecessor, which make his work in some respects more like that of Gregory of Tours. Although, like Eusebius and unlike Gregory, Bede rarely recorded secular affairs for their own sake, he had to devote considerable attention to them. Eusebius, writing under Constantine, had only one Christian emperor to deal with and so was concerned with the Church as opposed to the State. Bede had to describe a Church very much involved with the State and to show how Providence had affected the affairs of kings many of whom were Christian, some even saints. Secondly, while Eusebius had incorporated accounts of martyrs in his work much more of Bede's is devoted to the lives and particularly the miracles of saints. Belief in the miraculous had increased greatly between the fourth century and the eighth. The demand for it had been fed by hagiographies in the tradition which began with the life of Anthony by Athanasius (*c.* 296–373). Such lives were prominent among Bede's sources and he wrote some himself. Writing with a largely didactic purpose and for an audience which needed vivid and concrete demonstration of the power of God and of virtue Bede made his *Ecclesiastical History* a chronological hagiography as well as a record in the manner of Eusebius.[13] He is distinguished from most hagiographers of his time by his using miracle-stories only to reinforce religious teachings rather than to advertise the merits of a particular shrine.[14]

[12] J. M. Wallace-Hadrill, 'The Work of Gregory of Tours in the Light of Modern Research', *The Long-Haired Kings* (1962), pp. 49–70.

[13] Jones, *Saints' Lives and Chronicles, op. cit.*, pp. 82–5.

[14] Bede thought wonder-working shrines could diminish rather than increase faith when the unworthy were not healed (Carroll, p. 197) and he attributes to Cuthbert the view that when such a shrine became a sanctuary for evildoers it also became a nuisance to its keepers, *Two Lives of St. Cuthbert*, ed. and trans. B. Colgrave (Cambridge, 1940), p. 278.

The works of earlier writers provided Bede not only with models,
but with much of the information in the first book of the *Ecclesiastical
History*.[15] His account of the Romans in Britain came largely from
Orosius and the pagan historian Eutropius. The interest taken by
Gaulish historians in the Pelagian heresy enabled him to gain valuable
information from the *Vita Sancti Germani* of Constantius. These, with
an important British source – Gildas's *De Excidio* – a *Passio Sancti Albani*,
some English tradition and a certain amount of misinformation from
the *Liber Pontificalis* largely saw him through the twenty-two chapters
devoted to the period before Augustine's mission.[16] His task in
compiling his much fuller account of subsequent events was more
difficult. Much is known of his sources for this since he describes some
of them in his introduction and mentions others later. He obtained a
considerable number of documents, especially papal letters, from Rome
and Canterbury. Like a true successor to Eusebius he inserted many of
them into his text; they comprise about a fifth of it and provide the
backbone of his account of the conversion and of subsequent relations
with Rome. His contacts with Rome were good enough to allow him
access not only to such letters but also to the official history of the
popes, the *Liber Pontificalis*; he used its account of Gregory II even while
that pope was still alive. Otherwise his chief written sources were
biographical – mainly hagiographical. He had *Vitae* of Fursey,
Cuthbert, Wilfred, Ceolfrith, Aethelburh and perhaps of others. Some
annals, regnal lists and genealogies were available to him but they seem
to have afforded little information on events outside Kent and
Northumbria or, for the earlier part of the seventh century, within
them.[17] He was, for example, unable to record even the year in which
Augustine died.

The written sources of which we know leave the origins of much of
the *Ecclesiastical History* unaccounted for. Bede tells us that much of his
information came from oral tradition, either directly or through

[15] The best accounts of Bede's sources are those of Plummer, Levison and Laistner in
the works cited in notes 1, 3 and 10 above.
[16] For the *Passio Sancti Albani*, W. Levison, 'St. Alban and St. Alban's', *Antiquity*, XV
(1941), 337–59. Discussion of the possibility of at least part of the *De Excidio* being of a
date later than the mid-sixth century one usually accepted has recently been revived:
P. Gorsjean, 'Remarques sur le *De Excidio* attribué a Gildas', *Archivum Latinitatis Medii
Aevi*, XXV (1955), 155–87; 'Notes de hagiographie celtique', *Analecta Bollandiana*,
LXXV (1957), 185–226.
[17] English sources of an annalistic nature possibly used by Bede are discussed by Jones,
Saints' Lives and Chronicles, op. cit..; P. Hunter Blair, 'The *Moore Memoranda* on
Northumbrian History', *The Early Cultures of North-West Europe*, ed. C. Fox and B.
Dickins (Cambridge, 1950), pp. 245–57; 'The Northumbrians and their Southern
Frontier', *Archaeologia Aeliana*, 4th ser., XXVI (1948), 98–126; and P. Grosjean 'La date
du Colloque de Whitby', *Analecta Bollandiana*, LXXVIII (1960), 255–60. Some informa-
tion may have come to him from inscriptions, C. Peers and C. A. Ralegh Radford, 'The
Saxon Monastery at Whitby', *Archaeologia*, LXXXIX (1943), 40–6.

correspondents.[18] To determine, or guess, the value of such information it is necessary to consider the forms in which it may have been preserved. Mrs Chadwick has recently suggested that many of Bede's sources were 'ecclesiastical sagas'. These were, she thinks, sometimes transmitted orally, sometimes at some stage written down, but retaining the characteristics of oral saga style – 'leisurely, detailed, circumstantial and dramatic', often divided into three parts, recording proper names and retailing conversations verbatim.[19] In the extreme form in which she presents this theory – for example, maintaining that Bede's account of the Synod of Whitby is 'certainly an elaborate form of ecclesiastical saga' – it does not seem altogether helpful.[20] Her criteria appear to be capable of including very diverse works and hardly enable one to distinguish an 'ecclesiastical saga' from a *Vita* of a saint. Nevertheless, it is very likely that many of the traditions used by Bede had been transmitted in fairly defined and constant forms and this may have made them more reliable. How reliable is a matter for conjecture. Certainly even detail could be preserved from the fairly remote past. Bede was able to give a detailed description of the appearance of Paulinus from an oral tradition a century old.[21] Oral tradition can, however, be as false as it is circumstantial and if it is accurate in details may be so in nothing else. We cannot verify many of the traditions Bede records. He must himself have often lacked the means to do so, and sometimes, it may be, the inclination.

There is no doubt that Bede was exceptionally fitted to deal with such diverse and often bad sources. More learned in chronology and computation than any other scholar of his day he was well qualified to correlate chronological data which, although often scanty, were in diverse forms. His Biblical studies had involved the use of many of the techniques of the historian. He had taken particular care in the comparison of different texts of scriptures. His preference of Jerome's more recent Latin translation of the Old Testament to the Greek of the Septuagint led him radically to revise Eusebius's chronology.[22] His Biblical work naturally involved chronological problems and the comparison of divergent texts describing the same events.[23] The compilation of commentaries required, *inter alia*, the exposition of the literal meaning of scripture and so enquiry into topographical and other facts; this may help to account for the interest in imparting topographical

[18] *H.E.* pp. 6–7.

[19] N. K. Chadwick, in *Celt and Saxon, op. cit.*, pp. 138–85, esp. pp. 169, 177.

[20] Jones is equally confident that Bede's account of the synod is in a different genre, modelled on *Acta Synodi Caesareae, Saints' Lives and Chronicles, op. cit.*, 181.

[21] *H.E.* II, 16, p. 117.

[22] Levison, 'Bede as Historian', *op. cit.*, p. 117.

[23] C. Jenkins, 'Bede as Exegete and Theologian', *Bede, his Life, Times and Writings, op. cit.*, pp. 196–9.

information apparent in parts of the *Ecclesiastical History*. Spurious texts required the attention of a Biblical scholar. Bede showed himself able to expose at least one such, the *De Transitu Beatae Virginis*, partly on historical grounds.[24] In writing the *Ecclesiastical History* at the end of such a scholarly career Bede might have been expected to produce a work of more than ordinary reliability and it is agreed that he did.

This is not to say that the *Ecclesiastical History* is technically flawless within the limits of Bede's intentions. The most conspicuous faults are chronological; the dates he gives are not always mutually consistent. Although Bede was the most expert chronologist of his day his task in dating events in England was very difficult. He had to correlate dates given according to the regnal years of the kings of different kingdoms with one another and with dates from ecclesiastical sources expressed in imperial or consular years or in terms of the position of the year in a nineteen-year cycle, the indiction. He gives dates according to several systems, frequently as years A.D. – it was largely through him that this system became current. The correlation of different dates which Bede gives according to different systems reveals discrepancies. Various attempts have been made to explain and correct these but many of the problems involved remain controversial. There is disagreement on when Bede began the year and on how he calculated regnal years. Thus cases have been put for the battle on the Winwaed's having taken place in 655, which is the year Bede gives, in 654 and in 656. All the theories advanced require the assumption that Bede made some mistakes. It is doubtful whether some of the problems will ever be completely solved. We have little evidence beyond what Bede himself provides. For many secular events he was dependent on dates expressed in regnal years. These may have often been inaccurate or expressed in complete years only. Different systems of calculation may have been used in different kingdoms at different times and Bede may not have been well informed about them. He may have made corrections or alterations on the basis of information unknown to us.[25]

Other errors can be detected in Bede's work which are due to slips, or to the difficulties of his material. Dr D. P. Kirby has shown recently that although Bede clearly implies that the marriage of Edwin of Northumbria to a Kentish princess took place in 625 he provides other evidence which makes it very likely that the marriage took place in or very near to 619. Either Bede made a false assumption – that Paulinus was consecrated before he left for Northumbria – or else he wrote the passage concerned rather carelessly.[26] Arch-Abbot Brechter in an

[24] Laistner, 'Bede as a Classical and Patristic Scholar', *op. cit.* pp. 84–5; cf. Jenkins, *op. cit.*, pp. 160–1.
[25] For the literature on Bede's chronology, D. P. Kirby, 'Bede and Northumbrian Chronology', *English Historical Review*, LXXVIII (1963), 514–27.
[26] Kirby, 518, 522–3.

elaborate study of Bede's account of St Augustine's mission to Kent has alleged that Bede knowingly falsified its chronology, ante-dating Ethelbert's baptism, post-dating Augustine's episcopal consecration, reversing their order and discarding a papal letter which showed him to be wrong.[27] This is too dramatic. Brechter's arguments for what the course of events really was are not conclusive, though neither are they implausible, especially on the date of Ethelbert's baptism. The evidence he offers for Bede's dishonesty is unconvincing. Bede may have erred through carelessness in saying that Ethelbert received the faith in 597, if he meant by this that he was baptised then.[28] He may have been wrong about the time at which Augustine was consecrated and certainly confused the archbishop of Lyons with the bishop of Arles and misdated a journey to Rome.[29] He had difficult sources to deal with, could slip, and did not write in an age in which it was thought necessary to distinguish between known facts and deductions or assumptions.[30] There is no need to assume more.

Some of the discrepancies and awkwardnesses in Bede's text may be attributable to the method and circumstances of his writing. He does not seem to have gathered all his evidence before he began to write, but

[27] (H.) S. Brechter, *Die Quellen zur Angelsachsenmission Gregors des Grossen* (Beitr. zur Gesch. d. Alten Mönchtums u.d. Benediktinerordens, Heft 22), Münster i. W., 1941), pp. 228–52, critically discussed by F. A. Markus, 'The Chronology of the Gregorian Mission: Bede's Narrative and Gregory's Correspondence', *Journal of Ecclesiastical History*, XIV (1963), 16–30.

[28] It is likely that Bede did not know when Ethelbert was baptised. The use of *interea* with the perfect tense to introduce his account of Augustine's journey to be consecrated abroad suggests that when he wrote 1, 26 and 27, he was uncertain of the relationship of this event to the baptism of Ethelbert (cf. III, 20, p.169; III, 28, p. 194; IV, 4, p. 213). The absence of a date for the baptism from the chronological summary in V, 24, strongly suggests that his sources did not give him one. The phrase 'post XX et unum annos acceptae fidei' in II, 5 (p. 90), is not entirely unambiguous. It probably refers to the baptism or conversion of Ethelbert which Bede would therefore here place in 597. If so this may well be a slip on his part. There is other evidence that II, 5, was carelessly written (Kirby, *op. cit.*, p. 521).

[29] The dating of this journey is connected with the vexed question of the authenticity of the *Responsiones* to Augustine attributed to Gregory, for which see M. Deanesly and P. Grosjean 'The Canterbury Edition of the Answers of Pope Gregory I to St. Augustine', *Journal of Ecclesiastical History*, X (1959), 1–49; P. Meyvaert, 'Les "responsiones" de S. Grégoire le Grand à S. Augustin de Cantorbery', *Revue d'Histoire Ecclésiastique*, LIV (1959), 879–94; 'Bede and the *Libellus Synodicus* of Gregory the Great', *Journal of Theological Studies*, new ser., XII (1961), 298 n.; M. Deanesly, 'The Capitular Text of the *Responsiones* of Pope Gregory I to St. Augustine', *Journal of Ecclesiastical History*, XLI (1961), 231–4.

[30] It is not altogether clear that Bede's well-known account of the co-operation of Oswy of Northumbria and Egbert of Kent in choosing an archbishop of Canterbury is not a mere deduction based on the conflation of a letter from Pope Vitalian to Oswy and some account of Egbert's sending a candidate for the see to Rome, H.E. III, 29, pp. 196–9; IV, 1, p. 201; *Hist. Abb.*, ed. Plummer, *Baedae Opera Historica*, I, 366; cf. Plummer's note, II, 200–1.

rather to have made insertions in what he had already written as new material reached him. The type of text which Plummer calls C appears to preserve one recension slightly earlier than the last, differing from it chiefly in not including chapter XIV of the fourth book: traces of other insertions into an earlier version or versions appear in the text as we have it.[31] It may well be that Bede had to write under difficulties. He was fairly old by the time he wrote the *Ecclesiastical History*; the tone and nature of the last chapter suggest that he may have been ill. He may have been hindered by liturgical duties and shortages of writing materials and copyists. It was not perhaps easy for him to find his way about his own text or materials; indexes have been invented since his day. One may fancy the *Ecclesiastical History* as the last great work of an elderly and ailing scholar compelled to great labours by a sense of relgious duty. It is surprising, not that there are inconsistencies, ambiguities, or loose ends in the *Ecclesiastical History*, but that they are so few. It is to Bede's credit rather than his discredit that it is possible to criticise him largely on a basis of evidence he himself provides. The quantity of the information he records and the care with which he uses it are such that he may be regarded almost as if he were a modern historian. Almost and sometimes, but it is wrong to judge his work, or to use it, as if he really were one.

It is not Bede's competence which marks him as the product of a distant age, but his purpose. His general aim is explicit and inevitable, to describe men and their deeds so that the *religiosus et pius auditor* may be excited to imitate good and to shun evil.[32] Much of the *Ecclesiastical History* is devoted to inculcating through stories about the past the virtues and the dogmas which Bede had spent most of his life expounding, probably to a narrower and more learned audience, in his commentaries. For example, in the commentaries Bede says that there are two kinds of compunction with the same outward manifestations. One came from fear of hell and could develop into the other which came from the love of heaven. The story of Adamnan of Coldingham in the *Ecclesiastical History* gives an instance of this. Adamnan, thanks to an accident and his own scrupulousness, continued throughout his life a regime of mortification which had been intended to last for a shorter time and

quod causa divini timoris semel ob reatum compunctus coeperat, iam causa divini amoris delectatus praemiis indefessus agebat.[33]

Most of the doctrines which Bede dramatises and makes memorable in the *Ecclesiastical History* are naturally of more general application than

[31] For textual questions see Plummer, pp. lxxx–cxliv, *The Leningrad Bede*, ed. O. Arngart (Copenhagen, 1952), pp. 13–35; *The Moore Bede*, ed. P. Hunter Blair and R. A. B. Mynors (Copenhagen, 1959), pp. 11–37.

[32] *H.E.*, p. 5.

[33] *H.E.* IV, 23 (25), p. 264; Carroll, *The Venerable Bede* . . ., *op. cit.*, pp. 162–3, 234.

this. Thus his accounts of visions of the other world, which are perhaps the most obvious demonstrations of his homilectic intentions, drive home such points as the folly of depending on the chance of being able to make a death-bed repentance, the certainty that even the least thought or action will be taken into account after death, the purpose and frightfulness of purgatory and the much greater frightfulness and eternity of hell.[34] The value of such instruction remains, no doubt, *semper, ubique et pro omnibus*. But much of what Bede seeks to teach by giving examples in the *Ecclesiastical History* is directed towards the particular circumstances of England in his own day and the nature of his work can be fully understood only in relation to these.

The *Ecclesiastical History* was intended to reach a lay as well as a clerical audience. It is the only one of Bede's works to be dedicated to a layman, Ceolwulf, king of Northumbria 729–37 or 38; he had been sent a draft to comment upon. It is not known whether he or other laymen were capable of reading it.[35] A few may have been, but in any case Bede's references to those who were either to read or to hear it suggest that he did not expect knowledge of it to be confined to the literate but rather that it would be read out and, presumably, translated.[36] Offa, king of Mercia 756–97, had a copy of the *Ecclesiastical History* and it was the only one of Bede's works which Alfred had translated.[37] No doubt Bede knew and intended that its main audience would be clerical. But the English Church contained too many nobles and was too dependent upon kings to be indifferent to the needs and interests of secular rulers. Much of the *Ecclesiastical History* was intended to show how the needs of kings could be fulfilled and where their true interests lay.

England in Bede's day was divided into a number of kingdoms whose relative power fluctuated and whose rulers lacked security. In the course of the seventh century the dynasties of Kent, East Anglia, Mercia, Northumbria and Wessex had in turn been the most powerful in England. All at some stage fell from greatness, some to recover it later, others not. All kings had enemies inside as well as outside their kingdoms. Aethelbald of Mercia, whose superiority south of the Humber was recognised at the time when Bede completed the *Ecclesiastical History*, was to die at the hands of his own bodyguard. A major theme of the probably near-contemporary poem *Beowulf* is that the wages of greatness and heroism is death. The poet constantly reminds his audience that the great kings and kingdoms with which he is concerned all came to

[34] *Ibid.*, chapter IV; *H.E.* V, pp. 12–14.
[35] Aldfrith, Ceolwulf's predecessor, was literate; laymen brought up in such a household as Wilfred's might have become so, *Eddius*, ed. Colgrave, *op. cit.*, p. 44. Wilfred himself was literate well before he was ordained priest and could have gone on to a secular career, as others perhaps did after a similar beginning, *Eddius*, pp. 8, 10, 18.
[36] E.g. *H.E.*, p. 6; V, 13, p. 313.
[37] D. Whitelock, *After Bede* (Jarrow Lecture 1960, n.p., n.d.), p. 11.

disaster.[38] English kings had to struggle hard to stay successful, and alive, in a very dangerous world. It is a question what part the Church and Christianity played in this struggle and it was a question then what part they could and should play. The acceptance of Christianity in the seventh century was part of the process by which England grew more civilized under the influence of those parts of the Continent where the wreck of Roman civilisation had been less complete than it had been in Britain. The Church was successful in England partly because it suited the needs and aspirations of kings. It made some contribution to royal government, which may have had to face new problems in the seventh century as some dynasties built up kingdoms of a size unprecedented since the Anglo-Saxon conquest of England. It must in some degree have changed kings' views of themselves and of their functions. But if kings owed something to the Church, the Church was very dependent upon kings and by the time that Bede wrote some kings were seeing their interest in exploiting rather than in protecting it. Although the English Church had a unity which transcended the boundaries of individual kingdoms and although it always in some degree acted in accordance with its own principles rather than with royal demands it was, nevertheless, very much subject to royal power. Bishops were often or usually appointed in accordance with the will of a king. A monastery which lacked royal favour could hardly hope to prosper.[39] Kings were becoming covetous of the wealth of the Church and demanding a share of it. According to St Boniface, Ceolred of Mercia (709–716) and Osred of Northumbria (705–716) were the first kings to violate the 'privilegia ecclesiarum in regno Anglorum'.[40]

The *Ecclesiastical History* is in part an attempt to demonstrate the role of a Christian king, what the Church did for him and what he ought to do for the Church. Bede repeatedly emphasises the connection between Christianity and success. His account of the career of Cenwalh, king of Wessex 643–674, is a good example. When Cenwalh succeeded in his Christian father he rejected the 'fidem et sacramenta regni caelestis' and not long after 'etiam regni terrestris potentiam perdidit'. While in exile he became converted and then regained his kingdom. But when he expelled his bishop his kingdom became subjected to severe and frequent attacks by his enemies.

tandem ad memoriam reduxit, quod eum pridem perfidia regno pulerit, fides agnita Christi in regnum revocaverit; intellexitque, quod etiam tunc destituta pontifice provincia recte pariter divino fuerit destituta praesidio.[41]

[38] A. G. Brodeur, *The Art of Beowulf* (Berkeley, 1959), pp. 76–85, 103, 116, 119.
[39] *S. Bonifatii et Lulli Epistolae* (*M.G.H. Epistolae Selectae* I), ed. M. Tangl (Berlin, 1916), no. 14.
[40] *Ibid.*, nos. 73, 78, 115; cf. E. John, *Land Tenure in Early England* (Leicester, 1960), pp. 70–3.
[41] *H.E.* III, 7.

When Oswy of Northumbria was hard-pressed by his enemy Penda and was unable to buy him off he turned to God. '"Si paganus", inquit; "nescit accipere nostra donaria, offeramus ei qui novit, Dominio Deo nostro . . ."'[42] And so he won a great battle. This campaign is one of the rare events described by Bede of which we have an account in another source. The *Historia Brittonum* attributed to Nennius, a compilation made in Wales probably in the early ninth century, tells a rather different story. It too mentions an offer of treasure to Penda, but one which was accepted. Nennius is later than Bede and the value of his work a matter for speculation. But in this instance he seems to have had information which Bede did not have or use and his employment of the apparently archaic Welsh phrase *atbret Iudeu*, 'the restitution of Iudeu' (? Stirling), to describe the incident suggests that it did take place and was well known in Welsh tradition.[43] The whole truth of the matter will never be known. It is conceivable that there were two offers of treasure, one accepted and one rejected. The suspicion remains, however, that Nennius and Bede were describing the same incident and that Bede was retailing an inaccurate version which suited his didactic purpose. Here and constantly he is insistent that the benefits which the Church can confer come in this world as well as in the next.

The king to whom Bede gives most attention is St Oswald and his account of him is an excellent instance of how Christianity could be presented to suit the needs and feelings of the rulers of England. If the Church deprived the kings of Northumbria of the gods whom they had regarded as their ancestors it soon provided their dynasty with a royal saint, a hero of exactly the kind most appreciated by the Anglo-Saxons, a great and famous man who met disaster nobly. It has been said that the greatest of heroic German themes was that of the inevitable death of the great, the theme of *Beowulf* itself in which 'as in a little circle of light about their halls men with courage as their stay went forward to that battle with the hostile world and the offspring of the dark which ends for all, even the kings and champions, in defeat'.[44] Oswald was an improved version of this type of hero. He came to greatness through being a Christian:

non solum incognita progenitoribus suis regna caelorum sperare didicit; sed et regna terrarum plus quam ulli maiorum suorum, ab eodem uno Deo, qui fecit caelum et terram consecutus est.[45]

---

[42] *H.E.* III, 24, p. 177.

[43] K. Jackson, 'On the Northern British Section in Nennius', *Celt and Saxon, op. cit.*, pp. 35–9. Jackson argues convincingly that the *Historia* is partly derived from written sources embodying annals recorded during the seventh century.

[44] J. R. R. Tolkien, 'Beowulf, the Monsters and the Critics', *Proceedings of the British Academy*, XXII (1936), p. 18 of the offprint.

[45] *H.E.* III, 6, pp. 137–8.

Although he met his inevitable fate and died fighting bravely far from home he lived elsewhere and retained power, which was demonstrated in a concrete way by miracles. As a Christian saint he is a somewhat curious figure. No miracles performed during his lifetime were attributed to him (unless his victory at Heavenfield be counted such); he died fighting an army which, though Bede does not tell us so, may well have included Christians; as he died he was popularly thought to have prayed, not for his enemies, but for the souls of his own men.[46] As the product of interaction between Christianity and the needs of a dynasty in a certain climate of thought and belief his cult is perfectly intelligible. Oswald was not the only type of Christian king. A surprising number of others in the seventh and eight centuries abandoned their kingdoms in order to enter a monastery or to go to Rome. Christianity was by no means always to a king's earthly advantage. Aidan's remark when Oswine of Deira humbled himself before him was a pregnant one. ' "Scio", inquit, "quia non multo tempore victurus est rex; nunquam enim ante haec vidi humilem regem".'[47] Bede recognised that there was more than one way in which a king could be virtuous. But he makes the duty of a king while reigning clear. It is to protect the Church, to observe its teaching and to defend his people in battle. The happiest times since the English came to Britain were, he says, those 'dum et fortissimos Christianosque habentes reges cunctis barbaris nationibus essent terrori'.[48] In the period of which he is writing here, the last generation of the seventh century, the 'barbari nationes' – he was probably thinking chiefly of the Picts – were all more or less Christian. There is a point where his admiration for the leader and defender of a Christian people meets a less specifically devout delight in the *strenuitas* of a warrior king.[49] It was not that Bede was committed in a simple way to the interests of the kings of Northumbria: he approved of a Mercian rebellion against Oswy and disapproved of a raid made by Ecgfrith on Ireland. It was rather that he was writing for an audience which saw Christianity in heroic terms and which may have believed in a more than rational connection between the virtue of a king and the prosperity of his people.

Bede's account of secular affairs is nearly always intended to show how virtue and vice were rewarded in this world as well as hereafter, or to present models of Christian kingship, or is simply incidental. For example, we learn from him of one of Penda's attacks on Northumbria only because it was involved with a miracle of Aidan's. He does not

[46] *H.E.* III, 12, p. 151.

[47] *H.E.* III, 14, p. 157; cf. Sigbert, king of Essex, said to have been murdered because he would forgive his enemies, III, 22, 173.

[48] *H.E.* IV, 2, p. 205.

[49] Wallace-Hadrill, 'The Work of Gregory of Tours in the Light of Modern Research', *op. cit.*, pp. 60–2.

even tell us the names of the British kingdoms against which the kings of Northumbria fought. He says very little indeed about the political events of the early eighth century, which were those about which he must have known most. Indeed, he gives less space to his own times than he does to any other period after 597; of the four books and twelve chapters devoted to the period 596–731 the years from 687 to 731 receive one book only.[50] The contrast with Gregory of Tours is striking. Gregory devotes six of the ten books of his history to the period of his own greatness, *c.* 573–591. The more he knew the more he wrote. It seems with Bede the more he knew the less he wrote. A clue to the reason for this may be given by his remark on the reign of Ceolwulf – that it was so troubled that 'quid de his scribi debeat quemve habitura sint finem singula, necdum sciri valeat'.[51] This is partly, no doubt, an expression of his usual discretion, but also an intimation that he was waiting for the pattern of God's judgments on the past to emerge. Until it had done so he would not write.

If much of the *Ecclesiastical History* is directed towards the laity, more is directed towards the clergy. The English Church in Bede's day enjoyed a status within the universal Church which it was never to reach again. Bede's own work indicates its learning. During his lifetime Englishmen converted much of Germany and they were soon to reform the Church in Gaul. Bede was proud of English achievements and devoted much of his fifth book to describing the work of English missionaries on the Continent, though he strangely says nothing of St Boniface, who was becoming the greatest of them.[52] But it is not for nothing that much of the rest of the book consists of accounts of visions of hell. Bede felt that much was amiss with the Church and in particular in his own kingdom of Northumbria. We have the letter which he wrote at very nearly the end of his life to Bishop Egbert, of York, lamenting the ills which plagued the church.[53] His criticisms were, briefly, these. There were not enough bishops to ensure that pastoral duties (which then fell largely on the bishop in person) were properly discharged. Large dioceses were maintained because bishops were anxious to exact all the dues they could. Some bishops were surrounded by men given to laughter, jokes, tales, feasting and drink. Many priests were ignorant, many monks ill-conducted. Monasteries were often such in name only, being in fact the property of laymen who sought chiefly the rights and exemptions associated with the monastic tenure of land. The kingdom had become so demented with this 'mad error' since the death of Aldfrith that its security was threatened since there

---

[50] The period 596–687 occupies 239 pages of Plummer's edition, that after 687, 71.
[51] *H.E.* V, 23, p. 349.
[52] Wallace-Hadrill, *Bede's Europe, op. cit.*, pp. 11–12.
[53] Ed. Plummer, *Baedae Opera Historica* I, 405–23.

was not enough land left to support the young men who should have
defended it.

It is not, of course, unusual in any period for the clergy to be wicked
and neglectful or for the laity to seek to batten on the Church. These
evils then took particular forms reflecting the nature of the Church and
of society in the seventh century and the relations between them.
Christianity had, after a slow start, spread very quickly in England. In
630 there was only one kingdom in which it was established at all
firmly. By 660 it was established for good in all but one. The Church
had become a native one just as quickly. Until 644 there was no English
bishop. By 678 there was only one who was not English, Theodore
himself. As the Church grew, and grew acclimatised, much of its way
of life seems to have been assimilated to that of lay society and the *mores*
of its rulers to those of the aristocracy from which so many of them
came. The career of Wilfrid affords the best illustration of many of the
circumstances and difficulties.[54] Born in about 634 he entered the
monastery of Lindisfarne, thereafter going to Canterbury, Rome and
Gaul and returning to England in time to play a leading part at the
synod of Whitby in 664. He then became bishop in Northumbria,
exercising his functions there from 669 or somewhat earlier until 678
when king Ecgfrith expelled him. He remained a wanderer in England
and abroad for most of the rest of his life, with intervals during which
he was restored to some power in Northumbria from 686–7 to 691–2
and from 705–6 to his death in 709. He was certainly one of the greatest
ecclesiastics of his day. Ascetic, deemed a saint by some, the founder of
several monasteries according to the rule of St Benedict, he established
Christianity in Sussex and attempted to do so in Frisia. At the same
time his life and conduct were in some respects like those of a great
Anglo-Saxon nobleman. As he grew powerful he surrounded himself
with a great household, not only of clerks, but also of young men who
did not proceed to enter the Church.[55] Like many of the great of his day
he had to go into exile more than once and he went surrounded by his
followers. He served more kings than one and so became very rich.[56]
He gained much for the Church, but what he gained was organised as a
personal ecclesiastical empire. He owned many monasteries in several
kingdoms. To some he may not even have appointed subordinate
abbots; they were his and his alone.[57] Some abbots put themselves
under his protection in almost the way that a nobleman might enter the
service of a king.[58] He behaved towards those beneath him with the

---

[54] The most recent extended account of Wilfred is that of Duckett, *Anglo-Saxon Saints and Scholars, op. cit.*, pp. 101–216.
[55] *Eddius*, ed. Colgrave, *op. cit.*, pp. 44, 48, 50, 94.
[56] *Ibid.*, pp. 16, 36, 48, 82–4, 136, 140.
[57] *Ibid.*, p. 134.
[58] *Ibid.*, p. 44.

generosity expected of a ruler. When he went to visit all his abbots in the south he either increased their livelihood with grants of land or rejoiced their hearts with money.[59] He is difficult for us to judge, as Bede seems to have found him difficult to judge. Active, munificent and it may be holy he was nevertheless very much part of a noble society which cared greatly for power and show, the possession of a loyal *comitatus* and the opportunity to exchange rich gifts. His career was in some respects unparalleled and may have owed something to Merovingian example. But in its reflection of the relations between the Church and the world it is typical of much that went on in Bede's day. *Beowulf* was almost certainly written in a monastery, probably at some time in the eighth century. Its learned author was a Christian; the feeling which inspires it is only intermittently so and is very much that of a warrior nobility. Even Cuthbert, one of the most ascetic of saints, had as his pectoral cross a jewel worthy of a king, or else it was thought appropriate that he should be buried with one.[60] The Church in Bede's day was not one in which it is, or was always, easy to draw the distinction between the lay and the clerical or even between good or evil.

Bede offered it models. Of the many lives of saints included in his history three seem to be particularly intended to give guidance to monks and bishops in their relations with the secular world, those of John of Hexham, Cuthbert and above all Aidan. If the high ecclesiastics of Bede's day 'immensum rerum secularium pondus et vectigal exigunt' Aidan and his immediate successors at Lindisfarne had 'nil pecuniarum absque pecoribus'.[61] When he died Wilfrid had thought it necessary for his abbeys to have treasures with which to buy the favour of kings and bishops.[62] Aidan gave 'potentes' nothing but food when they came to see him. The money they gave him he gave to the poor or used to ransom captives. There was, Bede thought, all too much ecclesiastical drinking and entertaining in his own time, but in those days 'tota cura cordis excolendi, non ventris'. If the king and his followers came to a monastery 'simplici tantum, et cotidiano fratrum cibo contenti, nil ultra quaerebant'.[63] In the letter to Egbert Bede complained that there were many villages and hamlets 'in montibus . . . inaccessis ac saltibus dumosis positi' which had not so much as seen a bishop for years 'quorum tamen ne unus quidem a tributis antistiti reddendis esse possit immunis'.[64] But Aidan and Cuthbert had taken

---

[59] *Ibid.*, p. 140.

[60] *The Relics of St. Cuthbert*, ed. C. F. Battiscombe (Oxford, 1956), pp. 308–25.

[61] *In Esdram et Nehemiam . . . Expositio*, ed. Giles, *Bedae Opera Omnia* IX, 21 (qu. Carroll, *op. cit.*, p. 149n), *H.E.* III, 27, p. 190.

[62] *Eddius*, p. 136.

[63] *H.E.*, III, 27, p. 190–1.

[64] Ed. Plummer, p. 410.

pains to tour the country to preach and teach and it was to just such places that Cuthbert had particularly gone.

Solebat autem ea maxima loca peragrare illis praedicare in viculis qui in arduis asperisque montibus procul positi.[65]

Bede describes the lives of these saints and in particular that of Aidan not simply as good examples but as good examples in strong contrast to the conduct of the Church in his own day – 'vita illius a nostri temporibus segnitia distabat'.[66] It is noticeable how much he stresses those aspects of Aidan's conduct which defied the customs of Anglo-Saxon society which had so powerful and inevitable an effect upon the Church, in particular entertainment and gift exchange. Hospitality was of the greatest importance to the Anglo-Saxons. It was of the essence of kingship for the king to dine with his nobles in his great hall. In their turn nobles frequently entertained kings. At all levels of society public or communal entertainment was a most important part of life. Similarly with the exchange of gifts. Even Cuthbert thought of it in his last hours when he asked to have the priest with him who had been accustomed to serve him

ideoque donationum acceptationumque eius omnium conscius erat indubius. Quem ob id maxime secum manere voluit, ut si cuiuslibet acceptis muneribus digna recompensatione non respondisset, illius admonitione recoleret et priusquam obiret, sua cuique restitueret.[67]

Thus much of the *Ecclesiastical History* is by implication a criticism of the Church in Bede's own day and expresses his longing for a return to a primitive simplicity which he thought had existed only a short time before. He may well have realised that if the Church was to survive it had to involve itself more with the world than he would wish. He remarks of Putta, Bishop of Rochester, who after his church and its possessions had been ravaged by Aethelred of Mercia, retired elsewhere.

nihil omnio de restaurando episcopatu suo agens; quia, sicut et supra diximus, magis in ecclesiasticis quam in mundanis rebus erat industrius.[68]

It is a slightly curious but a revealing way of putting it. His sympathies clearly lay with Putta; he thought the world was bad and the Church too much part of it. He wanted a poverty, simplicity and devotion

[65] *H.E.* IV, 25 (27), p. 270.
[66] *H.E.* III, 5, p. 136.
[67] *Two Lives of St. Cuthbert, op. cit.*, p. 276.
[68] *H.E.* IV, 12, p. 228.

which, if they had ever characterised the English Church, were never to
do so again.

Bede's account of the Church in the *Ecclesiastical History* is
distinguished by great discretion. While his commentaries contain
numerous references to the shortcomings of the Church and in his letter
to Egbert he is open and violent in denunciation he has very little to say
directly about the sins of the clergy in his history. A few sinful clerics
are mentioned, but, Britons apart, almost always incidentally. His
account even of Ceolred and Osred, kings who, so we learn elsewhere,
oppressed the Church, is limited to the dates of their respective
accessions and deaths. The nearest he comes in the *Ecclesiastical History*
to the long account and denunciation of fictitious monasteries in the
letter to Egbert is the cryptic statement that so peaceful are the times
that many Northumbrians have preferred to enter monastries rather
than to exercise the arts of war. 'Quae res quem sit habitura finem,
posterior aetas videbit.'[69] Similarly in his *Lives* of the abbots of
Monkwearmouth-Jarrow Bede makes no reference to the incident
described in the anonymous biography of Ceolfrid – which he used – of
Ceolfrid's leaving the abbey partly because of the behaviour of certain
nobles, who could not endure his regular discipline.[70] Had we to rely
on the *Ecclesiastical History* for our knowledge of the Church in the first
generation of the eighth century we should know little of it, and still
less of Bede's severe judgment on it. There can be little doubt that
Bede's failure to describe the conduct of those of his contemporaries of
whom he disapproved was deliberate. In his commentary on the Book
of Samuel he is explicit that it is wrong publicly to denounce even evil
priests:

nos quoque in exemplum beati Samuhelis erga tales modeste agere neque eos
traducere oportet quos incorrigibiles et divino iam iudicio non dubitamus esse
damnandos, maxime si hos aliquo gradu ecclesiastico.

and

docet quanta reverentia sit divinis adhibenda sacramentis quamvis per
malorum manum dispensatis, quantus personis sacri altaris officio mancipatis
honor impendendus, quantum ab harum laesione quamlibet male viventium
propter insigne gradus sit cuiuslibet temperanda praesumptio . . . Cavendum
ergo ne episcoporum, presbiterorum, diaconorum famam passim lacerare et
attaminare praesumamus.[71]

He clearly did not think it appropriate to enlarge on the deficiencies of

[69] *H.E.* V, 23, p. 351.
[70] *Baedae Opera Historica*, ed. Plummer, I, 390.
[71] Ed. Hurst, *Corpus Christianorum Series Latine* CXIX, *op. cit.*, pp. 135, 244–5;
Carroll, p. 150.

the clergy in a work such as the *Ecclesiastical History* which was intended for a fairly wide audience. A letter to another cleric such as that to Egbert was another matter, though even there he mentions no names. Others of his day were not so backward, like the monk who wrote to a friend describing a vision of hell where many sinners had appeared in torment, among them 'your abbot'.[72]

Bede's discretion is most apparent in his treatment of Wilfred.[73] He had access to some and probably the whole of the biography of Wilfrid attributed to Wilfrid's clerk, Eddius Stephanus. His account differs, however, from that of Eddius. While he adds to Eddius's descriptions of Wilfrid's defence of Roman orthodoxy and of his conversion of Sussex he says nothing of the important part which Wilfred played in Merovingian politics after 658 and his account of the struggle for ecclesiastical power in Northumbria is shorter and differs in emphasis. Eddius maintains that Wilfrid was wronged not only by kings Ecgfrith and Aldfrith but by bishops, and, in particular by archbishops Theodore and Berthwald. Bede does say briefly that several bishops were involved in Wilfrid's expulsion in 691 but otherwise presents the disputes as between Wilfrid and the kings of Northumbria alone, saying nothing of the parts played by the archbishops of Canterbury. He omits any mention of the synod of Austerfield (?703) at which, according to Eddius, the bishops led by the archbishop behaved aggressively and disingenuously towards Wilfrid. He does not mention, as Eddius does, that Wilfrid was imprisoned for nine months by Ecgfrith, *c.* 680 and he gives a different account of the circumstances of Wilfred's appointment to a Northumbrian see in 664.

These differences have for long attracted the attention of historians. R. L. Poole, in what remains the standard account of them, came to the conclusion that in the matters at issue Bede was almost always right and Eddius almost always wrong.[74] But, while it is true that Eddius was committed to Wilfrid's cause and capable of misrepresentation to support it, Poole assumes rather than demonstrates Bede's greater veracity; and Bede's veracity is what is at issue, since Eddius is almost the only contemporary source of any length with whom we are able to compare him.[75] There is a consistency in the ways in which Bede's

[72] *S. Bonifatii et Lulli Epistolae, op. cit.*, no. 115.

[73] For Wilfrid, see pp. 16–17, above.

[74] 'St. Wilfrid and the See of Ripon', *English Historical Review*, XXXIV (1919), 1–24.

[75] Thus it is extremely likely that Aethelwalh, king of Sussex, was already a Christian before Wilfrid arrived, although Eddius implies that Wilfrid converted him (Poole, pp. 6–7). But most of Poole's arguments for Eddius's unreliability are no more than demonstrations that his account differs from that of Bede. His attempt to show that Eddius's account of Wilfrid's role in Merovingian politics gives independent evidence of his untrustworthiness is unconvincing. Eddius may well exaggerate the importance of his hero. The sources for the events in question are, however, so poor

account of Wilfrid differs from that of Eddius which suggests, not that
Bede was more truthful, but that he was more discreet and that his view
of the function of a historian was different.[76] Wilfrid's career must have
presented Bede with great difficulties. He always speaks of Wilfrid with
great respect, and had reason to respect him, not least as the great
protagonist of Roman orthodoxy. But he probably disapproved of some
aspect of Wilfrid's career, which diverged considerably from his ideal. It
was in Wilfrid's presence that Bede had been accused of heresy and his
accusers – whom he describes, with the approach to venom which
characterises him when his own orthodoxy is questioned, as wanton,
drunken bumpkins – were probably members of Wilfrid's household.[77]
In any case Wilfrid's contentious life presented incidents which it was
difficult to make edifying, disputes between bishops, two worthy kings,
Ecgfrith, 'venerabilis er piissimus', and Aldfrith, 'vir . . doctissimus',
flouting papal decisions, perhaps even two archbishops doing so.[78] Part
of Wilfrid's misfortunes probably sprang from his resistance to
Theodore's policy of dividing up large sees. Bede thought such division
was necessary, but Wilfrid appears to have gained some degree of papal

and Eddius so important among them that it is not possible to demonstrate this.
Modern historians of the Merovingians have accepted Eddius's account in general, *faute
de mieux* it may be (e.g. W. Levison in his edition of Eddius, *M.G.H.*, SS. Rer. Mer.,
VI, 163–263, L. Dupraz, *Le Royaume des Francs* (Fribourg-en-Suisse, 1948, chapter 4).
Poole's allegation that Eddius states Ebroin to have been alive when he was in fact dead
(p. 5) is not sufficient to discredit Eddius's general reliability on Merovingian affairs
even if it is justified and Eddius's account of Wilfrid's movements is in any case just
compatible with Ebroin's having been alive when he says he was (Dupraz, p. 352, n. 1).

[76] Bede may have omitted any account of the synod of Austerfield because, as Poole
suggests, he knew Eddius's account to be wrong, but did not know enough to correct
it; but this is a strange argument to justify complete silence. It seems likely that he
similarly omitted Eddius's story of Wilfrid's imprisonment by Ecgfrith, not because he
knew it to have been wrong, but because it was unedifying. Poole's argument that the
incident is chronologically unacceptable is not strong. It depends on taking Bede's
statement that Wilfrid was in Sussex 'usque ad mortem Ecgfridi' quite literally, while it
need be no more than a general indication (cf. Plummer, ii, 319) and if taken otherwise
leaves an unnecessary gap in Wilfrid's career between 685 and 686–7, when the sources
agree that he was restored in Northumbria. The most famous crux is in connection
with the events of 664. Eddius says Wilfrid was made Bishop of all Northumbria but
that Chad was intruded in his place while he was abroad to be consecrated. Bede clearly
implies, though he is nowhere perfectly explicit, that Northumbria was divided
between them. The considerations which might lead one to incline to one side or the
other are very evenly balanced; for the extensive literature see Duckett, *op. cit.*, p. 143
n. That Eddius was not alone in his view of Chad's position is suggested by a (? mid-
eighth century) verse martyrology mentioning all the bishops of York up to Wilfrid II
(718–732) except Chad, H. Quentin in *Dictionnaire d'archéologie chrétienne et de liturgie* II,
642–4.

[77] *Bedae Opera de Temporibus*, ed. C. W. Jones (Cambridge, Mass., 1943), p. 307, 'Sed
haec tristi mox admixtione confudit, addendo videlicet quod me audires a lascivientibus
rusticis inter hereticos per pocula decantari'.

[78] Plummer, ii, p. 316.

support.[79] It was a matter which was difficult to describe so as either to encourage the good or deter the bad, for it is likely that in Bede's view these disputes were between good men who were all in some degree in the wrong. We do not have enough evidence to be sure to what extent he or Eddius conceals or distorts the truth. The likelihood is that Eddius gives a better, though partisan, account of what really happened while Bede steers a careful course, giving additional information on the most edifying aspects of Wilfred's career while omitting or playing down those which were to the discredit of the virtuous; sometimes, perhaps, he 'through necessity concealed the truth by the use of very cautious words'.[80] It is worth observing that almost none of the passages in Eddius which enable us to see how closely Wilfred's life in some aspects resembled that of the secular nobility were used by Bede. He very probably did not approve of them and, fond though he was of facts, his tendency was to describe men and events that they appear timeless. If the names were changed it would often be difficult to tell of which century or of what kind of society he is writing.

A theme which stands out above all others in Bede's attempt to instruct and edify through the *Ecclesiastical History* is that of the struggle for the unity and orthodoxy of the Church. To record the nature and fate of heresy was one of the most important functions of an ecclesiastical historian. Eusebius had given much attention to so doing. As a theologian Bede was concerned to refute many heretics and heresies – Plummer collected references to twenty-nine.[81] As a historian he was concerned with one heresy, Pelagianism, and one group of errors, those of the Celtic Churches which departed from the orthodox custom, especially in the calculation of the date of Easter. Pelagius's heresy of the denial of the necessity of grace for salvation may have originated in the British Isles. Bede thought that it had been imported in the fifth century, and in his first book describes at some length two visits made by St Germanus to extirpate it. Pelagian views seem to have continued to be held in Ireland in the seventh and eighth centuries and it may well have been from Ireland that there came the two works of the Pelagian Julian of Eclana and the one of Pelagius himself to which Bede had access.[82] The first book of his commentary on the Song of Songs was devoted to the refutation of Julian. His account of Pelagianism and its defeat in the fifth century was then of more than historical significance; the evidence he

[79] This policy probably led to disputes of which Bede only hints, see c. ix of the decrees made at Hertford (*H.E.* IV, 5, p. 216) and Bede's reticent account of the deposition of Bishop Wynfrid, which may have been connected with the division of his see (IV, 3, p. 212; IV, 6, p. 218; ii, p. 216).

[80] As he thought King David might have done, Carroll, p. 152.

[81] Plummer, pp. lxii–lxiii n.

[82] Hughes, 'Irish Monks and Learning', *op. cit.*, pp. 62, 72; *H.E.* II, 19, pp. 122–4; Laistner, 'The Library of the Venerable Bede', *op. cit.*, pp. 252, 265.

gives of God's condemnation of it in the past was a useful lesson for his own day.

The errors which received most attention from Bede were those of the Celtic Churches which diverged from Roman customs. The most important difference was that on the calculation of the date of Easter.[83] It was regarded not as minor point of discipline, but as a rift in the unity of the Church with serious doctrinal implications. For such a theologian as Bede, always seeking mystical interpretations, the movement of Easter and its proper calculation – and no one knew the proper calculation better than he did – was loaded with the weightiest significance. Consider, for example, the words Bede attributes to the dying Cuthbert who warns his companions to have no communion with those who depart from the unity of Catholic peace 'vel pascha non suo tempore celebrando, vel perverse vivendo'.[84] A considerable part of the *Ecclesiastical History* is devoted to the subject. In the second book we are told how Augustine attempted to induce the Britons to accept the Roman usages or to assist the evangelisation of the English. He failed and prophesied that the recalcitrant Britons would perish at the hands of the English. Bede records with some relish the fulfilment of this prophesy when Aethelfrith massacred the monks of Bangor. Here, as in his use of Gildas's account of the Anglo-Saxon invasions in the fifth century, Bede is able to reconcile two loyalties by showing his pagan ancestors to have been the instrument of God's revenge. He goes on to describe later attempts to persuade the Britons to accept the Roman Easter. The climax of the third book is his famous account of the synod of Whitby at which Oswy agreed that Roman usages should prevail in Northumbria, while those who did not accept them left. In the fifth book Bede now explains how Iona, northern Ireland and the king of the Picts were converted to a proper view – southern Ireland had become orthodox long since. The emphasis given to the Easter controversy throughout the *Ecclesiastical History* is clear. It receives the longest chapter in the third book and the longest in the fifth. The chapter which describes the conversion of Iona is the last in the whole except for that which gives a final survey of the general state of Britain. It must have given particular satisfaction to Bede to record the acceptance of Catholic unity by the house whence had come Aidan and the Irish missionaries whom he so much admired, but whose adherence to unorthodox usages he so much deplored. The battle for Roman uniformity was still not completely won at the time when he wrote. The Britons remained 'inveterati et claudicantes'.[85] As with

---

[83] For what was at issue see e.g. J. K. Kenney, *Sources for the Early History of Ireland* I (New York, 1929), pp. 210–17.

[84] *Two Lives of St. Cuthbert, op. cit.*, p. 284.

[85] *H.E.* V, 22, p. 347.

Pelagianism, so with the Easter controversy, Bede was writing not only an account of the past, but a tract for his own times.

Bede's preoccupation with the defence of orthodoxy and his distrust of the Britons who had erred, and in his own day still and alone continued to err, may have influenced his selection of subject-matter and coloured his account of what he selected. As always the lack of other sources prevents reasonable certainty as to how far this was so. Thus Nennius gives an account of the conversion of Northumbria quite at variance with that of Bede; it was accomplished, he says, by the British Church, Edwin being baptised by Rhun, son of Urien, a member of the royal dynasty of the northern British kingdom of Rheged. Until recently most scholars have rejected this story. Nennius is later than Bede, less scholarly, and recounts much that is fabulous. A considerable part of Bede's account of the conversion of Northumbria must be broadly true; he can hardly have fabricated the letters of Pope Honorius to Edwin and his queen which help to confirm his account. But Professor Jackson and Mrs Chadwick have recently argued that Nennius's tale should be taken more seriously.[86] It is consistent with the fragments of knowledge which we have about the rulers of Rheged and about Edwin's relations with the Britons. Much of this information inspires more interest than confidence, but it is not negligible. In particular Nennius gives another piece of information about the relations between the royal houses of Rheged and Northumbria, namely that King Oswy had two wives, Riemmelth, whose descent is given and who seems to have been a member of the royal house of Rheged, and Eanfled, daughter of Edwin. Bede mentions the second, but not the first. That Nennius's information on this was accurate is suggested by the occurrence of what seems to be an Anglo-Saxon version of the first wife's name at about the right place in the 'list of names of the queens and abbesses of Northumbria' in the, presumably independent, *Liber Vitae* of Durham.[87] This fragment of evidence by no means proves Nennius's account of the conversion of Northumbria to have been true. But it does suggest relationships between Northumbria and its British neighbours of which Bede tells us, through ignorance or design, nothing; and it raises the suspicion that the British Church did play a more important part in the conversion of Northumbria than his account, which allows it none, indicates.

The problems involved in assessing Bede's account of the conversion of Northumbria are characteristic of those which arise in connection with the *Ecclesiastical History*. Bede was very learned and very

[86] K. Jackson, 'On the Northern British Section of Nennius', N. K. Chadwick, 'The Conversion of Northumbria: a Comparison of Sources' in *Celt and Saxon, op. cit.*, pp. 20–62, 138–66.
[87] Jackson, pp. 41–2.

intelligent. His aim was partly simply to describe the history of the Church in England and his care in collecting evidence and the methods, derived from those of Eusebius, with which he handled it enabled him to perform this task in a manner which makes this work more scholarly, in the modern sense, than that of any other Dark Age historian. This aspect of his work has always and rightly attracted attention and praise. But his principal intention was not just to record the past, but to use it to teach lessons to the present, mainly by treating seventh-century England as a gallery of good examples. Excellent instances of the reaction he sought are to be found in the work of Victorian historians, for example W. Bright – 'We think not only of the noble earnestness of Ethelbert, of the heroic sanctity of Oswald, of the sweet humility of Oswin but of the genuine conversions of Eadbald and Kenwalch . . .', etc.[88] The differences in the historiographical fortunes of the seventh-century England and seventh-century Gaul, the one often being regarded as moving and edifying, the other as repellent and vicious, are attributable not so much to one society's being nobler, or nicer, than the other as to Bede's aims and tastes being different from those of Frankish historians.[89]

Bede wrote then not only in the Eusebian tradition but also in that of hagiography. The principles of hagiographers were largely contrary to those of scholarship, though they sometimes adopted a misleadingly scholarly air, setting store by citing evidence for things which did not happen or which did not happen at the time or to the persons they alleged. They wrote in the attitude of mind with which the Bible is now often interpreted. Moral truth, not literal truth, was what mattered.[90] Emphasis was placed on the need for belief, not on the advantages of doubt. 'Vera lex historiae' is, says Bede, 'simpliciter ea quae fama vulgante collegimus ad instrutionem posteritatis litteris mandare.' He prides himself that he has used an earlier life of Cuthbert 'simpliciter fidem historiae quam legebam accomodans'.[91] Hagiographers tended to turn the men and events they described into types, 'Vous lui demandez un portrait', says Fr Delehaye of the hagiographer, 'il vous répond par un programme'.[92] Bede's account in the *Ecclesiastical History* of such

[88] *Chapters of Early English Church History* (Oxford, 1878), p. 435.

[89] If Grosjean is right in identifying Agilbert, bishop of Dorchester 650–60, with the Agilbert who helped to lure an enemy of Ebroin's to his death by swearing an oath on an empty reliquary ('La date du Colloque de Whitby,' *op. cit.*, p. 251) a Frankish historian could reveal other qualities in this man than the *eruditio* and the *industria* to which Bede refers (*H.E.* III, 7, p. 140).

[90] E.g. Jones, *Saints' Lives and Chronicles*, *op. cit.*, chapter 4; B. Colgrave, 'The Earliest Saints' Lives Written in England', *Proceedings of the British Academy XLIV* (1958), 35–60; and in general H. Delehaye, *Les légendes hagiographiques*, 4th ed. (Brussels, 1955).

[91] *H.E.*, pp. 7–8; Jones, *Saints' Lives and Chronicles*, pp. 82–3.

[92] Delehaye, p. 24.

saints as Aidan and Cuthbert is almost purely hagiographical and contrasts with the more factual and sober treatment of other biographies in his *Lives of the Abbots*.[93] It is a question how far what appear to be the more purely historical parts of the *Ecclesiastical History* are affected by his didactic purposes. These purposes certainly determined his selection of subject-matter; it can hardly be doubted that he was very discreet and sometimes suppressed that which could not edify. But one must wonder how far his account of the course of events is affected by his believing that he ought to give the version which best demonstrated the truth of his faith rather than that which best corresponded with the truth, and how far his judgment of what was likely was affected by his conviction of what was appropriate. He is so far our only source for so much of what he describes that no firm judgment on these matters is possible. But a comparison of Bede with such other sources as Eddius and Nennius, questionable though they are, suggests that the veneration which he has so long so rightly been accorded ought to be tempered by some mistrust. Historians have sometimes been too ready to assume Bede's reliability as axiomatic when it is the point at issue. It is not even safe to assume that the attitudes and emphases of the *Ecclesiastical History* fully reflect Bede's personal views. He thought it the duty of a teacher to suit his teaching to his audience.[94] Some of the apparant crudities in his approach to Christianity, for example the repeated emphasis on its connection with worldly success and on the importance of miracles, may indicate not so much his own view of his faith as his judgment of the limitations of his audience.[95]

Clear, almost simple, though the *Ecclesiastical History* is it is the product of a complex mind working under difficult circumstances. On the one hand Bede was concerned for the truth, interested in hard facts, excellently equipped technically and writing with the good model of Eusebius before him. On the other hand he was using history to teach lessons which he felt to be badly needed; he was writing partly not as a historian but as a hagiographer; he had to suit his work to his audience and present it in such a way that it moved men less learned and less subtle than he. He was a barbarian, one of the first handful of his people to have become literate, yet very learned in a tradition which sprang from the remote world of the Roman empire. He was very devoutly, indeed sternly, Christian, yet writing in and for a Church which had accommodated itself to the ways of its world. He sought to recall it to

---

[93] Jones, *Saints' Lives and Chronicles*, pp. 29, 54.

[94] Carroll, p. 245; *H.E.* III, 5, p. 137.

[95] The attitude towards physical miracles of some of the Fathers, including even Gregory the Great, who records so many of them, was one of some reserve, e.g. Jones, *Saints' Lives and Chronicles*, pp. 76–7, Carroll, pp. 196 ff.

what he thought to have been its primitive simplicity while treating it with the respect and discretion which any church deserved. Many of the difficulties in assessing the *Ecclesiastical History* derive from those inherent in Bede's intellectual position and in the nature of his task.

Whatever the difficulties, few of those who read his book and even fewer of those who work on it fail to come to admire it. Bede had and has the power to seize the imagination of his reader and to transport him to a strange world; strange because it is so distant in time and circumstances, even stranger because it is a world so directly dominated by God, where ordinary historical causality hardly applies. Most Dark Age historians provoke a sense, usually an overwhelming sense, of superiority. We know better, we are cleverer than they. Bede defies patronage. Remote, almost bizarre, though his view of history is he expounds it in the manner, and it is more than just the manner, of an educated, rational and moderate man. The *Ecclesiastical History* is not only the record of most of what we shall ever know of a century or more of English history, but a monument to the extraordinary skill and power of Bede.[96]

[96] I am very grateful to Mr M. W. Fredericksen, Mrs B. Mitchell and Mr J. M. Wallace-Hadrill for reading a draft of this paper and for their helpful comments. For a note on more recent work on Bede see pp. 47–8 below.

1. Frontispiece of the Codex Amiatinus, produced at Wearmouth or Jarrow before 716. *(Florence, Biblioteca Medicea-Laurenziana, MS. Amiatinus I, f. 4)*

2

Bede II

Bede was born about 673 and died in 735. He entered the monastery of Monkwearmouth (Wearmouth), in Northumbria, at the age of seven, and the remainder of his life was spent there and in the sister monastery of Jarrow. Today he is famous chiefly as the historian of the conversion of England. But he also wrote on almost every other branch of Christian learning; in his own day, and for long afterwards, his commentaries on the Bible and his treatises on chronology and other subjects were as much valued as his history.

It is remarkable that the most notable scholar the Western Church produced at that time should have lived in Northumbria, nearly at the extremity of the known world, and that he should have sprung from a people who had very recently been pagan and illiterate. In Bede's day, although most of the churches of Europe were very old, the English church was very new. In Gaul, Italy and Spain, Christianity survived the fall of the Roman Empire and won over the barbarian conquerors. But the English (Anglo-Saxon) people who, after the departure of the Romans in the early fifth century, occupied the southern and eastern parts of Britain, for long remained pagan and little affected by Roman civilisation.

Christianity had been quite strongly established in Britain while the Romans ruled there. It survived the Roman evacuation, in those areas of the west and north where the native British population remained free from Anglo-Saxon rule. The Christian Britons seem to have made little attempt to convert the invaders, Christianity was brought to the Anglo-Saxons by missionaries from overseas, most of them Italians or Irishmen.

The first mission of which we know is that of Augustine, who arrived from Rome in 597. He established Christianity in Kent, and he and his Italian followers attempted to convert other kingdoms. Their success was limited and insecure. For a generation the fate of Christianity among the Anglo-Saxons hung in the balance. Thereafter the faith spread quickly and prospered. By 660 it was established in nearly every kingdom. This success was due largely to the efforts of Irish misssionaries. Christianity had flourished in Ireland from the fifth century, and by the end of the sixth the Irish church was becoming notable both for its learning and for its missionary enterprise. The most important Irish mission to England was that led by Aidan, who came to

Northumbria in 635 from the Irish monastery of Iona, off the west coast of Scotland. Aidan founded the monastery of Lindisfarne in Northumbria. From this base the Irish evangelised Northumbria and much of the English Midlands. At the same time the Roman missionaries based in Canterbury remained active in the southeast; a few years previously they had even made an attempt to convert Northumbria, though with only temporary success. Meanwhile other missionaries, owing allegiance neither to Canterbury nor to Iona, appeared elsewhere in England.

Thus by 660 Christianity had been very successful in England; but English Christians were not united in reorganising a common ecclesiastical authority. Some acknowledged the authority of the archbishop of Canterbury in England and that of the Pope over the whole church. Others looked to Lindisfarne and to Iona. It may well be that some elements in the church recognised no superior authority at all. Before long, all were to recognise the supremacy of Canterbury and of Rome.

In 664 the Irish church in Northumbria accepted the Roman mode of calculating Easter, and an important cause of disunity was thus removed. Even more significant in the unification of the English church was the influence of the pontificate of Theodore, archbishop of Canterbury from 668 to 690. Theodore was a native of Asia Minor and about sixty-seven years old when he arrived in England. Despite these disadvantages he established the authority of Canterbury over all the other English sees. Other great changes came about at the same time. Centres of learning grew up at Canterbury and elsewhere, and many new monasteries were founded. The English church, which had been largely directed by foreign missionaries, became a native one, nearly all of whose bishops were English. By the end of the century the English were themselves sending missionaries to western Germany.

Bede's own monastery of Monkwearmouth-Jarrow played an important part in this prosperous and revolutionary period. Founded in 674 by Benedict Biscop, a Northumbrian nobleman, it was distinguished by its learning, its close connections with Rome and Canterbury, and its size. Its founder endowed it with a great library. A frequent visitor to Rome, he was closely associated with Theodore and was for a time abbot of the monastery of St Peter and St Paul in Canterbury. By 716 his foundation held six hundred or more monks. Monkwearmouth-Jarrow was outstanding among the monasteries of Northumbria, and there were few which could rival it in the whole of England.

Bede's work reflects the exceptional circumstances of his house. Its library enabled him to become very learned. The study of the literature of pagan Greece and Rome was unimportant for him, although he had access to at least a few of the Latin classics. His learning was in

Christian Latin literature, whose core was the works of the Latin Fathers: Ambrose, Jerome, Augustine, Gregory. This literature presented an account of God, of man, and of the universe which was complete, unified, and satisfying. Thanks to its double inheritance from Judaism and from Greece and Rome, Christianity had developed an intricate and sophisticated intellectual system. Centred on the elaborate interpretation of the Bible to reveal many layers of meaning, it established relationships between every kind of knowledge and showed how all proclaimed the same divine truths. By Bede's time few could read this literature with full understanding. Literacy was rare and unbroken traditions of learning much rarer. There were learned men in the seventh century, especially in Spain and Ireland, but they were not numerous – though it is true that we can learn much more easily of the minority of scholars who wrote than of the majority who simply read. During the Dark Ages Christianity might have lost its theology and have become for all what it became for nearly all: a collection of rituals, precepts, and crude arguments. That it survived as more than the barbarized detritus of a religion is thanks to the preservation of the Christian learning of the later Roman Empire and its continued study, however faltering and by however few. The continuance of that tradition was much more important in the intellectual history of Europe than the incidental preservation of the classics. Bede played an important part in continuing it. His wide range of works rested heavily upon, and was intended to transmit, the learning of his predecessors.

As a historian Bede found his models and sources in the histories written by Christians in and after the fourth century. Three features of Christian historiography should be noticed. First, it owed very little to the great historians of Greece and Rome. As Arnaldo Momigliano has written, 'No real Christian historiography founded upon the political experience of Herodotus, Thucydides, Livy and Tacitus was transmitted to the Middle Ages.' The Christian historians made a fresh start in new genres, and the change was not necessarily for the worse. Second, there was no clear division between history and theology. All knowledge was knowledge of God. Few, if any, learned men specialised in history and certainly Bede did not. Most histories were written by men who also wrote on other aspects of divine learning. Third, there were several kinds of Christian history, and the different genres were kept fairly distinct from one another. One author writing in two different genres can give very different impressions of himself.

Bede wrote in most of the historical genres known to him. The contrast between two of them may be seen by comparing his chronicles with his *Life of St Cuthbert*. His work in one genre is terse, packed with facts, and dry; in the other it is discursive, not containing so much as a date, and very readable. Bede wrote two chronicles, a short one which formed part of his book *On the Measurements of Time* (703) and a longer and better one which was included in *On the Computation of Time* (725). Chronicles were little more than lists of dates and events. Bede's short chronicle is an extreme example. A typical passage is this:

The third age contains 942 years. Abraham came into Canaan at the age of 75. At the age of 100 Abraham begat Isaac. For he first begat Ishmael, from whom the Ishmaelites. Isaac at the age of 60 begat Jacob. The kingdom of the Argives begins. Jacob begat Joseph at the age of 90. Memphis in Egypt founded. Joseph lived for ninety years. Greece began to have crops under Argos. The captivity of the Hebrews for 147 years. Cecrops founded Athens. Moses ruled Israel for forty years. Sparta founded . . .

Such works seem neither enlightening nor agreeable to the modern reader. Nevertheless they were very important in Christian historiography. The genre was established by Eusebius, bishop of Cæsarea (*c*.260–*c*.340), and thereafter numerous chronicles were compiled. They indicate one of the consequences of the spread of Christianity in the Roman world. Educated Christians knew two traditions of world history, one pagan and the other Christian and Jewish. Chronicles correlated the two so that the reader might learn, for example, what was happening to the Jews at the time of the foundation of Rome. One of the great distinctions between pagan and Christian scholars in history, as in much else, was that the Christians knew more, or thought they did; and they had a philosophy which enabled them to interpret all they knew. For example, the Bible afforded data which made it possible to calculate the date of the Creation.

More important, a chronicle, in summarising the whole history of the world, made it possible to display it as a Providential design. This could be done in various ways, but Bede was chiefly attracted by the doctrine of the Ages of the World. Each of his two chronicles was written as part of the chapter on Ages in a treaties on chronology. The history of the world so far was divided into six ages. Each corresponded to one of the six ages of a man's life and also to one of the days of Creation as described in Genesis. The sixth age had begun with the birth of Christ, and its termination would mark the end of the world. Bizarre though this theory now sounds, its comprehensiveness in establishing connections between the life of man, the course of history, creation, and judgement made it a very powerful one. Bede's concern with the exact length of each of the ages made him very careful about dates, and he was the first to correct the biblical chronology of Eusebius. The purpose of such a chronicle as Bede's first one was simply to sketch the history of the world in accordance with a Providential interpretation. His much fuller second chronicle shows how easily such a work could do more than this by serving as a vehicle for almost any kind of historical information.

The Life of St Cuthbert, which Bede wrote in about 720, is in a very different genre, that of hagiography. It consists almost entirely of beautifully told miracle stories and does not reveal even when its hero was born or when he died. Books of this kind were numerous and more influential than any other kind of history, if they can be called history. They derive from great changes which came about in the Christian church in and after the fourth century. In the third century, belief in contemporary, as opposed to biblical, miracles was not widespread, at least among the sophisticated. Belief in the frequent intervention of God to produce physical miracles and in the omnipresence of devils and angels became much more common from the fourth century. It seems to have been associated with the spread of monasticism from the east. Monks and miracles (together may have changed the Church as much as the Reformation did when it sought to expel them) came in together. One book, *The Life of St Anthony* by Athanasius, was of great importance in the proliferation. Written in about 360 (in Greek, but soon translated into Latin), it describes the life of Anthony, who lived as a hermit in Egypt until his death in 356. It is simply an account of virtues and marvels, vividly told. As the kind of Christianity which Athanasius described spread, so did imitations of his book. Such lives of the saints differed from one another in various respects but in general conformed to type. They record in some detail the circumstances of their subject's early life, his conversion to religion, his godly conduct, and the manner in which he died. Their main concern is not mundane details, but spiritual triumphs: the cures the saint wrought, the devils he put to flight. Hagiographers were often careful to state their evidence, as Bede does. The more remarkable the story, the more desirable it was that it should be supported. Such statements are not necessarily evidence of scholarly care, but went with this genre of writing. Saints' lives were for edification rather than for record (they were often read out, in whole or in part, on the saint's day), and their authors looked more to the effect they would have in the future than to what had actually happened in the past. Bede's *Life of St Cuthbert* is a typical and very skilful piece of hagiography. He took a previous 'Life of Cuthbert' by an anonymous monk, rewrote it, and modified it in certain respects, inserting additional miracles and giving a much longer account of Cuthbert's death. When he wrote in other genres he displayed great interest in facts and in detailed information. In writing this life he gave fewer facts, particularly topographical facts, than did his source.

Bede's greatest work, *The Ecclesiastical History of the English People*, completed in 731 or 732, represents yet another genre of Christian historiography. Its title recalls that of its model, *The Ecclesiastical History* of Eusebius. In this work Eusebius described the history of the Church from apostolic times until about 325. He sought to relate all the main events in the life of the Church, saying something of the outstanding Christians of each generation. Particular care was taken to record the succession of bishops in the principal sees, the details of heretics and heresies, persecutions and the passions of martyrs. As in his *Chronicle* so in his *History*, Eusebius was the father of a new kind of historiography. His works was distinguished from those of pagan historians not only by its content but also by its methods, in particular by his extensive citation of sources and his inclusion of many original documents. Here, too, Christian scholarship broke new ground. Bede sought to do for the church of England what Eusebius had done for the whole, and his *Ecclesiastical History* much resembles his predecessor's in content and in method.

Bede knew at least two other Christian histories of importance – *The Seven Books Against the Pagans* by Orosius and *The History of the Franks* by Gregory of Tours. They have to be considered beside his *Ecclesiastical History* not so much because of their contribution to it as because of their contrast with it. Orosius wrote his book in 417 to 418; it described and interpreted the history of mankind from the Creation to his own day and was intended as a riposte to those who accounted for the fall of Rome by pointing to the rise of Christianity. Orosius collected catastrophes and misfortunes to show that God had smitted the pagans hard, often, and deservedly. His own times he argued to be better. For him, history fell into a pattern, that of the Four Empires: Babylon, Macedonia, Carthage, and Rome. The history of each of them had followed a similar course; Rome and Babylon were especially alike, and 'the number seven by which all things are decided' was demonstrated to have been very important for both. The last empire, that of Rome, was shown to have been established by God in preparation for the advent of Christ. Orosius's scheme of explanation was crude, if elaborate. But his work was orthodox and popular, and his large store of information was drawn on by many, including Bede. Bede also followed him in beginning his work with a geographical introduction. He did not follow him in imposing a pattern upon history. For Orosius, Providence worked like a machine. Bede shows God's purpose and judgment always at work, but makes little attempt to schematize them.

Bede was not the first Christian historian to write on the history of one people. The only such national historian whose work was certainly known to him was Gregory of Tours (*c*.540–594). Gregory's history was in a sense an ecclesiastical history and has resemblances to Bede's. But it is his contrast with Bede which impresses. Gregory's work is very much that of a bishop of Tours, a great man who participated in great events. He provides a detailed, scandalous, and vivid account of affairs to indicate the power of St Martin and how he watched over his own see of Tours. Bede was very much more detached. His concern was to omit secular affairs and any kind of scandal. His descriptions of the miraculous are not intended to exalt his own monastery, and he makes no attempt to demonstrate that saints protect their shrines and followers in secular affairs. The temper of his work is entirely different from Gregory's, and the comparison brings home to us that one of the most remarkable things about *The Ecclesiastical History* is the number of things which one would expect an eighth century historian to say which Bede does *not* say.

In writing *The Ecclesiastical History* Bede looked back then to Eusebius and to the beginnings of Christian historiography. There are, indeed, important differences between his work and that of his predecessor. There is nothing in Eusebius to correspond with the geographical and historial introduction to his subject which Bede provides in the first book of *The Ecclesiastical History*. Bede's continual concern with the miraculous reflects a religious climate unlike that in which Eusebius wrote. Bede had to pay more attention to secular affairs, partly because the fortunes of Christianity were more closely involved with those of secular powers than they had been in the early days of the Church, and partly because Bede, and his sources, were more concerned than was Eusebius to emphasise the judgments of God on good and bad rulers. Furthermore, Bede is more concerned to be directly edifying, to use history to teach particular moral lessons. Nevertheless, Bede's history is, as its title implies, modelled on that of Eusebius. Its dominant concern is the same: to describe the principal events in the history of the Church, the succession of its bishops, its heresies, and its saints. His technique, in particular his extensive use of documents, often cited verbatim, also derives from Eusebius. Many of his virtues are those of his model.

Bede's account of the history of his church often leaves the reader admiring, but baffled. It is not hard to understand why *The Ecclesiastical History* should have become famous. Important and interesting events are described, and often made moving, by an extremely accomplished storyteller. Bede's citation of sources, his care with dates, and his inclusion of many documents argue his reliability. The impression is reinforced by his calm and moderate tone. Bede seems both pious and sound and has to a high degree the power of conviction. Nevertheless, *The Ecclesiastical History* seems oddly diverse and incomplete. The narrative of events is constantly broken by accounts of miracles and visions. Sometimes Bede rambles, as in the fifth book where, having mentioned Adomnan, abbot of Iona, he proceeds to devote two chapters to extracts from Adomnan's book on the Holy Places. Disproportionate space seems to be given to controversy over the date of Easter. Surprisingly little is said about Bede's own time, about which one would suppose him to have known most. His book seems a disjointed series of stories and documents held together by an accomplished style.

The unevenness of Bede's narrative is partly to be explained by the nature of his sources and by the way in which he used them. He was able to use the work of earlier historians for the first book, which describes the history of Britain from the time of Julius Cæsar until the coming of Augustine. In spite of the active search for materials, which he describes in his Preface, it was not easy for him to find them for more recent times. It was not normal in the seventh century for churches, let alone kingdoms, to keep records of their doings. Bede probably had some scanty annals from Kent and Northumbria, and a few royal genealogies and lists recording the lengths of the reigns of kings. For the most part, he was dependent on letters, chiefly from Rome, on a handful of saints' lives, and on numerous but doubtfully reliable oral traditions. He did not feel it to be his duty to criticise his sources as a modern historian would (although his theological work shows that he could have been acute in such criticism). The true law of history is, he says, simply to gather and record for the benefit of posterity such stories as are in circulation. It was a new experience for Bede to write a book on a subject about which no one had written before. His inclination was to follow what others had written, and the result was patchwork. Where we know what his sources were, and they have survived, he can be seen often to have followed them word for word, or very nearly so. This is the case in, for example I, xvii–xx, which comes from the life of St Germanus by Constantius, and in III, xix, which comes from an anonymous life of Fursey. One wonders how far Bede treated in the same way those of his sources which are unknown to us, and whether *The Ecclesiastical History* was not written by first establishing a chronological framework and then hanging to it by such verbal hooks as 'At that time', 'In the meantime', such materials as came to hand, frequently in the form in which they came to hand.

Nevertheless, it will not do to dismiss *The Ecclesiastical History* as no more than a collection of materials. Bede was both selective and subtle. His principles of selection were largely those of Eusebius. For example, like Eusebius he gave particular attention to heresy. But while Eusebius had had numerous heresies to record, Bede had to deal with only one heresy, Pelagianism, and one error, the adherence of some of the Celtic churches to the wrong mode of calculating the date of Easter.

Bede has a long account of the Easter controversy in each of the last four books of his history. It is at first sight not easy to understand why he should have given so much attention to what appears to us as a merely technical issue; for the practice of the Celts seems to have been simply that which had been used elsewhere in the past but which had become superseded. But Bede makes it very clear that the calculation of the date of Easter was not merely a technical or isolated issue. The movement of Easter was one of many things which argument in terms of symbols (as we would say, but *symbol* is for us a limiting word, *mysteries* they would say) showed to be loaded with significance. Easter had to be just at the equinox, for the lengthening days represented Christ's triumph over the powers of darkness. It had to be in the first month of the lunar year, for this was the month in which the world had been created and in which it ought to be newly created. It had to be as the moon was about to wane, for the moon turns from earth toward the sun as it wanes, just as we should turn from earthly to heavenly things. It was appropriate that Easter should always fall within a space of seven days, for seven was a number of divine significance. Considered from another point of view, Easter was to be calculated in such a way as to fulfil both the Old Law of the Jews and the New Law of Christ. If it was celebrated at exactly the right time, then all was in harmony. Nothing can illustrate the gulf between Bede's thought-world and ours more vividly than his views on Easter. Such views were not simple popular piety. They formed part of an elaborate and not unsophisticated system of thought, which brought all knowledge into unity and to divine ends, and whose power depended on the capacity to see an allegory as a mysterious truth rather than as an illustration or a coincidence. Divergence between churches on such a matter as Easter was not a trivial matter. It was a rent in the seamless garment, and it is not surprising that Bede, who was by far the most learned man of his day on computation, should have devoted much of his history to this issue.

Bede's concern was not just to record certain kinds of information and to refute certain kinds of error. His Preface emphasises that his concern is to edify, to describe the good so that it may be followed and the bad so that it may be shunned. *The Ecclesiastical History* was probably intended for a wider audience than were most of Bede's works, and is dedicated to a king. In his account of good kings (and no laymen other than kings have more than an incidental role), Bede shows how virtue was rewarded here and now as well as hereafter. It was not only heavenly but also earthly kingdoms which Oswald and Edwin gained. There are passages in which he makes his point in a way that is forceful to the point of crudity. He shows that just as those who adhered to the faith did well, so did those who abandoned it fail. Edwin, who brought Christianity to Northumbria, lived in unexampled peace and prosperity. His apostate successors perished miserably and soon. Nevertheless, Bede prefers to dwell upon the rewards of the good rather than on the punishments of the bad. Cadwallon, king of the Britons, is condemned in strong language, but briefly, and his violent and merited death is not dwelt upon. Even Penda, the pagan terror of England in the middle of the seventh century, is treated only incidentally, and Bede attributes worthy sentiments to him. There is no long account of any bad Christian king; indeed, no Christian English kings are said to have been bad, though one or two royal crimes are mentioned.

It is remarkable of Bede's picture of Providence at work in politics that, while he is clear that a causal connection between virtue and success was easy to observe, he makes little effort to explain the whole course of English history in Providential terms and to show God's rewards and punishments to whole peoples. He might, in the manner of Orosius, have chosen to show the pagan Saxon period as one of disaster and misery. In fact, he had almost nothing to say about it – though perhaps he did not know enough to say more. On only two occasions does he elaborate on the punishment visited in this world upon a sinful nation: in his account of Britain after the departure of the Romans and in the story of how the Britons were punished for not yielding to Augustine. In the first instance, his account and its emphasis came straight from the sixth century British historian Gildas, in the second, from some lost source. Although he adopted such views when they occurred in his sources, he makes almost no independent attempt to show that the Britons suffered for their persistence in the errors he detested. The opportunity was there. He could have described the great conquests made in the late seventh century by the West Saxons at the expense of the Britons, and have presented them as those of God's chosen people, accurate in their Easter reckonings. Instead, he merely mentions the subjugation of some of the Britons and associates it with their errors, very briefly, in V, xxiii. Similarly, although, as we know from his *Letter to Egbert*, he disapproved of much that went on in the Church in his own day, he does not elaborate on this in his history and draw the moral that punishment was at hand, as some historians would have done. Instead, Bede says nothing at all in his history about the sins of the Church, but emphasises the peacefulness of his own times in England. Even so, he does not say that the acceptance of Christianity and orthodoxy have brought peace and prosperity. If the connection is made it is by implication, and there are undertones of disquiet. Unlike many of his predecessors, he found it hard to see a clear pattern in God's judgments except where individuals were conerned. He is more reserved, less vehement, perhaps more troubled.

If the *Ecclesiastical History* has many lessons for the laity, it has more for the clergy. One of its principal functions is to set them good examples. Bede's account of what the church of England had been in the past is affected by his judgment of what it was and what it ought to have been in his own day. In *The Ecclesiastical History* Bede has very little to say about events in England after 690, and he does not make his views on the contemporary church explicit. But, thanks to the preservation of his *Letter to Egbert*, written to the bishop of York in 734, we know that some of them were unfavourable. The conduct of bishops, monks, priests, and laity all left much to be desired. Avarice, neglect, and ignorance were all too prevalent. His biblical commentaries shed further light on his attitudes. They showed him to have held strict views on the proper conduct of the clergy, and in particular on clerical poverty. How rich the clergy may properly be was, and remains, a subject for argument. Bede was adamant that they ought to be poor. Granted Bede's preference for praising the good rather than denouncing the bad, and his belief, made quite clear in his commentaries, that it is wrong publicly to denounce the clergy, be they never so wicked, it seems that his reticence in his history on the recent past of his church is largely to be explained by his disapproval of some of its members and their acts.

Modern knowledge of the early eighth century church is very incomplete, but the sources suffice to give some idea of those aspects of its life to which Bede objected. Some bishops had become powerful in the things of this world. Such a bishop as Wilfrid was wealthy in land, in treasure, and in followers. Bede says bishops levied dues from every village in their dioceses, and there is other evidence indicating that the church had significant power to tax. There is some reason to suppose that bishops exercised considerable jurisdiction over laymen. When Bede says that Wine bought the see of London in about 666 (III, vii) it is a fair deduction that episcopal office was already remunerative. Such examples of clerical power can easily be paralleled on the Continent. But there bishops had been established for centuries, had inherited power from the days of the Empire, and had added to it as the Empire collapsed. In England some bishops seemed to have gained a comparable position for themselves, having started with nothing. From Bede's point of view much was amiss with monasteries also. Monasteries were numerous, but were often treated as the hereditary property of the founder's family, and the fiscal advantages of monastic tenure seem to have led to the foundation of monasteries which were such in name only. This is not to say that Bede disapproved of all that went on in the church in his day, and we can see that if some elements in it were worldly others were rigidly pious, as he was. The codes of penances and secular laws of the period indicate a desire (there is no means of telling how far it was fulfilled) to make the Christian English observe the letter of a strict law. For example, 'If a freeman works on Sunday without his lord's command he is to lose his freedom.' Piety is not inconsistent with wealth, nor indeed are strict laws inconsistent with avarice, but it is likely that there were many like Bede who were both pious and unworldly. The English church was not only prosperous but diverse, containing Christians at very different levels of sophistication and, one may guess, sophisticated Christians whose views varied widely. It was faced with the opportunities and problems which occur when an ertswhile missionary church becomes part of society and changes its nature as it changes that of society.

If *The Ecclesiastical History* is read in the light of Bede's views on the church in his own day, it can be seen to be (among other things) an implicit commentary on it. In setting good examples from the past, Bede is especially concerned with bishops. Monks and monasteries are not neglected, but his long accounts are nearly all of bishops, and he has surprisingly little to say even of his own monastery. Bede's first account of a model bishop is that of Augustine in I, xxvi. Augustine is said to have lived in accordance with the mode of the Primitive Church in devotion, in poverty, in steadfastness, in practising what he preached. Emphasis on the same virtues recurs in Bede's accounts of later bishops such as Aidan, Chad, and Cuthbert. He lays particular stress on poverty. Pope Gregory told Augustine that he ought to live with his followers with all things in common as in the Primitive Church, and Bede later adopts this statement in describing Hilda. He admired a humble way of life, and points out that the bishops of the Celtic church preferred to walk rather than to ride – though Theodore made Chad ride in order to get about his diocese. The virtues of such men were in obvious contrast to the grasping bishops of his own day, to whose jolly parties he refers in *The Letter to Egbert*. Aidan's way of life was, he says, very different from the idleness of our days. In describing Cuthbert's reception when he went about preaching, he says that in those days people flocked to the preacher. The implication is that in his own day they did not.

Bede treats different bishops in different ways. For Aidan we have some account of the events of his life, a eulogy of the way in which he lived it, and a collection of miracles, for John of Hexham, miracles and almost nothing else; for Theodore a long account of his deeds, nothing of his way of life, and no miracles at all. It is possible to explain these striking differences as the reflection of the differences between Bede's sources and of Bede's difference to his sources. Bede was not concerned, one may think, to give a methodical account of the lives of each of these men, but simply inserted such useful and edifying material as he could find. Such an explanation is valid but not complete. Bede compiled where a modern historian would have edited, but he edited where a modern historian would have compiled.

The extent to which Bede was capable of editing his material in such a way as to exclude the unedifying may be seen from his treatment to Wilfrid. Most of what Bede says in *The Ecclesiastical History* is beyond criticism insofar as we have no other source describing the same events. But a contemporary biography of Wilfrid, probably by his follower Eddius, has survived, and it affords a rare opportunity of comparing Bede's treatment of a subject with that of another man, less able but also less discreet. An early supporter of Roman orthodoxy in Northumbria, Wilfrid was an active founder of monasteries, a successful missionary and, from 669, a bishop in Northumbria. His career was stormy. He seems to have hoped to make himself supreme over the church in the north, and so fell out with successive kings of Northumbria and archbishops of Canterbury. In spite of several periods of exile and one of imprisonment, he survived and prospered. Eddius was a very dutiful biographer and shows the great bishop in all his glory: ascetic, brave, and always right. His holiness was made evident by miracles. At the same time it is made clear that Wilfrid was rich and determined to preserve his riches, and his style of life seems to have been much like that of a great secular lord. His deathbed as described by Eddius is extremely instructive and very different from anything Bede tells us of a bishop. He divided his property into several shares. One of these was to reward the men who had followed him into exile and to whom he had not given land; they sound very like a *comitatus*, a band of warriors who followed a great lord. Part of his treasure was to go to his monastries to purchase the favour of kings and bishops. Never in his history does Bede give us to understand that a bishop might have a *comitatus* or a treasure, still less that there were bishops whose favour might be bought. His *Letter to Egbert* suggests that he knew perfectly well that such things happened, and two passages in the *Life of St Cuthbert* associate being made a bishop with becoming wealthy. But he did not regard such matters as a subject for history. It is nearly certain that Bede had Eddius's *Life of Wilfrid*, at least by the time he came to write V, xix; but he uses Eddius with discretion, and his survey of Wilfrid's career is very carefully edited. Nothing is said of Wilfrid's wealth and style of life. His quarrels are treated very discreetly; his imprisonment is not mentioned; his conflicts with other bishops are barely touched upon; a whole council is omitted. In describing such an edifying episode as the conversion of Sussex, Bede attributes near-miraculous powers to Wilfrid, but he relates none of the miracles which Eddius describes to show how God fought on Wilfrid's side in his struggle for episcopal power.

In the light of Bede's treatment of Wilfrid one begins to wonder about his account of Archbishop Theodore. He gives just a hint that he may not have approved of all Theodore's doings when he praises a bishop whom Theodore deposed (IV, vi). Although he usually refers to Theodore as 'of blessed memory', he has nothing to say of his personal holiness or of his way of life. No miracles are attributed to him. It is slightly surprising that Bede, who is willing to supply fifty-four lines of verse on an abbess about whom he has already had a good deal to say (IV, xx), should abbreviate the epitaph of so important a man as Theodore (V, viii). Can it be that he did not think well of all that Theodore did, and did the middle of the epitaph describe something of which he disapproved? The problem is typical of those which arise when Bede's history is analysed. Three kinds of answer are possible. First, it may be that the contrast between his treatment of Theodore and that of some other bishops simply reflects differences between his sources. In particular, the absence of miracles seems characteristic of Bede's Canterbury sources. He describes very few miracles performed by the archbishops or by other members of the Roman church in Kent. Second, it may be that the selection of material for his book was partly determined by incidental reasons of space, time, or chance. Either of these explanations could account for the nature of his treatment of Theodore. But they do not exclude the third, which is that he may have edited his sources, suppressing or abbreviating that which he found unedifying.

For all the superficial simplicity of *The Ecclesiastical History* it is not a simple book. Bede was a very intelligent, learned, and devout man, dealing with subjects which were very difficult (difficult not only because of deficiency of information, but because of the religious problems involved) and according to strongly held principles which were not always quite consistent with one another. The nature of his difficulties and some of the explanation of his power to move may be seen in his treatment of miracles. *The Ecclesiastical History* is full of miracles and visions. Their number may surprise the modern reader, but it is not hard to explain. They may be considered as the equivalent of Eusebius's account of the passions of martyrs. Bede sometimes tells us why he puts a particular story in; it will, he says, be useful (meaning spiritually useful) to his readers. A large part of what sources he had consisted of miracle stories. For all these reasons much of *The Ecclesiastical History* is hagiographical in style, content, and method. Wonder follows wonder. Now recent and contemporary (as opposed to biblical) miracles had for long raised severe difficulties for the thinking Christian. In sophisticated milieux there was the problem of incredulity. On the other side there was the danger (perhaps a worse one) of an endless hunger for the miraculous. Pope Gregory the Great warned more than once (for example, in the letter copied out in I, xxi) that not all saints performed miracles, that miracles could be performed by the wicked, that virtues were more important than wonders. Bede repeats his warnings. Yet both Gregory and Bede retail endless miracles. 'They seem to speak with two voices'. The difficulty may have been greater for Bede than it was for Gregory, for Bede lived among barbarian Christians and barbarised Christianity was largely a matter of wonders.

Although Bede was a devout believer in miracles and an assiduous collector of miracle stories, nevertheless he seems to have been selective in what he included in *The Ecclesiastical History*. A high proportion of the miracles he recorded there are the kind which are susceptible of a natural explanation, particularly miracles of healing. Clearly, he was not at all concerned to explain miracles away; but he does seem to have preferred to avoid the more flabbergasting of them. There are several analogues of scriptural miracles, but he never gives an instance of the raising of the dead. His miracles are usually to demonstrate the saintliness of a particular person or to reinforce some teaching. They are not random wonders. None has any political force; they do not demonstrate how God defended the rights of a particular shrine or of a particular man in a merely worldly struggle. In all these respects Bede is in sharp contrast to most of those who described miracles.

Perhaps the most influential collection of miracle stories was Gregory the Great's *Dialogues*. Bede knew this book and his style of narration may well owe something to it. But the differences between Bede and Gregory are more instructive than the similarities. Some of Gregory's miracles are brutal. For example, he tells of an unfortunate man who was struck dead because his playing on the cymbals disturbed a bishop at prayer. Others are trumpery, as in the case of Bishop Boniface's clearing his garden, by Divine aid, of caterpillars: 'I adjure you in the name of Our Lord Christ, depart and stop eating those vegetables.' It is fair to say that some of the animal miracles which Bede relates to Cuthbert, but only of Cuthbert, are not very different from this tale, though much more impressively told. But his miracles are never brutal and rarely have the anecdotal triviality of many of Gregory's.

Bede's stories contrast even more strongly with those of Gregory of Tours and other Frankish writers. A recurrent theme in Gregory of Tours is the defence of the interests of Tours by God and St Martin. There is nothing of this kind in Bede. In *The Ecclesiastical History* we never meet such common incidents of life in the Dark Ages as the alleged intervention of saints to protect their shrines and followers against all comers, or violent struggles for the possession of the body of a saint and the useful protection which was thought to come with it. It could be that such things did not happen in England. But this is unlikely and there is some evidence to the contrary. It is much more likely that Bede belonged to a school of thought which was uneasy about such aspects of Christianity among the barbarians and did not think it appropriate to record them. He tended to omit just the kinds of miracles and just the kinds of incident which most jar modern taste. There are exceptions to this. In particular, his accounts of visions of the next world indicate a harshness in his religion, which his preference for describing the good rather than the base generally conceals.

Selective though Bede was, his deference to his sources sometimes led him to introduce material which differs considerably in tone and emphasis from anything he himself wrote. This is most obvious in a comparison of the doctrinal disputes which he records in *The Ecclesiastical History*. His description of the repulse of Pelagianism by Germanus comes almost verbatim from Constantius's *Life of Germanus*. This is a fine example of a hagiographer's view of a theological dispute. We are informed simply that the heretics filled the air with empty words, whereupon the venerable prelates poured forth the flood of their apostolical and evangelical discourse and made them confess their errors to the cheers of the audience. Reasoning was of little significance to Constantius. What mattered most was divine demonstrations that Germanus was right: he could vanquish demons, work cures, and win victories. The account in Bede of Augustine's meeting with the Britons (II, ii) is in a similar vein. The power to cure is used as the touchstone of orthodoxy – 'Let some sick man be brought'. This account probably came straight to Bede from a source lost to us. Very different indeed is Bede's account of the later progress of the Easter controversy, which is almost certainly much more his own work, and where we do not find miracles, devils, and cures, but solid and lucid arguments.

Thus Germanus, as described by Constantius, appears as a thaumaturge, not much above the level of a witch doctor; while Wilfrid, in his defence, as Bede describes it, of the Roman Easter, and Ceolfrith, in his letter to Nechtan, appear as the intellectual heirs of the Fathers and ultimately of the civilised learning of Greece and Rome. Germanus was debating subjects which are still thought important and probably always will be: the problems of sin and grace. Constantius's account disregards the issues and debases the subject. The protagonists of the Roman Easter were fighting for a cause which not even Rome now cares about. Bede's account of the case is so skilful that he exalts it to a point where one can almost believe it matters. Bede could, had he wished to do so, have put able arguments against Pelagianism into Germanus's mouth. He chose simply to take over Constantius's account: it was edifying, unexceptionable, and he was bound to give it simple faith. The unevenness of *The Ecclesiastical History* is partly due to Bede's devout acceptance of Christianity as it was expressed at different levels of sophistication.

If *The Ecclesiastical History* is much affected by the nature of Bede's sources it should be possible to see him more by himself in his account of the abbots of his own monastery, *The Lives of the Abbots*. This did not belong, as did most of his other works, to a more or less established genre, though another monk of Bede's monastery had written a *Life of Ceolfrith* which Bede used and which much resembles his own work in style and in content. It is the style of *The Lives of the Abbots* which first impresses the reader. Bede's extreme skill in emotive description can nowhere be better seen than in his accounts of the deaths of Benedict and Eosterwine, and of the departure of Ceolfrith. In using the work of his anonymous predecessor, he sometimes made an addition to heighten the pathos as, for example, when in saying that some of Ceolfrith's followers stayed beside his tomb at Langres, he adds that they were among a people not even whose language they knew. The book is in strong contrast with the *Life of St Cuthbert* in including numerous facts and no miracles. Bede supplies a remarkable amount of information about the property and buildings of the abbey, and much chronological detail. There are many edifying stories, but not a single miracle. What little there is of the miraculous in the anonymous life of

Coelfrith is excluded. Bede does not say, as the Anonymous does, that his body remained uncorrupted and a light shone above it, and that miracles were reported at his tomb.

It may be that Bede did not regard this as the kind of book in which miracles were to be recorded. But no abbot or monk of Monkwearmouth-Jarrow is credited with miraculous powers in *The Ecclesiastical History* either; perhaps the relgous atmosphere there was different from that at Lindisfarne or at Barking. As in *The Ecclesiastical History* Bede's purpose in *The Lives of the Abbots* is continuously didactic: only here he is showing the way to monks and abbots rather than to bishops and kings. Humbleness and simplicity are again emphasised. He is very concerned that it should be understood that the abbacy was not to descend by hereditary succession (as was common in other abbeys). There is just enough evidence to suggest that, for all the lavish detail of *The Lives of the Abbots*, it is edited to give the right impression. The anonymous life of Ceolfrith says that he once left Jarrow 'because of the jealousies and most violent attacks of certain nobles, who could not endure his regular discipline'. Bede says nothing of this, but it is to be observed that in his account of Eosterwine he is careful to emphasise that he did not expect unusual privileges because he was noble. *The Lives of the Abbots* is unlike *The Ecclesiastical History* in its consistency in style and content and in its exclusion of the miraculous. It is very like it insofar as its purpose is to teach lessons and to do so by dwelling upon the good and saying nothing of the bad.

Any judgment on Bede as an historian must be tempered. We do not know enough about his sources to be able to say even how much of *The Ecclesiastical History* is his in the sense of being more than a selection of stories incorporated much as they came to him. It is impossible to be certain how far there is an element of randomness in its composition. Above all, there are too few other authorities with which to compare him. There is no means of telling whether most of what he says about English history is right or wrong. Our relative ignorance of what the church was like in his own day makes it difficult to assess his attitude and purposes.

Despite the reservations which such difficulties impose, Bede can be seen to be a great historian. Modern historians often praise him because he seems much as they themselves are. Interested in his work mainly as a source, they value those qualities which are thought to vouch for his reliability. Such praise is justified only in part. Bede's greatness comes not only from qualities which would have made him a good historian by modern professional standards, but also from others which would have made him an extremely bad one. Certainly his extensive collection of material and his care for documents and dates make him more reliable than most Dark Age historians. Few, if any, brought such ability and expertise to their task. But to ability and expertise was added high moral purpose and the task Bede set himself was not to describe the history of the English church just as it had happened. It was to describe it in such a way as to illustrate and support the principles of faith and conduct in which he believed. As a consequence *The Ecclesiastical History* is in part an ably constructed record and in part a history idealised to the point of becoming visionary.

Bede was the first important Christian historian to have been a monk. Most of his predecessors had been great men in the secular church. Bede considered events with more detachment or with a different commitment than theirs. His demand for humbleness and poverty among the clergy stands in a tradition which, although always present in the church, had gained new strength with the advent of monasticism from the fourth century. Eusebius had not placed so strong an emphasis on the simple way of life of model bishops. A bishop himself, and basking in the favour of the Emperor Constantine, he had not, perhaps, seen the need so clearly. Bede's views on episcopacy are much more like those of the monk-bishop St Martin of Tours, who, ascetic, devoted, and disheveled, was until his death in 397 an example and something of a threat to the prelates of Gaul. Bede's views on the proper conduct of the clergy made him opposed to much that went on around him. He stood for episcopal poverty and elected abbots at a time when at least some bishops were rich and powerful and some, perhaps many, abbots had inherited their offices. Soaked in the learning of the Fathers, who were very civilised, he lived among barbarian Christians whose beliefs and practices were often crude. Like Gregory the Great, he was both a devout believer in the frequent manifestation of miracles and mistrusted the consquences of that belief in others.

His history of his own church reflects the complications of his position. Characteristically, he looked a long way back for his model. Just as he had written a chronicle when that genre had been disused for nearly a century, so he wrote a history, not in the manner of his more immediate predecessors, but in that of Eusebius. He was too judicious to impose a simple Providential scheme as Orosius had done, and too reserved and discreet to make his work like that of Gregory of Tours, largely an account of recent events with moralising commentary. He chose to infuse his record with his beliefs not in these obvious ways, but by emphasis and selection. He dwelt upon the good and passed lightly over the bad, in particular omitting almost everything that might be to the discredit of the church. Bede's views on the miracles, their importance and their dangers, appear by his insertion of numerous miracle stories and also, I think it fair to assume, by his omission of others of kinds popular with other believers and writers, but distasteful to him. His work is so full of awareness of God that it gives a very strange picture of Man. Bede seems to lack almost all interest in human character except in so far as it could be represented in religious stereotypes. He had no taste for idiosyncracy. While *The Ecclesiastical History* is full of very memorable incidents, there is hardly a character in it who appears in any degree individual. Bede's principles and his caution led him to sheer away from his own times and from the complications and ambiguities of men and events as they really were and are.

These qualities are not those of a good historian in the modern sense. His history reflects not so much the nature of the past he described as his own nature. The impression which his work gives of calm, moderation, and judiciousness is justified. But, while these virtues led him to write history which was more accurate and technically more sophisticated than that of lesser men, they also made it less real and less revealing than theirs. Bede's power of mind, his narrative skill and, one might almost say, his good taste are employed to transmute the past and to carry the reader into a world which was partly of his own creation. Bede's greatness derives partly from the competence and usefulness of his history as record. Even more impressive is the learning, power of mind, and skill with which he made his account of the past a testament to his beliefs and a lesson to his church.

Additional Bibliographical Note

The study of Bede has made considerable progress since the publication of these papers in 1966 and 1968. A new edition of the text has been published by B. Colgrave and R. A. B. Mynors, *Bede's Ecclesiastical History of the English People* (Oxford, 1969). Plummer's text was already a very good one but Mynors's history of the manuscript history is important. The most significant emendation of the accepted text is that of J. O. Prestwich, 'King Aethelhere and the Battle of the Winwaed', *English Historical Review* lxxxiii (1968), pp. 89–95. Admirable guides to Bede's world have been provided by the late Peter Hunter Blair and by Henry Mayr-Harting; for these see chapters 3 and 4 below. Two important collections of essays on Bede are: *Famulus Christi. Essays in Commemoration of the Thirteenth Century of the Birth of the Venerable Bede*, edited by Gerald Bonner (1976) and *Bede and Anglo-Saxon England*, edited by R. T. Farrell (British Archaeological Reports, 46, Oxford, 1978). Among the most significant of fairly numerous articles are the following: J. N. Stevens, 'Bede's Ecclesiastical History', *History*, lxxii (1977), pp. 1–14 (which contains some criticism of what is written above); Roger Ray, 'Bede's Vera Lex Historica', *Speculum* lv (1980), pp. 1–21; H. E. J. Cowdrey, 'Bede and the "English People"', *Journal of Religious History* xi (1981), pp. 501–23; A. A. M. Duncan, 'Bede, Iona and the Picts', in *The Writing of History in the Middle Ages: Essays Presented to Richard William Southern*, ed. R. H. C. Davis and J. M. Wallace-Harting (Oxford, 1981), pp. 1–42; G. Tugène, 'L'histoire "ecclésiastique" du peuple Anglais: réflexions sur le particularisme et l'universalisme chez Bede', *Recherches Augustiniennes*, xvii (1982, pp, 129–72; Jan Davidse, 'The Sense of History in the Works of the Venerable Bede', *Studi Medievali*, 3rd ser. xxiii (1982), pp. 647–95; and the following contributions to *Ideal and Reality in Frankish and Anglo-Saxon Society: Studies Presented to J. M. Wallace-Hadrill*, ed. Patrick Wormald and others (Oxford, 1983); Judith McClure, 'Bede's Old Testament Kings' (pp. 76–98); Patrick Wormald, 'Bede, the *Bretwaldas* and the Origins of the *Gens Anglorum*' (pp. 99–129); Alan Thacker, 'Bede's Ideal of Reform' (pp. 130–53). A number of important studies on Bede and on the insular churches in the seventh and eighth centuries appear in *Peritia*, iii (1984): J. N. Hillgarth, 'Ireland and Spain in the Seventh Century' (pp. 1–16); D. O'Cróinin, 'Rath Melsigi, Willibrord and the earliest Echternach Manuscripts' (pp. 17–49); J.-M. Picard 'Bede, Adomnan and the Writing of History' (pp. 50–70); J. McClure, 'Bede and the Life of Ceolfrid' (pp. 71–84); E. James, 'Bede and the Tonsure Question' (pp. 85–98); M. Richter, 'Bede's *Angli*: Angles or English?' (pp. 99–114); P. Ní Chatháin, 'Bede's Ecclesiastical History in Irish' (pp. 115–30). The study of chronological matters has been much advanced by K. Harrison, *The Framework of Anglo-Saxon History to A.D. 900*, (Cambridge, 1976); and Susan Wood, 'Bede's Northumbrian Dates Again', *English Historical Review*, xcviii (1983, pp. 280–96, settles disputes about Bede's dates which needed settling. D. P. Kirby has made important contributions, in particular, 'King Ceolwulf of Northumbria and the *Historia Ecclesiastica*', *Studia Celtica*, xiv/xv (1979–80), pp. 168–73 and 'Bede, Eddius Stephanus and the Life of Wilfrid', *English Historical Review* xcviii (1983), pp. 101–14. See also G. Musca, *Il Venerabile Beda storico dell'Alto Medioevo* (Bari, 1973). On particular points above it should be noted that weighty arguments now suggest that *Beowulf*, as we have it, cannot be so probably allocated to the eighth century as is suggested above (p. 13) see *The Dating of Beowulf*, ed. Colin Chase (Toronto, 1981).

3

The First Century of Christianity in England

The achievements of the Church in England by the time of Bede (d. 735) are often, and justly, marvelled at. It is a matter for surprise that until last year no scholar had written a book about Bede and his environment. Mr Hunter Blair's recent book has filled that gap, providing a learned and judicious assessment of most aspects of Bede's life and work, apart from his theology.[1] It depends to a very great extent on Bede's own writings. This has to be so, for Bede's works, above all the *Historia Ecclesiastica*, are far and away our best source. But it may be that necessary dependence on Bede for information and justifiable respect for Bede's virtues have led to a tendency among some historians to see the first century of Christianity in England too much as Bede saw it, or rather, as he thought it best that readers of the *Ecclesiastical History* should see it. The merits of Bede's work as a historian are beyond question. He had, nevertheless, to work under great limitations and his purposes differed from those of modern historians. On some subjects he lacked information which, we may fairly assume, he would have liked to include. On others he fails to provide information which he had, but did not feel to be appropriate to the genre in which he was writing. He was concerned to edify, and thought it his duty to say much of the good and little of the bad. Bede did not simply present a straight narrative of events as he knew them, he selected, omitted, and emphasised for reasons some of which can be known, others only guessed at. To say this is, of course, simply to say that he was a historian writing in his own terms for his own world.

Bede's purposes in writing his history led him to under-emphasise, for different reasons, two important aspects of the English Church as it was in his own lifetime. One is the power and wealth of the Church; the other the number of its monasteries. Of some kinds of ecclesiastical power Bede much approved, and he tells us of them, indicating the remarkable extent to which Theodore was able to unite the English Church and to establish some degree of independence of the power of the kings. An aspect of episcopal power which Bede has much less to say about is the wealth of at least some bishops. He was fully aware of the connection between episcopacy and money; but disliked it and so says little of it. His reticence has been imitated by most later historians. Bede seems to have regarded avarice as high among the besetting temptations and sins of

[1] P. Hunter Blair, *The World of Bede* (1970).

bishops. In his letter to Egbert he says that although there were remote villages which had not so much as seen a bishop for years nevertheless not a single one of these places was immune from rendering *tributa* to its neglectful pastor.[2] *Tributum* is referred to in Theodore's *Penitential* where it is indicated that the term was a general one and included tithe and it is stated that it is to be levied according to the custom of the province and is not to be such as to burden the poor, which inclines one to think it was burdening the poor.[3] It is not possible to be positive that any particular clause in the *Penitential* refers to English conditions. The same objection does not apply to clause 61 of Ine's laws:

Church-scot is to be paid from the haulm and the hearth where one resides at midwinter.[4]

Not only had the Church in England established something like a right to tax, but it seems to have been concerned to get its share of what may have been the most important part of any successful king's income: the spoils of war. The *Penitential* of Theodore says that a third part of the *pecunia* taken from a conquered king shall be given to the Church or the poor.[5] Again, one cannot be quite certain that this refers to England. But probably it does and a famous letter from archbishop Berhtwold to the bishop of Sherborne attempting to regain a noble Kentish girl who was being held in captivity by the abbot of Glastonbury would fit easily into a context in which ecclesiastics were indeed getting their share of the booty.[6] The worldly greatness of a successful bishop is made sufficiently plain by Eddius. His story of Wilfrid's division of his treasure not long before he died is a revealing one. He had it brought before him at Ripon, 'gold and silver with precious stones' and had it divided into four parts. Of these one went to his abbots at Ripon and Hexham 'so that they might secure the friendship of kings and of bishops with gifts.' Another was to go to those followers who had served him long in exile and to whom he had not given land.[7] Here Wilfrid appears very much like a great secular lord with his treasure and his *comitatus*. The reference to buying the favour of bishops is an indication of their power and of how some of them used it. Wini had found it worth his while to buy the see of London as early as *c* 666.[8] Small wonder that when Bede described Cuthbert's attitude towards

    [2] *Opera Historica*, ed. C. Plummer, (2. vols., 1896), i, 410.
    [3] A. W. Haddan and W. Stubbs, *Councils . . . relating to Great Britain and Ireland* (3 vols., 1869–78), iii, 203; cf. G. Constable, *Monastic Tithes* (1964), 25ⁿ.
    [4] *Eng. Hist. Docs.* i (ed. D. Whitelock, 2nd ed. 1979), 406. For the literature on church-scot see F. Barlow, *The English Church 1000–1066*, 160–2.
    [5] Haddan and Stubbs, iii, 182.
    [6] *Eng. Hist. Docs.*, i (as at n. 4 above), no. 166.
    [7] *The Life of Bishop Wilfrid by Eddius Stephanus* ed. B. Colgrave (1927), 136.
    [8] Bede, *Op. Hist.*, i, 141.

the prospect of a bishopric he says that it was the perils of the love of money of which the saint was most afraid.[9]

In the *Ecclesiastical History* Bede does not draw episcopal wealth to the attention of his readers. He was very well aware of, and alarmed by it. He chose to avoid drawing attention to it but to lay great stress on the good example set by *poor* bishops in the past.

No such concern to avoid scandal and to emphasise the edifying can account for Bede's failure to give much weight to another important aspect of the English Church in his day, the very large number of monasteries (though he did mistrust some monasteries or pseudo-monasteries). He indicates that monasteries became numerous during the second half of the seventh century, describes the foundation of some, and mentions a considerable number of others. But monasteries are not his main concern; that is with bishops, the foundation of sees and the conversion of kingdoms, and with certain kinds of miracle story. In so far as he had a model it was that of Eusebius, who could have nothing to say about monasteries. It is clearly not part of Bede's design to record the foundation of monasteries, except in special cases or incidentally. The number of passing references to monasteries in his text indicates that they were numerous;[10] other sources suggest that they were very numerous. Many English monasteries of Bede's day are known only from a stray reference or so. For example, we should not know that there was a monastery of some note at Nursling, were it not mentioned in Willibald's life of Boniface.[11] The only incontrovertible early reference to the house at Much Wenlock comes from a letter of Boniface's.[12] The existence of the double monastery at Wimborne is known only from Rudolph of Fulda's life of Leofgyth.[13] There are many other such cases. When many monasteries are known only from isolated references in scanty sources it is a fair deduction that there were many others to which our sources do not refer at all. There must have been scores of monasteries by the time Bede died; possibly there were hundreds. It is an important possibility that Bede's not being concerned to record the foundation of monasteries except in special circumstances may give an inadequate impression of the importance of Irish foundations other than those made directly or indirectly from Iona. He mentions only two such: Fursey's in East Anglia[14] and Dicuill's at Bosham.[15] There is a fairly strong *a priori* case for supposing there to

[9] *Two Lives of St. Cuthbert*, ed. B. Colgrave (1940), 184, cf. 236.

[10] D. P. Kirby, 'Bede's Native Sources', *Bull. John Rylands Library*, xlviii (1965–6), 356.

[11] *Vitae Sancti Bonifatii Archiepiscopi Moguntini*, W. Levison (M.G.H. Script. Rer. Germ. in usum Schol. 1905), 9.

[12] Ed. M. Tangl, *S. Bonifatii et Lullii Epistolae* (M.G.H. Epistolae Selectae i, 1916) 8.

[13] Ed. G. Waitz (M.G.H. Scriptores, XV, 1887), 123.

[14] *Op. Hist.*, i, 163f.

[15] *Ibid.*, i, 231.

have been other such houses unmentioned by Bede, granted that so many Irishmen went abroad as missionaries and hermits in this period. It is strengthened by there certainly having been one Irish monastery which he does not mention as such. This is Malmesbury, founded by Maidubh, probably by about the middle of the seventh century, possibly before 640.[16] To judge from the rank and attainments of its most eminent son, Aldhelm, it was a house of some note and some learning. It is hard to believe that it did not play a part in the conversion of Wessex; and Bede's saying nothing of it in that context is a warning that there may have been important elements in the conversion of England as a whole of which he does not tell. Indeed we have only to reflect upon how little he tells us of his own monastery. All the detailed information he gives us about it comes from his *Lives of the Abbots*; it is from there alone that we can surmise the relative magnificence of the monastic buildings of Jarrow.

Of course 'monastery' at this period is a comprehensive term, denoting institutions of rather various kinds. Some no doubt were small and by later standards anomalous institutions. Others were establishments of some considerable grandeur. Monkwearmouth/ Jarrow was not only a very numerous community, some six hundred strong, but was also very well housed. Bede describes Benedict Biscop's building activities; and the important excavations which Miss Cramp has been carrying out demonstrate that the monks of these monasteries were indeed housed *more Romanorum*, in large regularly built buildings, plastered inside and out, the inside walls being painted, the floors made up of an imitation of *opus signinum*, and the windows filled with clear and coloured glass.[17] Bede was living in physical surroundings very different indeed from the rustic simplicity of Aidan's accommodation a couple of generations earlier. Other monasteries had noble buildings; Wilfrid's foundations of Ripon and Hexham are obvious examples. More impressive still is the great church at Brixworth, belonging to a monastery which, if we had only written sources to go by, we should not think likely to have been of more than minor importance. There were other monasteries of which our sources tell us little which had buildings of some splendour. Aldhelm's poem on the abbess Bugge's church (possibly at Withington, Gloucs.) refers to its glass windows. He also lays some stress on the beauty of a golden chalice inlaid with gems which adorned this monastery and on its other treasures.[18] This is a reminder that the Church of his day was rich not

[16] A. Watkin in *VCH Wilts.*, iii (1956), 210–3.

[17] R. Cramp, *Early Northumbrian Sculpture* (1965), 3; *Medieval Archaeology*, vi–vii, 315; viii, 232.

[18] Ed. R. Ehwald (M.G.H. Auct. Antiquiss., xv, 1919), 17, 18. I owe this reference to the kindness of Dr. Henry Mayr-Harting. Cf. M. Bateson, 'The Origin and Early History of Double Monasteries', *Trans. Roy. Hist. Soc.*, new ser., xiii (1899), 178.

only in buildings but in gold and silver. Great ecclesiastics like great laymen expected to be surrounded by rich and splendid objects. Ethelbert II's idea of a present to send to Boniface was a silver cup lined with gold and weighing three and a half pounds.[19] If the gold and garnet pectoral cross and the silver-covered travelling altar found in Cuthbert's tomb were actually his, as it seems reasonable to suppose, then even that ascetic saint had magnificent possessions.[20] There is evidence to suggest that rich objects were manufactured in English monasteries; for example Miss Cramp's discovery of an unused stick of millefiori enamel at Jarrow.[21] There was much wealth and much grandeur in the English Church in Bede's day. He is not concerned to draw such things to the attention of readers of the *Ecclesiastical History*.

It is probable that the relationships between England and Gaul were of much more importance in determining the progress of the Church in England in the seventh century than emerges directly from Bede's text. Our evidence on the closeness of those relationships before 597 is inconclusive.[22] The marriage of Ethelbert of Kent to the daughter of the Merovingian king Charibert (before 590) may have been part of a more extensive connection. Certainly the Frankish kings Theudebert (534–48) and Chilperic (561–84) at least liked to be thought to have had overlordship beyond the Channel and may have had it.[23] Although a recent argument that the Frankish objects found in southern England indicate that the fifth century invasions south of the Thames were largely Frankish has not met with general support the archaeological evidence does suggest some Frankish settlement in Kent.[24] Bede says that among the peoples from whom the Anglo-Saxons were derived were the *Boructuari*; this people is generally counted as Frankish.[25] All told there is a fair case for supposing there to have been Franks in England. Furthermore it is more or less certain that there were considerable Saxon settlements in north Gaul: round Boulogne (by the

[19] Ed. M. Tangl, 230.

[20] Ed. C. F. Battiscombe, *The Relics of St. Cuthbert* (1956).

[21] R. L. S. Bruce Mitford, 'The Reception by the Anglo-Saxons of Mediterranean Art', *Settimane di Studio del Centro Italiano sull'Alto Medioevo*, xiv (1967), 818.

[22] Dr. J. M. Wallace Hadrill, from whom one hesitates to differ, in 'Rome and the English Church: some Questions of Transmission', *Settimane . . .*, vii (1960), 526–8, regards it as being under a misapprehension to hold that Frankish-Kentish contacts had been established on a wide front before 597, but it is hard to see how the evidence can justify so firm a conclusion.

[23] F. M. Stenton, *Anglo-Saxon England* (2nd edn., 1947), 4, 7, 14; A. R. Burn, 'Procopius and the Isle of Ghosts', *Eng. Hist. Rev.*, lxx (1955), 258–61.

[24] V. Evison, *The Fifth Century Invasions South of the Thames* (1965); C. F. C. Hawkes in *Dark Age Britain*, ed. D. B. Harden (1956), 91–111.

[25] *Op. Hist.*, i, 296. This passage is generally regarded (as Mr. Hunter Blair regards it, *World of Bede*, 23–4) as giving a list of peoples living in Germany. But the sense of the Latin is that these are the peoples from whom the Anglo-Saxons living in Britain were derived.

shortest crossing from Kent); in the neighbourhood of Bayeux, where a
body of Saxons was recognised as a distinct entity in the sixth century;
and near the mouth of the Loire.[26] In some ways Franks and Saxons
probably merged into a kind of *continuum*. Consider the lands which
Augustine would have passed through on his way to England; we do
not known his exact route but it probably ran up the Rhone valley to
Autun and then to Quentovic for the crossing. He would have gone
through, first, lands which were still in important ways part of the
Roman world, where the descendants of the senatorial aristocracy
survived and provided the bishops and where some sort of urban life
was maintained; and then lands where the institutional Church survived
but where Roman survival was less marked and Frankish settlement
thicker; and then lands still within the sphere of influence of the
Merovingian kings but where the population was not only largely
German but pagan, and where bishoprics had not survived; and then a
part of that area in which the German inhabitants included Anglo-
Saxons; and finally, across the Channel to Kent where there may have
been Frankish settlers and which some Frankish kings at least chose to
regard as under their power. The Channel was not necessarily the most
important of the boundaries he crossed; so far as religion and culture
went the crucial divide was further south.

Deficiency of information leaves a wide area for doubt in assessing
the closeness of the relationship between the Franks and the Saxons. For
example insufficient is known of the Frankish language in this period
for us to tell whether it would have been fairly intelligible to Saxons.
Bede's reference to Augustine's use of Frankish *interpretes* suggests that
it could have been.[27] Our knowledge of Anglo-Saxon society in the
period of conversion is not sufficient to enable us to estimate how
similar Saxon kings were to Frankish kings. A curious parallel between
a story of Bede's and a text probably describing the Merovingian court
suggests more similarity than one might guess. The story is one of
Oswald. He was, Bede says, sitting down to dinner one Easter Day.
Before him was set a silver dish, laden with good things. Then in came
his *minister*, whose task it was to relieve the poor, and said that many
poor men were asking for alms from the king. Oswald not only gave
them his food but ordered the silver dish to be broken up and given to

---

[26] For the literature on these settlements see W. Levison, *England and the Continent in
the Eighth Century* (1947), 4; D. A. White, *Litus Saxonicum* (1961), 56–72 and note. It is
of some interest that the first Saxons known to have become Christians anywhere were
living in the diocese of Nantes, c. 560 (Levison, *England and the Continent*, 4 and n.) and
that there is archaeological evidence to suggest direct contact between this area and
Kent at the time, most recently H. Vierck in K. Haucke, *Goldbrakteaten aus Sievern*
(1970), 390–3 (I owe this reference to Mrs. S. C. Hawkes.)

[27] *Op. Hist.* i, 45. *Interpretes* may possibly mean no more than 'emissaries' but could
indicate Franks who knew the language spoken in Kent.

them in little pieces, *minutatim*.[28] The Merovingian text describes officials called *consules* whose function it is to make the king's gifts. The *consul*, it says, sprinkles little pieces of silver on the ground which the poor scramble for as best they can, while the happy king looks on, smiling.[29] It may be that the coincidence is a chance one; but the appearance in both sources of an officer whose function it is to make gifts and of the business of scattering little pieces of silver to the poor does not seem more likely than not to be by more than chance and does something to justify entertaining the supposition that the Northumbrian court was not unlike that of a Merovingian king. There are further indications in the early seventh century of fairly close relationships between England and Gaul. After Edwin of Northumbria's death his son and grandson were sent to Gaul to be brought up by their relation Dagobert.[30] Sigbert of East Anglia went into exile in Gaul. Ethelbert's son Eadbald, himself half-Frankish, seems to have married a Frankish princess.[31] Men described as Saxons were sometimes prominent in Gaul; though here there is the difficulty that we cannot tell whether, for example, the Saxon *dux* who went with Dagobert's army to Gascony in 635 or the Saxon servant of St. Eloi were English or Continental Saxons.[32]

The secular connections between England and Gaul were reinforced by and help to explain the relationships between the English and Gallic Churches. Bede has quite a lot to tell us about these relationships. Three bishops of English sees came from Gaul: Felix (of East Anglia c 630–?647) and Agilbert and his nephew Leutherius (both of Wessex 650–660 and 670–676).[33] Wini, bishop of Wessex (662–666) and later of London (666–666 x 675) was consecrated in Gaul.[34] Wilfrid spent three years in the service of Archbishop Annemundus of Lyons (655–8) and had other close relationships with Gaul.[35] The connection with Lyons may have been of particular significance in view of its importance as a centre of learning in the period. Berhtwald, archbishop of Canterbury, was consecrated there in 693.[36] Englishmen going to Italy usually went via the Rhone valley and Benedict Biscop is unlikely to have been the only Englishman to have taken the opportunity to acquire books there. In

---

[28] *Op. Hist.* i, 138.

[29] J. M. Wallace Hadrill, *The Long Haired Kings* (1962), 217–8. Various explanations of the coincidence other than that mentioned above are, of course, possible; e.g. that Bede's story derives in outline from some lost piece of Continental hagiography.

[30] Bede, *Op. Hist.* i, 126.

[31] Ibid., i, 116; F. M. Stenton, *Anglo-Saxon England* (2nd edn., 1947), 60.

[32] Ed. J. M. Wallace Hadrill, *Fourth Book of the Chronicle of Fredegar* (1960), 65; W. Levison, *England and the Continent in the Eighth Century*, 9 and n.

[33] Bede, *Op. Hist* i, 116, 140, 141.

[34] Ibid., i, 140.

[35] Eddius, *Life of Wilfrid*, ed. Colgrave, caps. vi, xii, xxviii.

[36] Bede, *Op. Hist.* i, 295.

the time of Earconberht, king of Kent (640–64) there were, according to a famous and very important passage in Bede's *Ecclesiastical History*, few monasteries in England and those seeking the monastic life went to houses in Gaul, especially to Chelles, Faremoûtier-en-Brie and Andelys. Among those who went to these monasteries were Earcongota (daughter of Earconberht of Kent), Saethyrth and Aethelburh (daughter and step-daughter of Anna of East Anglia), who went to Faremoûtier, the last two becoming abbesses, and Hereswith, who went to Chelles, where her sister Hilda, later abbess of Whitby, at one time intended to follow her.[37]

It is possible to add details from other sources to what Bede tells us of the relations between the Church in England and the Church in Gaul. The weight to be attached to some of these is uncertain; they do no more than raise possibilities. For example, we know that Justus, bishop of Rochester, and Peter, abbot of St Peter's Canterbury, attended the great council at Paris in 614.[38] Many explanations of their presence are possible, from chance to their having been summoned as an indication of Clothar II's having some kind of overlordship in Kent. But some of the additional information which we have, put together with what Bede tells us is of more definite import. It draws our attention to the great importance in relation to the history of the Church in England of the monastic movement led by Columbanus and his disciples in Gaul.

Columbanus came to Gaul from Ireland in about 590. He first went to Burgundy where he founded the monasteries of Luxeuil and Annegray. He was expelled from Burgundy by Theuderich II in 610 and, shortly afterwards, went to Lombardy (612). He founded the great monastery of Bobbio before his death in 615. He seems to have had a great impact on the Frankish courts and nobility. His monasteries, above all Luxeuil, flourished and there were many daughter houses. He, his disciples, and his monasteries seem to have been largely responsible for the great changes which came over the Church in northern Gaul in the seventh century. At the time of Columbanus's arrival from Ireland the Church in much of northern and eastern Gaul was in a poor way. Little had been done to convert the pagans of Flanders and Picardy and paganism was probably still strong in other northern areas. In the north and north east of Gaul the Gallo-Roman ruling class had not survived to provide a means for the survival of something of the Roman world as they had in the south and centre. Monasteries were very few and in large areas there were, so far as we know, none. What Pierre Riché calls the *zone barbare*, an area including lands to the north of the lower Loire, much of Normandy, Picardy, Flanders; and a good deal of north eastern Gaul was probably in many

[37] P. Hunter Blair, *World of Bede*, 144–5.
[38] Ed. F. Maassen (M.G.H. Legum Sectio III Concilia), i (1893), 192.

ways more like England than it was like southern Gaul.[39]

In the seventh century all this changed very much. Missionaries such as St Amand and St Ouen laboured in the north east and sees were established or re-established there.[40] A very large number of monasteries were founded; the seventh century foundations of northern Gaul provide a long list of famous names: Corbie, Chelles, Jumièges, St Bertin, St Riquier, Fontenelle, to name only a few. It seems that among the impulses which started these movements the influence of Columbanus and his followers was the most important. It is true that much of what happened can be known only through hagiographical sources which can often only be checked by the crude process of making assumptions about plausibility, which in the nature of the case, we do not have adequate means of making. Nevertheless it seems certain that many of the active bishops and monastery founders of the period had come directly or indirectly under the influence of Columbanus; and that most of the new monasteries were either daughter houses of one of his foundations, above all Luxeuil, or were at least founded by or under the influence of men and women associated with him or with his immediate disciples. The churches of Ireland and Gaul became involved in a fairly close relationship. A considerable number of Irish came to Gaul and a considerable number of Franks went to Ireland to study.

It is clear that many of the English relationships with Gaul were with the, so to speak, Columbanian connection. This is certainly true of two of the three monasteries to which Bede says the English went. Faremoûtier was a daughter house of Luxeuil itself.[41] Jonas, Columbanus's biographer, spent some time there *c* 644 and mentions a nun there to add to the list of those of whom we otherwise know.[42] Chelles was refounded by Balthildis, who was by origin an English slave, had married Clovis II and was for some years after his death in 657 regent of Neustria. She brought the first nuns for it from Jouarre, which had been founded by Adon, apparently under the influence of Columbanus.[43] Chelles, Jouarre and Faremoûtier are fairly close together in an area somewhat eastwards of Paris. Jouarre is less than 20

[39] P. Riché, 'Les foyers de culture en Gaule Franque du VIᵉ au IXᵉ siècle', *Settimane . . .*, xi, (1964), 298–301; P. Riché, *Education et culture dans l'occident barbare* (2nd edn., 1962), 220–26.

[40] For summary accounts E. de Moreau, *Histoire de l'Eglise en Belgique*, i (2nd edn., 1945) and G. Tessier, La conversion de Clovis et la christianisation des Francs', *Settimane . . .*, xiv (1967), 171–89.

[41] *Dictionnaire d'Histoire et de Géographie Ecclésiastiques*, xvi, under Fare and Faremoutiers.

[42] Jonas, *Vitae Columbani . . . Libri II* ed. B. Krusch (M.G.H. Script. Rer. Merov., iv, 1902) 136–7.

[43] W. Levison, *England and the Continent in the Eighth Century*, 9–10; *Vita Bertilae*, ed. W. Levison, (.M.G.H. Script. Rer. Merov., vi, 1913) 104–5.

miles from Chelles and less than 15 from Faremoûtier. The connection between Chelles and Jouarre is an important one in relation to English history. Agilbert, bishop of Wessex, seems to have been related to Adon, founder of Jouarre, and to Telchildis its first abbess and the sarcophagus in which he was buried in the crypt there is still to be seen.[44] Agilbert's having spent some time in Ireland strengthens the other evidence for his connection with the heirs of Columbanus.[45] Bede indicates the importance of Agilbert and that of Chelles, but he does not indicate that there was a connection between the two. The number of people who came to England from Gaulish milieux under Irish influence was probably considerable. The *Vita* of Bertila, first abbess of Chelles (probably written a hundred years after the events it describes) says that she sent holy men and women and books to England in response to request from Saxon kings for aid in founding monasteries.[46] The *Testament of Mildburg*, a source which inspires reserve infused with mistrust, says that the first abbess of Much Wenlock was called Liobsynde, apparently a Frankish name; and she could have been one of the women Bertila sent, perhaps.[47] In any case the similarities between the double monasteries of England and their Gaulish counterparts are sufficiently great to make the *Vita Bertilae*'s story plausible. Ronan, the Irishman whom Bede mentions at the council of Whitby and who was in *Galliae vel Italiae partibus regulam ecclesiasticae veritatis edoctus* sounds very much as if he came from a Columbanian context; and Bede tells us there were others in England who came *de Galliis*.[48] St Riquier, according to his *Vita* went to England for a period to preach and to redeem captives.[49] St Amand is said to have wanted to go to preach in England.[50] Both had connections with the Irish. It is possible that there was Columbanian influence on the conversion of East Anglia. Sigbert was converted in Gaul *c* 630 at a time when the influence of Columbanus's followers was

[44] For the early history of Jouarre, see J. Guerout in Y. Chaussy, et al., *L'Abbaye Royale Notre Dame de Jouarre* (2 vols., 1961), i, 1–67. It was founded c. 635 by Adon, St. Ouen's brother. But the family which provided the first abbesses and whose property Jouarre probably became was that of Adon's step-mother. Agilbert was almost certainly Telchildis's brother. He probably built the crypt in which he and the early abbesses were buried and one tradition actually regarded him as the founder of the monastery.

[45] Bede, *Op. Hist.* i, 140.

[46] Hunter Blair, *World of Bede*, 145, 153.

[47] H. P. R. Finberg, *The Early Charters of the West Midlands* (1961), 208–9.

[48] *Op. Hist.* i, 181.

[49] Ed. B. Krusch, *Vita Richarii* . . . (M.G.H. Script. Rer. Merov., vii, 1920) 448. This is the first *Vita*, which, although in Krusch's judgment unreliable and not as nearly contemporary with its subjects as it claims to be, cannot be of later than eighth century date. If the story is true the saint would have gone to England some time before *c* 640.

[50] *Vita Amandi* ed. B. Krusch, M.G.H. Script. Rer. Merov., v, 440, n. 3. Not a contemporary observation.

strong and his bishop Felix came from Burgundy.[51] Even in the case of
the mysterious Birinus, first bishop of Wessex, it is fair to say that a
plausible context for a missionary coming from northern Italy at this
period is a Columbanian one.[52] There are scraps of evidence to show that
there were English members of monastic communities in Gaul other
than those which Bede mentions.[53] The career of St Fursey provides
further evidence of the interconnections between England, northern
Gaul and Ireland in this period. Having come to East Anglia from
Ireland, apparently in the 630's and established a monastery there, he left,
probably early in the next decade, for Gaul. There he settled at Lagny on
the Marne (between Chelles and Jouarre). He seems to have been in the
favour of Erchinoald, mayor of the palace in Neustria, who founded the
monastery at Péronne to which Fursey's body (he died in 649 or 50) was
moved and which became the head of an important family of
monasteries which included Gertrude's at Nivelles. A generation later
Aldhelm was in direct communication with Péronne.[54] It is true that
some of the evidence for the relations between the Churches of England
and of Gaul in the early and middle seventh century is of a particularly
difficult kind. That a very late life of an English saint says he went to
Chelles, or an earlier but still not contemporary life of a Frankish saint
says he went to preach in England are susceptible of explanations other
than that we are being told the truth. But granted how much fairly solid
information our sources do provide, and granted that much of the
Gaulish (and Irish) influence would have found expression in the
foundation of monasteries and the arrival of missionaries who did not
become bishops (things which Bede's scheme did not enable him to
devote very much attention to) then it is reasonable to suppose that Gaul
and particularly the milieux in Gaul under Irish influence had a very great
deal to do with the progress of the Church in England.

It is likely that the development of the churches in England and in
northern Gaul in the seventh century took place upon the same lines and
for the same reasons, and that the interconnections between them were
sufficient to mean that we ought to think of the transformations through
which the Church went in England not as insular, but as the English part
of changes which were taking place over a much wider area.

The most important developments in the history of the English
Church in the seventh century seem to have been as follows. First, the
conversion of most of the royal houses in the generation from *c* 635.
The Italian mission to Kent appears to have been relatively unsuccessful

[51] J. M. Wallace Hadrill, art. cit., 530.

[52] Bede, *Op. Hist.* i, 139–40. The Revd. H. E. J. Cowdrey pointed this possibility
out to me.

[53] E. John, 'The Social and Political Problems of the Early English Church',
Agricultural History Review, xviii (1970), Supplement, 58f.

[54] J. F. Kenney, *Sources for the Early History of Ireland* (reprint 1966), 500–508.

after its first few years and the leading role in conversion from the 630's seems to have been taken by the Irish mission which had come to Lindisfarne from Iona. Second, the acceptance of the authority of Rome and of Canterbury; here the crucial event is the arrival of Theodore in 669. But the way had been prepared for Theodore by developments in the 650's and 660's, by the turning towards Rome of such men as Wilfrid and Benedict Biscop and by the defeat of the proponents of the Celtic Easter. In this development Canterbury seems to have played little part. It was men who had been brought up in Northumbria, where the influence of Iona was strongest, and the Frankish bishop Agilbert, who were largely responsible. Third, the foundation of very large numbers of monasteries in the second half of the century whereas in the first half there had been very few. Fourth, the development of learning in the last generation of the seventh century. Before the coming of Theodore we know of no book composed nor of any manuscript written in England. The age of Bede was very different. Fifth, the great increase in power and wealth of the church by the end of the seventh century. The rich bishops of Bede's day with their apparently well-established powers must have been very unlike the foreign missionaries of the early days of Christianity in England and the well-built monasteries with their rich treasures unlike the simple accommodation of such as Aidan.

The same changes can be seen taking place in Gaul. In both England and Gaul Irish missionaries can be seen to have had astonishing power. They really do seem to have changed the way of life of many members of formidable barbarian aristocracies. Those whom Columbanus affected were Christians already, but his impact seems little less striking than that of Aidan and his followers. The *modus operandi* of the Irish in England and in Gaul seems to have been much the same and what happened in one country throws light on the other. In the case of Columbanus much seems to have been accomplished by force of character expressing itself in defiance of the *convenances* of noble life. In a famous incident he refused to bless the bastard sons of Theuderich, delivering instead, before striding out, the remark that they would never become kings, having been born in adultery. As he crossed the threshold there was a great clap of thunder. Theuderich reflected that it was unwise to provoke the Almighty by offending his servant and, like a true barbarian king, concluded that the occasion called for a timely and generous proffer. So he sent Columbanus rich gifts. All his *ministri* got from the saint for their pains was the information that *munera impiorum reprobat Altissimus* and they were *pavifacti* while the rich vessels tumbled on the ground. Columbanus was *ferox*; he was *audax et animo vigens*. He was also frightening in his power of prophecy, successfully foretelling the doom of the kings.[55] Refusal to conform to the ways of the

[55] Ed. Krusch (as at n. 42 above), 87–8, 106.

world, and a demeanour towards the great which was aggressive to the point of menace seem to have been, not the only elements, but certainly important elements in his approach. Bede's story of Cedd's treatment of Sigbert, king of Essex, is in the same genre. Cedd met the king coming away from dinner with a *comes* whom he had excommunicated. Sigbert dismounted and fell trembling at the saint's feet. Cedd, *iratus*, touched him with his staff and told him that because he would not avoid the house of a man who was damned 'in this same house shall you meet death'. So Sigbert did.[56] Notes of anger and defiance are recurrently struck in our accounts of the Irish. Aidan, the most successful of the Irish missionaries in England, was a man of milder spirit. But his conduct seems to have been in essential ways the same. He too acted contrary to the ways of the world. He rarely dined with the king; when he received gifts he gave them to the poor and he did not give gifts to nobles who visited him. Such a line of conduct may have seemed almost shocking to a society accustomed to gift exchange. He too was the master of the stern word and the frightening prophecy.[57] Of course such incidents occur in the hagiography of many different times and places. The general similarity to, for example, some incidents in Sulpicius' life of St Martin is clear. For all that they probably do tell us something about how Irish missionaries gained success partly by adopting the role of Old Testament prophets.[58] That Jonas, who was nearer at the time he wrote to Columbanus than Bede was to Aidan and Cedd, tells the same kind of story about Irish missionaries as does Bede strengthens the case for there being a considerable degree of realism in what Bede tells us.

In both England and Gaul, especially northern and eastern Gaul, the successes of missionaries were followed by the establishment of very numerous monasteries. It has been calculated that forty monasteries were founded in the dioceses of Thérouanne, Cambrai, Tournai, and Liège between 625 and 700, that is to say in an area which was largely pagan until the seventh century.[59] Elsewhere in Gaul there were many new foundations. In both England and Gaul nunneries were prominent among the new foundations, and the women who entered them were often of very high birth. Such nunneries were in both countries, often 'double', that is to say they had an attached community of monks under the rule of the abbess. This peculiar institution was characteristic both of England and of Gaul and seems to have spread from Gaul to England. It was not Irish in origin, nor, so far as it known, was it Italian. Its origins must probably be sought in Gaul itself, or perhaps in Spain.[60] Why monasteries should have become so numerous in both

[56] Bede, *Op. Hist.* i, 173–4. [57] Bede, *Op. Hist.* i, 136, 156.
[58] Cf. A. Mirgeler, *Mutations of Western Christianity* (trans. Quinn, 1964), 67.
[59] E. de. Moreau, *Histoire de l'Eglise en Belgique*, as at n. 40 above. i, 131.
[60] S. Hilpisch, *Die Doppelklöster* (1928); M. Bateson, 'Origin and History of Double Monasteries', as at n. 18 above, P. Hunter Blair, *World of Bede*, 135–36.

England and Gaul and why nunneries should have been so important in both is not clear. But it is clear that the social circumstances in both countries were very favourable to monasticism and that English monasticism owed very much to that of Gaul.

In both England and in Gaul noble monks and nuns seem often to have expected to be nobly housed and surrounded by rich objects, however severe their personal mode of life may have been. The same contrast which can be drawn between the physical surroundings in which Aidan lived and those of English ecclesiastics a couple of generations later can be drawn between Columbanus, who lived in simple huts, and the greater grandeur in which monasteries founded somewhat later under his influence were housed. Most of the building associated with the monastic movement in northern Gaul has been lost. Such basilicas as that which Wandrille built of squared stone at Fontenelle do not survive. But it is clear from descriptions and from such surviving monuments as the crypt and tombs at Jouarre that, as in England, the new monasteries were not infrequently provided with buildings of some splendour. That there are similarities between some English and some Merovingian architecture of the period is unsurprising; Benedict Biscop got his masons from Gaul. It is likely that further work will strengthen the evidence for the connection. For example excavations at Deux Jumeaux and at Evrecy (dép. Calvados) have uncovered remains of monasteries of the seventh and eighth centuries bearing considerable resemblance to Monkwearmouth/ Jarrow at the same period. Sculpture (sometimes painted) was used as architectural decoration in the same way as at Monkwearmouth/Jarrow and, as is the case there, the motifs used are both those of Mediterranean origin and barbaric beasts such as are found on the metalwork of the period. A more precise parallel is the use at Evrecy of incised baluster shafts very similar to those used at Monkwearmouth/ Jarrow.[61] The Gaulish monasteries, like the English ones, were provided with rich treasures. For example we have a seventeenth century engraving of a wonderful chalice from Chelles. Of gold, a foot high, inlaid, probably with garnets, in a cloisonné style similar to that of some of the Sutton Hoo jewellery; it must have been such a chalice as Aldhelm praises in his poem on Bugge's monastery.[62]

The remarkable developments in learning and in the production of manuscripts in England in the age of Bede should probably, as Riché

---

[61] I have not seen L. Musset's *Deux Jumeaux. Résultats des fouilles sur le site de l'ancien prieuré* (Caen, 1963) and know of these sites only from his articles in *Bull. de la Soc. des Antiquaires de Normadie*, liii (1955–56), 116–68, 405–19; liv (1957–8), 571–82; and in *Art de Basse Normandie* No. 23 (1961). It is believed that the finds at Deux Jumeaux date from the seventh or eighth centuries while those at Evrecy seem somewhat later, but no clear evidence of date seems to have been found.

[62] A. de Saussay, *Panoplia Sacerdotalis* (Paris, 1681), 198–200.

has argued, be seen as part of a much wider movement.[63] The parallel
between what happened in England and what happened in northern and
north eastern Gaul is again close.

So far as it known no manuscripts were written in England until the
late seventh century. Similarly in northern Gaul; there is nothing until
the second half of the seventh century. In that period Luxeuil becomes
'the first great writing centre of Merovingian Gaul'.[64] Of the two major
foundations of Balthildis Corbie became a very important centre of
manuscript production, certainly in the eighth century and probably in
the seventh and Chelles was probably also the source of an important
series of manuscripts.[65] If we include Chelles these three were easily the
most important sources of manuscripts known of in Gaul. Previously
Lyons and Autun had been the main centres of manuscript
production.[66] But by 700 new monasteries in the north were taking the
lead from old Gallo-Roman episcopal centres further south, and their
scriptoria are the counterpart of the new monastic scriptoria in
England. It does not appear that books were composed in England until
about the beginning of the eighth century. We then have a considerable
number, not only the works of Bede and Aldhelm but a number of
lesser works, particularly saints' lives, from various centres. Similarly
in northern Gaul where in the last generation of the seventh century
books start to be composed in areas where they had not been composed
before. We have saints' lives from Rebais, Remiremont, Fontenelle,
Nivelles and Laon from between *c* 670 and 710 and the poems of
Theodfrid, first abbot of Corbie.[67] This is not, it is true, a very
impressive body of literature, but it is not unlike what England
provided if we exclude the quite extraordinary achievement of Bede.

One is looking at the same kind of development taking place in the
same kind of new monastery in England and Gaul. Compare, for
example, Whitby and Chelles. Whitby was founded in 657 by Hilda,
who had been intending to go to Chelles which was refounded at about
the same time. Both monasteries were double. The most striking thing
about Whitby, particularly by comparison with the nunneries of later
centuries, is the intellectual activity there. Six bishops, Bede says, were
educated at Whitby. The first life of Gregory the Great, one of the first
books to have been composed in England, was written there.[68] The
number of styluses etc. found in the excavations at Whitby is an
indication of how much writing went on.[69] The evidence for

[63] P. Riché, *Education et culture*, op. cit., 410–19.
[64] E. A. Lowe, *Codices Latini Antiquiores*, vi (1953), pp. xv–xvii.
[65] Ibid., pp. xxii–xxvi.
[66] Ibid., pp. xiii–xv.
[67] Riché, *Education et culture*, op. cit., 412.
[68] *Op. Hist.*, i, 254–5.
[69] C. Peers and C. A. Ralegh Radford, 'The Saxon Monastery at Whitby',
Archaeologia, lxxxix (1943), 64–5.

comparable activity at Chelles is not absolutely watertight. One is dependent on suppositions, though they are the suppositions of Lowe and Bischoff.[70] If they are right Chelles was the source of a series of manuscripts in the late seventh and the eighth centuries, including the earliest manuscript of the Gelasian sacramentary and a group of manuscripts written for Hildebald archbishop of Cologne (785–819) by nuns who wrote their names at the end of their work. It looks as if the monastery Hilda founded was of much the same kind as the one she nearly joined and as if both were of an unusual kind.

An important part in the development of learning in northern Gaul, as in England, was played by direct contacts with Italy. St Gertrude, St Ouen and St Amand looked to Italy for books in the same way as did Benedict Biscop.[71] That contact with Italy was important for milieux in the Gaulish Church which were also under strong Irish influence is a reminder that we should not be led by Bede's concentration on the influences of Iona and of Canterbury and by his great concern with the Easter controversy to regard the contrasts between the 'Roman' and 'Celtic' churches as being generally sharp or invariably present. 'Italian' and 'Irish' influences were not mutually exclusive. England came under Irish influences not only directly, but indirectly, via Gaul. It came under Italian influence not only directly, but indirectly via the Irish. As Mr John has recently emphasised some of the things which have been frequently discussed as if they were characteristic of the 'Roman' as opposed to the 'Celtic' church were, in fact, particularly associated with the Irish.[72] The Irish were as often the friends as the enemies of papal authority. Columbanus's fracas with Gregory the Great arose through his trying to induce the Pope to impose the Irish Easter on the bishops of Gaul. It seems to have been the Irish who were responsible for the diffusion of the cult of St Peter in Gaul and it seems virtually certain that it was largely through monasteries under the influence of Columbanus that knowledge of the Benedictine rule was diffused in Gaul in the seventh century.[73] Columbanus's foundation of Bobbio (for which a papal exemption from the authority of the diocesan bishop was early obtained) helped to give his successors a continuing and close connection with Italy. The conflict over the calculation of the date of Easter did indeed set some Irishmen and their disciples at odds with the rest of western Christendom, and this conflict was by no means a trivial one. But very many Irishmen both at home and abroad did not stick to

[70] B. Bischoff, 'Die Kolner Nonnenhandschriften und das Skriptorium von Chelles', *Karolingische und Ottonische Kunst* (1957), 395–411; E. A. Lowe, *Codices . . .*, vi, pp. xxi–xxii.

[71] P. Riché, *Education et culture*, op. cit., 382, 399.

[72] E. John, 'The Social and Political Problems of the Early English Church', as at n. 53 above p. 59.

[73] P. Riché, *Education et culture*, op. cit., 382–3.

their traditional reckonings; the dispute was quite as much one between Irish and Irish as between Irish and non-Irish. The majority of the Irish had probably abandoned the Celtic Easter by 650. In the seventh century the Churches of England, Gaul and Ireland formed in some ways one interconnected world and one in which the influence of Italy and of Rome was strong and growing stronger. In such a world there is nothing surprising in the demand for the adoption of the Roman Easter in Northumbria having come from a man such as Wilfrid, who had been a member of the community at Lindisfarne, or from Agilbert, a Frank educated partly in Ireland. 'Italian' and 'Irish' influences remained almost inextricably entwined together in the age of Bede. Theodore's *Penitential* was largely based on Irish models and Wilfrid's combination of episcopal power with that over a scattered family of monasteries looks as if it was derived from Irish example.[74]

In general when English historians have discussed the development of the English Church in the seventh century they have explained it largely in terms of Italian and Irish influences, with those from Gaul regarded as noteworthy, but secondary; and when they have looked over the Channel they have been inclined not to focus their gaze until it reaches somewhere about Lyons.[75] There is a good case for giving more weight to the relationships and similarities between England and northern Gaul, and for regarding many of the developments which took place in England as being part of wider movements which were also affecting Gaul, and were such as to establish numerous connections between England, Gaul and Ireland. Bede's interests and emphases have in some degree obscured the extent to which this was so. His concern with Canterbury and Iona and the importance which he attached to the Easter controversy have not infrequently led to the differences between the Irish and other churches being overstressed. Because he looked so earnestly to Italy and to Rome historians have tended to follow him, not always giving due weight to the extent to which this impulse to turn towards Rome was something which had come to England from Gaul and Ireland. In so far as it was not part of Bede's intention in the *Ecclesiastical History* to seek to give anything like a full account of the foundation of monasteries he does not bring home to its readers how large the number of monasteries founded in later seventh and early eighth century England was. This wave of monastery-founding corresponds to and is clearly connected with a similar wave in northern

[74] E. John, 'Social and Political Problems . . .' as at n. 53 above, 59–61; Mr. John compares Wilfrid's position with that of Columbanus; that of the bishops of Armagh may present a closer parallel, K. Hughes, *The Church in Early Irish Society* (1966), 69, 86.

[75] This is not, of course, true of the important articles by Dr. Wallace Hadrill and Mr. John already cited; and cf. M. Deanesly, 'Early English and Gallic Ministers', *Trans. Roy. Hist. Soc.*, 4th ser. xxiii (1941), 25–70.

Gaul. Quite what the social forces were which led to the establishment of so many monasteries in England and in Gaul in this period is not at all clear, but it is a reasonable assumption that these forces were the same on both sides of the Channel. Bede's reticence on aspects of the life of the Church in his own way obscures the extent to which its bishops and abbeys were like those of Merovingian Gaul. It would be absurd to maintain that the English Church was exactly like the Church in Gaul. To take only the most obvious differences: the Church in Gaul did not produce a Bede and did not have a Theodore. All kinds of influences, some of them from very distant places, helped to mould the Church in England. But amongst them that of Gaul was of primary, not secondary, importance.

The establishment and burgeoning of the Church in seventh century England can be seen as part of a wider movement in which lands on the northern and eastern fringes of Gaul regained some of the Roman civilisation which they had lost in the barbarian invasions. In that movement the influence of Gaul must have been very important. After their conquests of the late fifth and early sixth centuries the Merovingian kings were the only rulers north of the Alps and Pyrenees who ruled states in which much of Rome survived. To the peoples on the borders of Gaul the Merovingian régime must, whatever it appears like to modern readers of Gregory of Tours, have been the most impressive and the most Roman they knew. The influence of Frankish Gaul was wide. Theudebert was gaining power over much of western Germany at the same time as his ambassadors were trying to demonstrate at Byzantium his authority in Britain. At just the same time there is evidence for Gaulish influence in Wales while pottery apparently of Frankish origin, evidence it may be for trade, is found round the northern shores of the Irish Sea.[76] While Frankish objects of luxury were in demand in sixth century England warriors in Norway seem to have been changing their weapon kit in accordance with Frankish practice.[77] At the time in the seventh century when Frankish ecclesiasts were venturing in England in search of souls or of preferment a Frankish adventurer, Samo, was establishing some kind of authority in Bohemia. How like some of the kings of England were to Merovingian kings at the beginnings of the seventh century is an open question: what is certain is that they were far more like Merovingian kings by the end of that century. They were Christians, they had

[76] V. E. Nash Williams, *Early Christian Monuments of Wales* (1950), e.g. p. 104; C. Thomas, 'Imported Pottery in Dark Age Western Britain', *Medieval Archaeology*, iii (1959), 89–111.

[77] H. Shetelig and H. Falk, *Scandinavian Archaeology* (1937), 262–3.

bishops, some of them had written law-codes,[78] some of them were issuing coins modelled on Merovingian coins. An English king such as Aldfrith was literate, and could receive a treatise from such a scholar as Aldhelm, advising him on the art of metrical composition.[79] Like some Frankish or Visigothic rulers he could have, or be deemed to have, a taste for literary amusements derived from those of Rome. There is even evidence to suggest that the great of England in the seventh century came to dress themselves in the styles of late antiquity.[80] The English kingdoms were becoming as it were sub-Roman states at second remove. It is hard to believe that the models they imitated were not, for the most part, those of Gaul.

[78] For important remarks on the law codes, J. M. Wallace Hadrill in *Settimane*, vii (1960), as at n. 22 above, 528, 539.

[79] Ed. R. Ehwald, *Opera* (M.G.H. Auct. Ant., xv, 1919), pp. 61–204.

[80] E. Crowfoot and S. C. Hawkes, Early Anglo-Saxon Gold Braids, *Mediev Archaeol.*, xi (1967), 64, quoting Aldhelm *De Virginitate*. It is possible that Aldhelm derived this description of female dress from a continental source but the authors mention archaeological evidence also.

Additional Bibliographical Note

I should have referred to F. Prinz, *Frühes Mönchtum in Frankenreich* (Munich, 1965), a mine of information. At the time of writing I had not seen F. Krüger, *Königsgrabkirchen der Franken, Angelsachsen und Langobarden bis zur Mitte des 8. Jahrhunderts* (Munich, 1971) which raises many questions about England's relationship to a wider world. For Wilfrid, G. Isenberg, *Die Wüordigung Wilfrieds von York in der Historia Gentis Anglorum Beadas und der Vita Wilfridi der Eddius* (Weidenau/Sieg 1978) is of special importance. See also M. Gibbs, 'The Decrees of Agatho and the Gregorian Plan for York', *Speculum*, xlviii (1973), pp. 213–46 and D. P. Kirby's article of 1983 (for which see the bibliographical note to Chapter 1 above). Two significant articles on the relations between England and Gaul are: P. Sims-Williams, 'Continental Influences at Bath Monastery in the Seventh Century', *Anglo-Saxon England*, iv (1975), pp. 1–10 and E. Fletcher, 'The Influence of Merovingian Gaul on Northumbria in the Seventh Century', *Medieval Archaeology*, xix (1980), pp. 69–86.

2. Scenes from the life of Christ. This sixth-century Italian Gospel book may well have been brought to England by St. Augustine. *(Cambridge, Corpus Christi College, MS. 286, f. 125)*

4

Observations on the Conversion of England

It is appropriate that the 1300th anniversary of Bede's birth should be marked by the publication of the best account so far written of the conversion of England. Dr Henry Mayr-Harting's *The Coming of Christianity to Anglo-Saxon England.*[1] Learned, perceptive and eloquent, it illuminates its subject in innumerable ways. The main focus of its author's concern is, he says, with the clergy rather than with the laity. He is above all concerned to describe 'how Christianity itself was fashioned in this island, how churchmen prepared themselves by prayer, study and travel as well as by social awareness, to Christianise their world, and how they conceived their task'. His emphasis is 'rather on those who spread the Gospel than on those to whom it was spread'. While his work is more comprehensive than his own account of it might suggest, it is true that there are aspects of the conversion of which he has little to say. The purpose of the present article is to offer some passing and incomplete observations on some of the problems of when, how and with what effects the English became Christians. They are made partly in the light of Dr Mayr-Harting's account, partly in some degree to supplement it.[2]

The first question is, when did the conversion of the Anglo-Saxons begin? Bede's answer is clear: in 597. It would be absurd to question the substantial truth of what he says in so far as it applies to the arrival of the institutional Church and the beginning of the main stream of conversion; but it may not be the whole truth. Bede does not appear well informed on sixth century England. He knew relatively little even of Augustine's mission beyond what the letters of Gregory the Great told him. When he wrote *De Temporibus*, in 703, before he was familiar with those letters, he appeared unaware even of the true date of the English mission and it is 'at least doubtful whether he knew anything about Gregory's connection with the mission or about Augustine'.[3] It may be that the full story of the conversion of the English begins earlier than Bede's straightforward account would suggest. We do know of two Englishmen who were Christians before the coming of Augustine. Their names were Pilu and

[1] 1972.

[2] Among the important and relevant themes not even touched on below are those of the development of the cult of royal saints and of the development of the independent power of the Church in the later seventh century.

[3] P. Hunter Blair, *The Age of Bede* (1970), 68–9.

Genereus, and they were at Iona before the death of Columba, who died in 597.[4] Beyond this we have to depend on the speculative assessment of possibilities and plausibilities.

Some of the German settlers in Britain arrived before Roman rule ended. Of those who came later some, and perhaps many, were from peoples who had been active within or on the borders of the Empire. Bede's account of the origins of the Angles, Saxons and Jutes should not lead us to suppose that all the invaders came more or less directly from such insipid milieux as those of Kiel or Cuxhaven. The archaeological and literary evidence strongly suggests that some came from the Rhineland and from other areas in western Germany.[5] Some Saxons had long been associated with Franks; some settled in Gaul; and of these some may ultimately have come to Britain.[6] England did not become isolated after the period of invasion. It is clear that East Kent in particular had connections and intercourse in many directions. So some of the invaders were probably men who were familiar with the Roman, or a Romanised, world and some parts of England remained fairly closely connected with the Rhineland and with Gaul. That is to say that to some extent Anglo-Saxon England formed part of an interconnected German world in other parts of which Christianity was known. It has, for example, become clear during the last generation that even in the Rhineland strong Christian communities survived the fall of the Empire.[7] The first Saxons we know to have become Christians did so in about 560. They were living in the diocese of Nantes, in an area which we know to have had commercial contact with England.[8] It may not be irrelevant to observe that the great increase in the later sixth and early seventh centuries in the number of bishops in northern and central Gaul, and in the Rhine and Moselle valleys, who bore Germanic names suggests that the German ruling class in these areas was becoming more committed to or involved in the Church than had previously been the case.[9] We can feel fairly sure that there were Anglo-Saxons before 597

---

[4] *Adomnan's Life of Columba*, ed. A. O. and M. O. Anderson (1961), 486 and 512. Genereus was the community's baker.

[5] E.g., J. N. L. Myres, *Anglo-Saxon Pottery and the Settlement of England* (1969), 77. Bede, *H. E.*, V, ix (above, p. 53, n. 25) would be consonant with a movement from the Rhineland and from western parts of Germany in the fifth century. In view of the odd reference in this passage to Huns it is not without interest that according to Priscus, Attila boasted that he ruled over 'the islands in the ocean'. C. E. Stevens, 'Gildas Sapiens', *Eng. Hist. Rev.*, lvi (1941), 363, n. 9.

[6] Above, p. 54.

[7] For an indication of the strength of the archaelogical evidence see e.g., *Frühchristliche Zeugnisse in Einzugsgebiet von Rhein und Mosel*, ed. T. F. Kempf and W. Reusch (Trier 1965).

[8] Above, p. 54, n. 26.

[9] H. Wieruzowski, 'Die Zusammensetzung des gallischen und fränkischen Episkopats', *Bonner Jahrbücher*, cxxvii (1922), 1–83, esp. 14. While it cannot be assumed that nomenclature is necessarily a secure guide to racial origin (ibid., 15, 25) the

to whom the sight of a basilica, or of a bishop, would not have come as a surprise. We may think it likely that German Christians came to England and perfectly possible that Englishmen became Christians. We should perhaps look at the conversion of Kent in the context of some general change in the relationship towards the Church of German peoples living in areas of the Continent with which that kingdom certainly had contacts and which it may have resembled more closely than it did most of the rest of England.

Adomnan's reference to Saxon monks at Iona is a reminder that the missionaries to Northumbria in the 630's may not have been the first Irishmen to seek English souls. A late life of St Columba of Terryglass, thought to contain early materials, at least says that he visited an (unnamed) English kingdom about the middle of the sixth century, and adds the circumstantial detail that cremation was practiced there.[10] An ogham inscription of Silchester bears witness to the presence of two, presumably Christian, Irishmen there at about the time of Augustine.[11] It is not an impressive body of evidence. But if Irish monks came to England at or before the time of Columbanus's venture to Gaul in 590 it is not only uncertain, but even unlikely, that our sources are good enough to have informed us of this.[12] We do happen to know, thanks to Bede's preservation of part of a letter from Archbishop Laurentius, that an Irish bishop, called Dagan, came to Kent at some time in the first or second decade of the seventh century.[13] That we have this incidental reference to one such visit strengthens the case for entertaining the possibility that there were others.[14]

The most difficult and important problems in relation to Christianity

contention that very marked increases in the proportions of bishops with Germanic names is significant seems just; and at the very least it must be significant of a great increase in the acceptability of Germanic names. It is of some interest that the appearance of the first Bishop of Cologne to bear a Germanic name (in 590) marks the point from which the series of bishops is continuously known, *Frühchristliches Köln* (Romisch-Germanisches Museum, Cologne 1965), 11.

[10] J. Morris in *Christianity in Britain, 300–700*, ed. M. W. Barley and R. P. C. Hanson (1968), 66; J. F. Kenney, *Sources for the Early History of Ireland* (1929), 385–6.

[11] If one may so paraphrase Professor K. Jackson's reported opinion on the date of the inscription: 'the form of the lettering probably precludes a date significantly earlier than the seventh century although the linguistic forms could suit better a rather earlier date', *Mediev. Archaeol.*, iii (1959), 87.

[12] The evidence suggests that even in the seventh century there could have been Irish monasteries in England of which our sources say nothing, see above, pp. 51–52.

[13] Bede, *H. E.* II, iv.

[14] It has to be borne in mind that in this period Irish immigration into western parts of Britain was on a large scale. Professor C. Thomas goes so far as to say that 'It is by no means improbable that, during the fifth and sixth centuries A. D., the sum total of Irish settlers and their families in western Britain equalled or even exceeded that of the various Germanic tribes on Britain's eastern and southern shores', *Britain and Ireland in Early Christian Times* (1971), 66.

among the English before 597 have to do with their relationship to the Britons. They thus involve the great issue of "continuity". This is hardly the place to venture into that desert where one man's mirage is another's oasis. At least it can be said with confidence that of the Christians living in England in Bede's day very many owed their faith to traditions which went back beyond Augustine to the British Church. This must have been true of Wessex where Britons conquered after 658 were living under English rule, where it is not unlikely that British religious houses were absorbed into the West Saxon Church and where relations with the British Church may have been more friendly than they were elsewhere. It is highly probable that Northumbria contained considerable numbers of British Christians. The same could be true of parts of Mercia.[15] Within south-eastern England a considerable area north and north-west of London remained in British hands until within a generation of 597.[16] It may have included St Alban's, where, Bede says, and the weighty authority of Levison accepts, that the cult of the saint was maintained from Roman times until the eighth century.[17] If so, when Saeberht, King of Essex, was converted by Augustine's mission he had already had a Christian shrine within his kingdom.[18] The presence of two place-names in Norfolk and one in Kent containing the element 'eccles' (which seems to derive from the British word for a church) is suggestive of the survival of British churches in the south-east.[19] The survival, or possible survival, of Christian Britons under Anglo-Saxon rule does not, in itself, contradict Bede's adamantine insistence that the Britons did nothing to convert his countrymen.[20] It does suggest that he is unlikely to have been entirely right.

Until the last generation of the sixth century and the first of the seventh we have little knowledge of the deeds of Anglo-Saxon kings. As soon as, thanks to Bede, we have more information than the curt annals of the *Chronicle* afford, we find that kings have close relationships with their Christian neighbours. The king of Kent married a Christian princess.[21] The sons of a king of Northumbria went into exile among the Christian Scots.[22] A pagan war-lord in Mercia allied with a

---

[15] Mayr-Harting, *The Coming of Christianity*, 118–20; H. P. R. Finberg, *Lucerna*, (1964), 4–6, 85, 98; K. Jackson, 'Angles and Saxons in Northumbria and Cumbria' in *Angles and Britons* (O'Donnell Lectures, Cardiff, 1963, no editor), 60–84, cf. G. W. S. Barrow, 'Northern English Society . . .', *Northern History*, iv (1969), 1–17.

[16] F. M. Stenton, *Anglo-Saxon England* (1947), 27.

[17] *H. E.* I, vii; W. Levison, 'St. Alban and St. Alban's', *Antiquity*, xv (1941), 350–9.

[18] On the assumption that Hertfordshire was within the kingdom of Essex.

[19] K. Cameron in *Christianity in Britain, 300–700*, op. cit., 87–92.

[20] Cf. K. Hughes, *The Church in Early Irish Society* (1966), 43 for British ecclesiastical legislation tending to bear out what Bede says.

[21] Bede, *H. E.* I, xxvi.

[22] *H. E.* III, i; cf. IV, xxiii.

Christian king in Wales.[23] Such relationships of marriage, exile and alliance may have been new, happening for the first time at just the period when we have a source which will reveal them. The assumption is defensible, but a large one. It is equally likely that they were not new and that Anglo-Saxon kings had for long had relations with Christians and Christian relatives.

It is possible then that the arrival of Augustine begins not the first, but a later, stage in the conversion of England. The English were exposed from more directions than one to Christian influences which may have been growing in strength during the sixth century. In England, as elsewhere in the former Empire, we should perhaps imagine a kind of proto-Christianity preceding the re-establishment of an organised Church. It may have been a world in which there were a considerable number of Christian survivals or half-survivals, one in which Christians and the Church were not universally unfamiliar, and in which individual Christians and conversions were known. The possibility of there having been both Churches and missions of which our sources tell us nothing has always to be borne in mind. To be convinced of this one has only to contrast the written and the archaeological records for Christian survival in parts of the Rhineland, or to reflect how numerous are the seventh century missions of which, were it not for Bede, we should know nothing.

Whatever may have happened before 597 there can be no doubt that the series of royal conversions which began with Augustine's mission was of the utmost importance. What persuaded English kings to become Christians? In the first place argument, no doubt. Our only indication of the arguments brought to bear on Ethelbert comes in Gregory's letter to the king.[24] The Pope stressed that God could make the king's 'glorious name still more glorious even to posterity' (citing the example of Constantine) and drew attention to indications of the imminence of the end of the world. In the appeal to the love of glory, to Roman example and to fear may be recognised the experienced touch of one whose dealings with the Lombards must have made him an old hand at coping with barbarian potentates. Bede's fullest account of a conversion is of that of Edwin of Northumbria.[25] Here two main emphases appear. One is that of the famous account of the nobleman who compared a man's life to a small bird flying through a hall in winter, in one door and out the other, from the unknown to the unknown: Christianity explains the mysteries of life and death. The second emphasis (it is one which appeared time and again in the

[23] *H. E.* II, xx.
[24] *H. E.* I, xxxii (written after Ethelbert had accepted the faith). (For a detailed account of the sources relating to the arguments used in preaching to the Germans see R. E. Sullivan, 'The Carolingian Missionary and the Pagan', *Speculum*, xxviii (1953), 703–40, esp. 715–8).   [25] *H. E.* II, ix–xiv.

'Ecclesiastical History') is that God will reward his followers with victory and wealth here on earth. Edwin put this contention to a successful trial before he undertook to renounce idols. A third line of argument appears in Bede's account of the conversion of King Sigbert of Essex.[26] Here the inanities of idol-worship alone are stressed. The longest account from an English context of arguments for use in conversion comes in Bishop Daniel's letter to St Boniface (723–4) advising him on how to approach the pagan Germans.[27] He advises two lines of argument. One is to tie the heathen in dialectical knots 'calmly and with great moderation', so making them ashamed of the illogicalities and follies of paganism 'more out of confusion than exasperation'. The other is to demonstrate that pagan gods looked after their servants ill. Ask them, Daniel says, why their gods have left them in 'the frozen lands of the north', 'while the Christians are allowed to possess the countries that are rich in wine and oil'. It would be quite wrong to assume that missionaries saw, or kings came to see, their faith as confined to such coarse simplicities.[28] It is, however, a fair assumption that the initial arguments often enough relied heavily on the contentions that pagans were fools and Christians prospered.

Kings, being kings, were influenced by considerations of power. They could be taught to fear and enlist the power of the Almighty. They did not need teaching to respect that of a great overlord. It has long been recognised that the first expansion of Christianity from Kent to Essex and East Anglia reflected the authority of Ethelbert as overlord of southern England and that its first retreat from those kingdoms was a consequence of Kent's loss of power. Dr Mayr-Harting carries this line of argument further in his account of the conversion of Edwin. He suggests that it is significant both that Edwin was not converted until after the death of Redwald of East Anglia (who had been his protector and whose power derived from 'his shaking off the overlordship and the Christianity of Ethelbert') and also that, once baptised, the first thing Edwin did was to secure the baptism of Eorpwald, Redwald's successor. 'He made sure to set the tune for the East Anglian king to play'.[29] The connection between the power of a Christian overlord and

[26] *H. E.* III, xxii.

[27] *S. Bonifatii et Lullii Epistolae* (M. G. H. Epistolae Selectae, i), ed. M. Tangl (1916), No. 23. I have used the translation by C. H. Talbot, *The Anglo-Saxon Missionaries in Germany* (1954). The arguments suggested contain little that is specifically Christian, and could have been employed by an Arian, or a Jew.

[28] See p. 11 above. Cf. *H. E.* III, v, for the lack of success of a missionary who failed to begin by offering the milk of simpler teaching.

[29] *The Coming of Christianity*, 66–7. Dr Mayr-Harting's acceptance of Dr. D. P. Kirby's argument that Paulinus went north as early as 619 needs reconsideration in the light of P. Hunter Blair's discussion of the issues of *England before the Conquest*, ed. P. Clemoes and K. Hughes (1971), 5–14. The details, but not the main lines, of Dr. Mayr-Harting's argument are affected.

the conversion of other kings is most obvious in the time of the Northumbrian overlords, Oswald and Oswy. The conversion of the kings of Wessex, Essex and Middle Anglia was in whole or in part the responsibility of one of these rulers.[30]

It is possible that the relationship of godfather to godson was of special importance in these conversions. We know that Oswald stood godfather to Cynegils of Wessex. It is likely, though not stated by Bede, that Oswy was godfather to Sigbert of Essex and to Peada of Middle Anglia, since both were baptised in Northumbria. When Bede tells us of the baptism of a king in England and names a godfather, the godfather is also a king.[31] His most revealing account of such a baptism is of that of Aethelwalh of Sussex, which took place at some time before the death of Wulfhere of Mercia (658–674) and presumably at a time when Wulfhere was overlord in southern England. Aethelwalh was baptised in Mercia 'in the presence and at the suggestion of King Wulfhere who, when Aethelwalh came forth from the font, accepted him as a son. As a token of his adoption Wulfhere gave him two provinces, namely the Isle of Wight and the province of the Meonware'. Here, apparently, is an overlord standing godfather to a lesser king (though one cannot be quite sure that the godfathership is what Bede means to imply) and this relationship associated with that of adoption. Adoption was important to the Anglo-Saxons. For example, in 'Beowulf', after the hero has killed Grendel, King Hrothgar says he will regard him as his son, and the language used ('henceforth keep well this new kinship') suggests that this statement was more formal and carried more weight than a mere figure of speech.[32] Furthermore the laws of Ine illustrate how a godfather-godson relationship could be regarded as establishing ties comparable to those of blood.[33] Such relationships may have had importance in linking overlords and lesser kings because they created such ties and provided means of uniting dignified subordination with mutual obligation.

In stressing the connections between Christianity and overlordship (and there are others besides those mentioned here) we must beware of being positive that the courts and the policies of these kings were so strongly coloured by Christianity as Bede may wish us to believe. For example, his account of the conversion of Sigbert of Essex shows that Sigbert was a frequent visitor to Oswy's court before he became a Christian, that is to say into the 650's.[34] The marriage of Oswy's

[30] *H. E.* III, vii; III, xxii; III, xxi.

[31] *H. E.* III, xxii; IV, xiii.

[32] Lines 946–9, translation by J. R. Clark Hall revised by C. R. Wrenn (1950), 69; cf. lines 1, 175–6.

[33] Ine, c. 76. (On the compensation payable to a godfather for the killing of a godson, and conversely.)

[34] *H. E.* III, xxii.

daughter to Penda's son (653), Oswy's son already having married Penda's daughter, justifies the supposition that Penda himself was for a time among Oswy's pagan allies. Bede does not say so in so many words, but his readers would hardly have missed the implication, and it is presumably for this reason that Bede, who otherwise has hardly a good word to say for Penda, at this juncture thinks fit to present him to the role of Good Pagan, one who tolerated missionaries and despised Christians who did not obey the precepts of their faith.[35]

Kings might be convinced by the arguments advanced by missionaries and they might take these more seriously to heart if they were backed by the power of a *bretwalda*. However the initial step was taken, some kings can hardly have failed to notice the advantages which the Church offered to rulers. The acceptance of Christianity was often followed by the introduction of more sophisticated means of government and the Christianization of England may be seen as part of a process whereby the English kingdoms became more like those of Gaul.[36] The Church may have provided means to power even more important than those associated with, for example, the introduction of written laws. Looked at very generally the political development of England in the seventh century can be seen as marked by two great movements, which provided new opportunities and new problems for certain kings. The first is the creation or wide extension of the three frontier kingdoms of Mercia, Northumbria and Wessex and their gaining power at the expense of those of the south and east. The second, largely associated with the first, is the absorption, by fair means or foul, of small kingdoms into larger ones. In both movements Christianity had a part to play. The new or newly enlarged kingdoms of the frontier were of the unprecedented size. The Church may have been of great service to kings in reaching and controlling their peoples. The most obvious case is that of Northumbria. There is little reason to doubt that by the time of Aidan a considerable proportion of the inhabitants of Northumbria were Britons.[37] If so it may have mattered to its kings to be associated with Celtic ecclesiastics. The monastic movement which began to affect the Celtic world in the sixth century seems to have aroused great enthusiasm and its effects may sometimes have amounted almost to the reconversion of peoples whose Christianity had become dormant.[38] When such a movement was brought to Celtic population by English kings, upon whom the holy

[35] *H.E.* III, xxi.

[36] Pp. 65–67 above.

[37] P. 72 above.

[38] J. Morris, 'The Celtic Saints', *Past and Present*, No 11 (1957), 1–14 and 'The Dates of the Celtic Saints', *Journ. of Theological Studies*, new ser., xvii (1966), 342–91, for a fairly extreme view. J. Ryan, *Irish Monasticism* (1931), 104–45, and L. Gougaud, *Les Chrétientés Celtiques*, 2nd ed. (Paris 1911), chapter 3, for others less so.

men looked with favour, the kings presumably gained. In general kings needed obedience and veneration from kingdoms to large parts of which their dynasties were new and which contained tracts of wild country inhabited by men hardly less so; areas as such as men like Cuthbert set themselves to penetrate.

With some English kings in the seventh century as with Frankish kings in the eighth conquest went hand in hand with Christianity. Bede provides extensive materials for the study of Christian conquerors. It may suffice here to consider one extreme and sordid example. It is his account of the conquest of the Isle of Wight by Caedwalla, King of Wessex, in 686.[39] Wight was an independent or semi-independent kingdom with a dynasty of its own and it was pagan, probably the last kingdom to remain so. Caedwalla attacked it and sought to wipe out its inhabitants. Though not yet baptised he acted in association with St Wilfrid, to whom he promised a quarter of the island. When he captured two boys, brothers of the island's king, he killed them, acting no doubt according to the practical wisdom of the day which saw that the only safe member of a rival dynasty was a dead one. He did, however, allow them to be baptised first so that 'they gladly submitted to temporal death'. Wilfrid duly received his share of the island and assigned it to one of his clergy, a nephew of his, as it happened. He associated a priest with him to teach and to baptise. The men of Wight had lost their independence, but gained the faith. It is likely that in such a conquest as this, as with conquests made by the Franks, conversion was an aid to subjection. It may well be that there was an association in minds of men such as those of Wight between their old rulers and their old gods. A new power established a new faith; and a new faith may have helped to establish a new power.

The mere presence of ecclesiastics, almost irrespective of what they did, may have been of advantage to kings. If one of the signs of and means to royal power was to have a great hall full of noblemen, drinking hard and royally entertained, then the presence of important strangers, equipped with luxurious objects and performing unusual ceremonies, may have been in itself of value, not only, though perhaps principally, because it indicated connection with distant powers, but also as a source of interest and entertainment. The king who took a Columbanus or a Cedd on with such a end in view would, of course, have got more than he bargained for. But the attraction to barbarian kings of things which to us may seem trivial appears, for example, in Bede's account of the behaviour of the sons of Sæberht, King of Essex, after the death of their father (616 or 617).[40] They were pagans, but they nevertheless demanded from Bishop Mellitus the communion bread. 'Why don't you offer us

---

[39] *H.E.* IV, xiv.
[40] *H.E.* II, v.

the white bread which you used to give to our father Saba?' The bishop said they would have to be baptised first. They replied, 'We are not going into that font, for we do not know that we stand in any need of it. All the same, we will eat that bread'. Whether they wanted the bread because it was magic bread, or simply because it was white bread, we cannot tell. In either case Bede's little story suggests the attractions of the unfamiliar things which were the incidentals of Christian worship.

To turn from the piety and power of kings to the conversion of the mass of Anglo-Saxons is to pass from a flickering light to greater darkness. Bede tells us that the conversion of kings was followed by the conversion, sometimes the mass conversion, of subjects. It is clear, however, that many could remain pagan for long afterwards. The first English king to forbid the worship of idols was, he says, Earconberht, King of Kent, 640–64.[41] He does not tell us who the next was and leaves us in the dark as to when it was that all the English became at least nominally Christian. The general tenor of the 'Ecclesiastical History' suggests that this stage had been reached by the time he was writing it, in *c.* 731. The last pagan kingdom was probably Wight, whose conversion did not begin until 686.[42] It is strange that Bede should not provide more than approximate means of knowing when the public exercise of pagan cults ended. It is easy to imagine that many of the nominally Christian had only a limited knowledge of their faith and remained in many ways pagans, and this must have been so. Yet even here much of the evidence turns in the hand as one seeks to use it. For example, Bede, in his 'Life of Cuthbert', has a famous story of how a *vulgaris turba* watched some monks drifting out to sea on rafts and said 'Let no man pray for them, and may God have no mercy on any of them, for they have robbed men of their old ways of worship and how the new worship is to be conducted, nobody knows'.[43] This painful scene can be taken to show 'how slow was the progress of Christianity in the more remote districts and in fact everywhere'.[44] But was this *turba* one of imperfectly converted pagans? Is it not more likely that they were Christians objecting to changes which had been brought about in their worship by the monastery from which the monks came? Their remarks as quoted would be more consonant with their being Christians and few students of ecclesiastical history can regard more than a moderately extensive change in modes of worship as required to ensure that some of the conservative faithful would allow the innovators to drift beyond the horizon on rafts of fire-wood. Again, we may deduce from much of what Bede says that the Church was, for a

---

[41] *H.E.* III, viii.
[42] P. 77 above.
[43] *Two Lives of St. Cuthbert*, ed. B. Colgrave (1940), 163–5.
[44] Ibid., 343 (Colgrave's commentary); cf. Mayr-Harting, *The Coming of Christianity*, 240–1.

considerable time, short of manpower. Priests were few and much depended on the bishop himself, touring his diocese and bringing the sacraments to his flock, it may be annually. No doubt this was sometimes or often so. But it is not easy to estimate how far it was so at a given date. It may be that Bede's concentration upon bishops and saints gives us a misleading impression that what may be called rank and file missionaries and priests were fewer than in fact they were. Certainly there were by the end of the seventh century numerous, it may be very numerous, monasteries, very many of which would have some degree of pastoral responsibility.[45]

We cannot doubt that there were many pagan survivals and that pagan and Christian beliefs and attitudes naturally became very much involved together.[46] Here again our evidence fails in chronological precision. One of the essential difficulties is that such survivals and interactions went on for so long. It is legitimate to point to the mid-seventh century Finglesham brooch with its heathen figure, perhaps of Woden, or to the persistence of pagan place-names as evidence for the strength of paganism.[47] But pagan pictures are with us yet (of immense size, and brazenly flaunted on hill-sides)[48] and so, too, are pagan place-names. Once these things stood for living paganism; now they are interesting survivals. In between lies a whole series of transitions of attitude towards them. But how can we tell whether one of the generations after the initial conversion saw a more decisive change in attitude than another, or whether such a generation was early or late? The period was one of drastic and rapid change, yet our sources are such as to drive us to blur the distinctions between generations, very different from one another though we know they must have been.

In determining the chronology of the conversion of the mass of the population archaeology is becoming increasingly helpful. In recent years attention has been drawn to a series of cemeteries in many parts of the country which appear to mark a transition from paganism to Christianity in the seventh century.[49] The graves do not normally contain grave-goods except in so far as the dead were buried in their ordinary dress with fastenings and ornaments with such adjuncts of everyday wear as knives. In Kent some of these cemeteries begin in the early seventh century, but generally the period of use appears to have

[45] Above, pp. 51–52.

[46] W. A. Chaney, *The Cult of Kingship in Anglo-Saxon England* (1970) contains an extensive account of much of what is involved.

[47] As Dr. Mayr-Harting does, *The Coming of Christianity*, 64.

[48] E.g. the Cerne Abbas giant is a pagan figure if ever there was one.

[49] M. Hyslop, 'Two Anglo-Saxon Cemeteries at . . . Leighton Buzzard', *Archaeolog. Journ.*, cxx (1963), 161–200 and, most recently, A. L. Meaney and S. C. Hawkes, *Two Anglo-Saxon Cemeteries at Winnall* (Society for Medieval Archaeology, Monograph Series, no 4, 1970). Miss Hyslop suggests that such cemeteries can be identified in Beds., Berks., Cambs., Hants., Oxon., Somerset, Surrey and Yorks.

been from about the middle of the seventh century until about the middle of the eighth. A number of these cemeteries are near earlier pagan cemeteries, suggesting a deliberate move from an old to a new site. Although the study of these cemeteries is not yet fully developed and the inferences on which they are judged to be Christian are not absolutely secure it does look as if they provide evidence for the conversion of the communities concerned. In the course of the eighth century the deposit of grave-gods of any kind ceased and it appears that cemeteries were then generally moved to sites beside churches within towns and villages.[50]

Perhaps the most important, but by no means the least difficult, source for the extent to which England was converted by the early eighth century is the secular and canon law of the period. The implications of some of this material are to a surprising degree other than what one might *a priori* have expected. They suggest strict royal control in the interests of the Church and extensive ecclesiastical control over the life of the laity. For example, the laws of Ine impose heavy penalties for failure to have a child baptised within forty days of birth or for working on a Sunday.[51] Earconberht of Kent, Bede tells us, not only forbade the worship of idols but also, more remarkably, enforced *principali auctoritate* the observance of the forty days Lenten fast. The relationship between royal and ecclesiastical laws and powers was close, and important both to kings and to the Church. For example, it has recently been fairly convincingly argued that Ine of Wessex's enforcement of rights of sanctuary would have been of great advantage to the king in so far as it could have ensured that fleeing criminals who took sanctuary would either have become royal slaves or paid heavily to the king. On this argument a sanctuary was *inter alia* a royal slave-trap.[52]

The *Penitential* of Theodore and the *Dialogue* of Egbert seem to show an elaborately organised Church and priests exercising close control over their flocks, above all through penance. Not the least of Dr. Mayr-Harting's virtues is that he uses these canon law sources, of which some of his predecessors have tended to fight shy. 'It is,' he says, 'in the field of penance that we see most clearly the attempt to project an ideal monastic life on to society as a whole.'[53] Laymen, like monks, were expected to put the whole of their moral lives under the close direction

[50] For the importance of the study of cemeteries in the Celtic lands and for important observations upon certain English cemeteries see C. Thomas, *The Early Christian Archaeology of North Britain* (1971), Chapter 3.

[51] Ine, c.2, c.3. For sabbatarianism in the period see *Adomnan's Life of Columba*, ed. Anderson and Anderson, op. cit., 25–8.

[52] C. H. Riggs, *Criminal Asylum in Anglo-Saxon Law* (University of Florida Monographs, Social Science No 18, 1963), Chapter 1.

[53] *The Coming of Christianity*, 257.

of a priest. The penitential codes which developed in the Celtic churches and spread, above all via the collections made under the influence of Theodore in England, to the western Church as a whole, were to guide confessors. Occasionally such a code may be seen to temper the wind to the shorn barbarian lamb, as in the extremely light penance imposed in Theodore's *Penitential* on a man who slays at the command of his lord – forty days abstention from church, while accidental killing required a year's penance and other kinds of killing far more.[54] But in general they speak of a minute and rigorously puritanical rule of conduct and of conscience.

The great question in regard to both secular and ecclesiastical codes is that of how far they were expressions in the main merely of aspirations and much more honoured in the breach than in the observance, and how far, on the contrary, they were genuinely effective forces in determining the lives and beliefs of the people. The general tendency of English historians is to leave the question on one side, while rather assuming that the first answer is more likely to be true (especially of the ecclesiastical codes) than the second. Such an assumption is understandable, for it is not easy to reconcile much of what is said in and implied by the laws and penitentials with our other information on Anglo-Saxon society. For all that, these codes probably tell us about a great deal which really happened. Certainly if the penitentials express mere aspirations their popularity shows that such aspirations came to be widely held. Dr Mayr-Harting interestingly draws attention to a passage in Egbert's *Dialogue* which at least professes to speak not of intention, but of fact.[55] Egbert says that from the time of Theodore the English people practised fasts, vigils, prayers, and the giving of alms for the full twelve days before Christmas, as if this were prescribed by law. Not only the clergy in the monasteries but also the laity with their wives and families would resort to their confessors and 'wash themselves of carnal concupiscence by tears, community life and alms in those twelve days' so preparing themselves for the Christmas communion. This surprising picture is, at the very least, a reminder of how little we can be sure of about the religious, as about all other, aspects of the life of the early English.

The safest principle in the study of the conversion of England is one of doubt, of the acceptance of the widest range of possibilities. To take two questions touched upon above: we do not know whether England was in some degree Christianised before 597; we cannot be certain how elaborated, sophisticated and secure the organisation of kingdoms and of the Church was by 700. In both instances there is a better case than is commonly accepted for at least a suspension of disbelief in what may

---

[54] Hadden and Stubbs, *Councils*, i, 180.
[55] *The Coming of Christianity*, 257.

appear *prima facie* the more extravagant possibilities. Two generalisations, safe because very general, can be made about seventh century England and its Church. The first is that the success of the Church was associated with and helped to cause very important changes in area with which religion has nothing directly to do. Some of these have already been mentioned. There are others. One of the most obvious was in which the Church helped, directly or indirectly, to change the nature of English politics was through the introduction of bookland, land held by charter. If Mr. Eric John is right (and his case is a powerful one) in arguing that in early England nobles held land only by precarious tenure and that perpetual, heritable tenure came in with the charter, then English noblemen getting charters, by covert means from about the end of the seventh century and openly from the later eighth, could have meant a major transformation in the life and relationships of the English ruling class.[56] The conversion could have had very extensive economic effects. The largest communities of any kind which we know to have been living in one place in early Anglo-Saxon England were those inhabiting the twin monasteries of Monkwearmouth and Jarrow. Bede says that in 716 the brethren of the two monasteries numbered nearly 600.[57] Our only evidence for the size of secular communities comes from cemeteries; not even the largest of these would suggest a population of 300 in one community. The scale of Monkwearmouth-Jarrow's agricultural activities is suggested by the fact that the three great manuscripts of the Bible written there in the time of Abbot Ceolfrith (688 or 9 to 716) would have required the skins of 1,550 calves.[58] Monkwearmouth-Jarrow was an altogether exceptional monastery, but there were other big ones, and by the end of the seventh century it is likely that monasteries of all kinds were very numerous. Thus there is quite a strong possibility that the development of monasticism brought about major changes in the pattern of settlement, and that by 700 in much of England the nearest approximation to a town was a major monastery. We know that certain new techniques were introduced by the Church: for example, building in stone and the use of glass windows. Bede provides an instance of the Church introducing a technique at a more basic level. When Wilfrid was engaged in converting Sussex in the early 680's he taught the inhabitants how to catch fish; previously they had only been able to catch eels, but the bishop showed them how to use eel nets for catching other kinds of fish, with encouraging results.[59] It was in the nature of

---

[56] E. John, *Land Tenure in Early England* (1960), 1–63; cf. F. M. Stenton, *Latin Charters of the Anglo-Saxon Period* (1955), 60–62.

[57] *Opera Historica*, ed. Plummer, i, 382.

[58] R. L. S. Bruce Mitford, 'The Art of the Codex Amiatinus', *Journ. Archaeolog. Assoc.*, 3rd ser. xxxii (1969), p 2 of the off-print.

[59] *H.E.* IV, xiii.

the monastic life that men of wide experience, who might rise to positions of great authority, became involved in manual labour with which otherwise those of such birth as theirs never sullied their hands. It may well be supposed that Wilfrid owed his expertise in fishing to experience gained at Lindisfarne and one is entitled to guess that the particular case involving him of which we know may be one of many instances, of which we do not know, of ecclesiastics introducing new techniques.

The analysis of the apparently Christian cemeteries of the seventh century had revealed other possible implications of the conversion which extend beyond religion. The ornaments and objects found in them are, we are told, very different from those which appear in earlier cemeteries. The brooches and necklaces are, by and large, of new kinds. There are differences in weapons, when they appear. Objects of kinds almost unknown before, for example 'thread-boxes' become fairly common.[60] These transformations might signify no more than a change in fashion. But it said that not only are the new objects and styles derived in the first instance from Kent but also that 'for the first time in the Anglo-Saxon period parallels for our material are not found in North Germany and Scandinavia but in South Germany, Switzerland, and more particularly Italy!'.[61] The diffusion of the new style looks as if it was associated with the conversion and it appears possible that a religion which had much to do with Italy and fashions in ornament which had much to do with Italy came in at the same time. T. C. Lethbridge suggested that conversion was accompanied by both men and women becoming 'much less ostentatious and barbaric in their dress than they had a century earlier'. He went on to hint that a transition from Teutonic to classical dress may have accompanied the conversion.[62] He did not press, nor should we, the idea that one of the first duties or inclinations of a convert was to throw away his trousers and replace them by something in the nature of a toga, or kilt. But it does look as if the conversion may have been accompanied by, or have caused, changes in dress. It could be an expression of that association of *Romanitas* with religion which one seems to see in another way in, for example, the regular buildings of Monkwearmouth and Jarrow, much more like Roman villas than anything which had been built in the north for nearly three hundred years.[63] The attitude of mind of African and Asian converts in the nineteenth century who may have found difficulty (so reflecting something about their mentors) in distinguishing top hats and the Early English style in architecture from

[60] Hyslop, 'Two Anglo-Saxon cemeteries . . .', op. cit., 190–2.
[61] Ibid., 191.
[62] T. C. Lethbridge, *Merlin's Isle* (1948), 144–6, cf. p 00 above.
[63] R. Cramp, 'Excavations at the Saxon Monastic Sites of Wearmouth and Jarrow: an Interim Report', *Mediev. Archaeolog.*, xiii (1969), 21–66.

the essentials of the Christian religion, is one which *mutatis mutandis* may easily have appeared in seventh century England. Compare the ruling, in what Miss Hughes regards as a sixth century Irish canon, that clerics must (in her words) 'conform in three ways to civilised Roman conditions: by wearing a tunic, shaving their heads, and seeing their wives go veiled'. A comparable ruling of a Welsh synod requires that no *catholicus* should let his hair grow *more barbarorum*.[64]

Our second safe generalisation is that England and its Church contained much diversity. Dr Mayr-Harting lays justified stress on the variety of the traditions of the Church and on the continuing and valuable strength of 'localism'. The English Church was full of contrasts: between Monkwearmouth/Jarrow with its daily masses and Lindisfarne with its less frequent celebration,[65] between the learning of Bede and the very different learning of Aldhelm,[66] between monasteries where miracles were believed to be regularly performed and others where they hardly occurred.[67] The Church contained genuinely holy men of very diverse kinds. It came to include men whose learning was strangely applied. It is hard to believe, in the light of recent studies revealing the elaborate sophistication of the inscriptions on the Franks casket, that they are not the work of a cleric.[68] What are we to make of the mental world of one who related the Christian, the classical, and the very barbarously pagan as they are related on this casket? The Church also came to include some strange institutions, for example, the 'righteous man' who would perform penances for others for a consideration.[69] The conversion of England has to be understood in relation to societies almost as complex and to views and beliefs quite as diverse as those found in later centuries. In seeking to understand it we should beware (it may well be that in what is written above I have bewared insufficiently) of taking a striking or moving instance as a guide to the whole; and we should always be ready to be surprised.

---

[64] K. Hughes, *The Church in Early Irish Society* (1966), 47–8.
[65] *The Coming of Christianity*, 163.
[66] Ibid., 214–9.
[67] Above pp. 41–43.
[68] Most recently M. Osborn, 'The Grammar of the Inscription on the Franks Casket, Right Side', *Neuphilologische Mitteilungen*, lxxiii (1972), 663–71.
[69] J. T. McNeill and H. Gamer, *Medieval Handbooks of Penance* (1938), 236 (though this may not be English).

The 'Additional Bibliographical Note' at the end of Chapter 3 applies to this chapter also.

5

Bede's Reges and Principes

Bede dedicated his *Ecclesiastical History* to a king, and it is in a degree a mirror for princes. Yet he by no means sought to tell all that he knew about kings. On the contrary, to the extent that he sought to typify and to edify he was both discreet and selective. The description of secular institutions was alien to his intention. His book was written for the purposes which do not conform to all the needs of our curiosity. So, often it proves a reticent or an ambiguous witness. To ask of it so superficially simple a question as 'What is a *rex*?' is not to gain a simple answer. Bede uses the the word for rulers of widely differing power. He refers regularly to *reges* of Northumbria, Mercia, Essex, Wessex, Sussex, Kent and East Anglia.[1] No grander noun is employed for the great overlords enjoying power over most of Britain. At the other extreme he mentions *reges* apparently of lesser status than those of the major kingdoms. Thus once, but only once, he mentions a king of Wight.[2] Another lesser *rex* appears in his account of Penda's son Peada, ruler of the Middle Angles and 'iuvenis optimus et regis nomine et persona dignissimus'. Most worthy of the title of king Peada may have been; all the same Bede does not seem too sure about giving it to him. He does so once, but twice elsewhere Peada is *princeps*[3] *Princeps* in his usage is not easy to define; it is not for him an ordinary synonym for *rex*, though it can include *reges*; sometimes it denotes important men

---

The notes have been kept to a minimum and are by no means fully comprehensive. The following abbreviations have been used in them.

B.	*W. de Gray Birch, Cartularium Saxonicum*, 3 vols, and index (1885–89).
OH	*Venerabilis Baedae Opera Historica*, ed. C. Plummer, 2 vols. (Oxford, 1896).
S.	*P. H. Sawyer, Anglo-Saxon Charters. An Annotated List and Bibliography* (1968).
Two Chronicles	*Two of the Saxon Chronicles Parallel*, ed. C. Plummer and J. Earle, 2 vols. (Oxford, 1892, 1899).

The numbers given in references to B. and S. are those of the charters.

[1] Also for those of Bernicia and Deira. For Bede's usages of *rex* and of other words discussed below see P. F. Jones, *A Concordance to the Historia Ecclesiastica of Bede* (Cambridge, Mass. 1929) *s.v.*

[2] *OH*, i, p. 237.

[3] *OH* i, pp. 169, 354.

subordinated to kings, but possibly such as had independent authority.[4] Bede uses other terms related to, but not synonymous with *rex*. After the death of Cenwalh, Wessex was, he says, divided among *subreguli*.[5] In describing Penda's forces at the battle of the Winwaed he first says they included 'xxx legiones ducibus nobilissimis', but a moment later calls these *duces* not *nobilissimi* but *regii*.[6] It appears that to Bede some potentates were indubitably *reges*, while others did not unambiguously deserve such a description, but nevertheless had something regal about them.

His vocabulary for kingdoms and peoples is no more clear-cut. For royal authority he uses *imperium* and *regnum*, synonymously, and sometimes with territorial implications.[7] Like others he distinguished between *gens*, *populus*, and *natio*, but not sharply or always, for he applies all three to the Mercians.[8] Generally he uses *natio* only for large ethnic groups and particularly to denote racial origin as in 'de natione Anglorum'. Conversely *populus*, when used for a particular people, almost always indicates that of a single kingdom.[9] *Gens* is the term Bede uses most commonly, and he uses it indifferently for either a large ethnic group, e.g. *gens Brettonum* or for the men of a particular kingdom, e.g. *gens Merciorum*. His normal word for what we think of as a kingdom is *provincia*: *provincia Merciorum* etc.; but he also uses it, if rarely, for lesser divisions: *provincia Gyruiorum . . . Meanuarorum . . . Undalum*.[10] His normal word for an area less than a *provincia* (in its larger sense) is *regio*. Northumbria and Mercia are made up of *regiones*.[11] Ely is a *regio*, so too are the lands of the *Girvii*, Surrey, *Loidis*, *Incuneningum*, and *Infeppingum*.[12] Only once does he use *regio* for an area

[4] See Jones, op. cit., *s.v.*, and esp. *OH*, i, pp. 111, 180, 182, 243.

[5] *OH*, i, p. 227.

[6] *OH*, i, p. 178.

[7] For the synonymous uses of these words see e.g. *OH*, i, p. 89 lines 13, 27, cf. pp. 89, 97, 229 with 180, 267 for the equivalence of *imperium Anglorum* with *regnum Anglorum*. Cf. H. Vollrath-Reichelt, *Königsgedanke und Königtum bei den Angelsachsen* (Cologne, 1971), pp. 79–80 .

[8] Vollrath-Reichelt, pp. 40–48; for the Mercians *OH*, i, pp. 125, 170, 171, 180.

[9] The slightly aberrant use of *populi* for the Angles, Saxons and Jutes on their coming to Britain (*OH*, i, p. 31) reinforces the impression given by the fact that here only does he call the South Saxons *Meridiani* rather than *Australes* and the West Saxons *Occidui* rather than *Occidentales* that this famous passage came to him from a written source, possibly a letter. It is likely that variations in Bede's usage are often to be explained similarly.

[10] *OH*, i, p. 169, 230, 322, 330.

[11] *OH*, i, pp. 158, 302 (*regio* is used in a probably very general sense in both cases).

[12] *OH*, i, pp. 244, 246, 218, 218, 179, 304, 171. (The usage of early charters is like Bede's in that it draws no clear line between *regio* and *provincia*) thus Kent is mentioned both as a *provincia* in which a *regio* lies (e.g. B. 254 (S. 128)) and as a *regio* (B. 291 (S. 1258)); Surrey is both *provincia* (B. 34 (S. 1165)) and *regio* (B. 275 (S. 144)). But, as with Bede (the one reference to *regionem Genissorum* (p. 87 below) excepted), though a *regio* may be within a *provincia* the converse is never the case.

which normally he would call *provincia: regionem Geuissorum*.[13]

While most of the words which he uses for what we think of as a kingdom, or its people, are also used for larger or smaller entities, a fairly coherent, if smudged, pattern emerges. In particular, though he uses *gens* both for the people of a kingdom and for wider groupings, and *provincia* both for a kingdom and for a smaller unit, the *provinciae* which he regards as having a *gens* or *populus* he also mentions as having a *rex*. In some contexts he regards the territorial *provincia* as equivalent to the non-territorial *gens* and *populus* and attributes to the entity which can indifferently be described by any of these words something like a national identity. 'Huius industria regis Derorum et Berniciorum provinciae quae eatenus ab invicem discordabant in unam sunt pacem et velut unum compaginatae in populum'.[14] 'Ossa . . . noluerunt . . . excipere . . . quia de alia provincia ortus fuerat et super eos regnum acceperat'.[15] If the convergences of his usage are suggestive, so too are its divergences. A kingdom such as Mercia or Wessex is presented as inhabited by or equivalent to a *gens*, which is to suggest that its people were an entity in some way comparable to, say, *gens Anglorum*. At the same time such an entity is a *provincia*, a word also applied to units of lesser significance. Such ambivalences may indicate more than simply what was inevitable when the new wine of Germanic circumstances was poured into the old bottles of a Latin vocabulary which in any case lacked precision. The messiness and ambiguities of Bede's usage may reflect something of the world he described.

They hinder us in answering two obvious and plain questions about the kings and kingdoms of early England: How many? Of what kind? A number of *reges* other than those of the 'Heptarchic' kingdoms and Bernicia and Deira may be collected. Best known are those of the Hwicce, whose line can be traced from the later seventh century to the later eighth.[16] Bede calls one of these rulers *rex*,[17] this description is also used in certain charters, but the Hwiccian kings almost always appear in subordination to those of Mercia, as *subreguli, reguli, comites* or *ministri*. Still, there was a sense that the Hwicce were a distinct people; they had a *provincia* and a bishop as well as a *rex*. The origins of the dynasty are unknown, but are possibly Northumbrian. That the presence of a *rex* for the Isle of Wight in the late seventh century should be known only from one reference in Bede strengthens the case for supposing there to have been other *reges* whom he does not mention at all.[18] One such line,

[13] *OH*, i, p. 238.
[14] *OH*, i, p. 138.
[15] *OH*, i, p. 148.
[16] H. P. R. Finberg, *The Early Charters of the West Midlands* (Leicester, 1961), pp. 167–180.
[17] *OH*, i, p. 255.
[18] *OH*, i, p. 237.

that of the *reges* or *subreguli* of the Western Hecani (later Magonsæten),
can be dimly but convincingly traced, almost entirely in late and
doubtful sources, from the mid-seventh century to the mid-eighth,
with authority in Herefordshire and Shropshire. They may have
descended from a son of Penda.[19] That Lindsey is called by Bede
provincia and that it had bishops of its own strengthens Stenton's
argument (based largely on an eighth century genealogy) for supposing
it to have had kings.[20] We know of one *rex* of the Middle Angles,
whom Bede regarded as a *populus*, inhabiting a *provincia* and entitled to
a bishop of their own, but that is the ambiguous case of Peada and it is a
question whether Middle Anglia was an old entity or not.[21] In a charter
of 672 × 674 Frithuwold, 'provinciae Surrianorum subregulus regis
Wlfarii Mercianorum' grants land.[22] Surrey's name and size suggest it
to have been an important early unit, though also that it was part of a
larger one. It is more than once mentioned in the *Chronicle* as if it were
of the same kind as Kent and Sussex.[23] This charter is the only evidence
for there having been someone of something like royal status at its
head. One may wonder how many other such areas had such rulers and
whether they belonged to dynasties which had once been independent.
Three other *subreguli*, we are not told of what, witness the charter.

Special problems are posed by the *reges* and *subreguli* of Wessex and
the *principes* of Mercia. Bede says that after the death of Cenwalh (674)
Wessex was divided among *subreguli*. A version of the *Chronicle* states
that Edwin killed five *reges* in Wessex in 626. In a number of early
charters relating to Wessex appear *reges*, *reguli* or *subreguli*, sometimes
granting land, who were not rulers of Wessex as a whole. Some of these
charters are questionable. Still, as Chadwick said 'unless the authors
had at least a tradition to go on they would hardly have chosen names
which were otherwise unknown and given them titles which were not

---

[19] Finberg, *The Early Charters of the West Midlands*, op. cit. pp. 217–224.

[20] F. M. Stenton, *Preparatory to Anglo-Saxon England* (Oxford, 1970), pp. 127–37. It
is curious that the only *provinciae* for which Bede uses the forms '*provincia Lindissi*',
'*provincia Cantiae*', with a genitive singular rather than a plural, as in e.g. *provincia
Nordanhymbrorum*, are the only two whose names are known to go back to Romano-
British past, in the sense of deriving from names certainly in use in Roman Britain.

[21] W. Davies, 'Middle Anglia and the Middle Angles', *Midland History* 2 (1973–4),
pp. 18–20 (cf. H. E. Walker, 'Bede and the Gewissae', *Cambridge Historical Journal* 12
(1956), pp. 176–7) argues that Middle Anglia is highly unlikely to have been an entity
existing before Peada had authority there. Her arguments depend on the assumption that
princeps and *ealdorman* are words signifying royal officers and no more, which is not
certain (cf. pp. 85–86 above and pp. 89, 91 below); on the silence of the sources on
anything about the Middle Angles other than Peada's ruling them, which is not
conclusive (cf. p. 90 below); and on the fact that in the 'Tribal Hidage' the Middle
Anglian area is divided among several 'peoples'; this is indeed suggestive, but could mean
no more than that after Peada's time Middle Anglia was divided up.

[22] B. 34 (S. 1165).

[23] E.g. *Two Chronicles* . . . i, pp. 43, 61.

used in Wessex after the eighth century'. His argument that it was probably normal for this kingdom to be divided among *subreguli* under a 'main king' and that these were, or often were, identical with the *ealdormen* of Ine's laws is powerful.[24]

We meet in Bede one *princeps* from the area of Mercian authority, Tonberct, 'princeps . . . Australium Gyruiorum.[25] The *regio* or *provincia* of the Southern Gyrvii, was not large – 600 hides – but Tonberct was a man of high status, for he married a daughter of the king of the East Angles (the only marriage Bede records of the offspring of one *rex* to someone who was not the offspring of another). Other Mercian *principes* are met in charters, as witnesses, and sometimes more revealingly. In memoranda of between 675 and shortly before 691 'Friduricus principus Aedilridi regis' is recorded as granting lands to Medeshamstede.[26] In ninth century charters *principes* appear as having rights over extensive lands coordinate with, but inferior to, those of the king. In 836 when Wiglaf of Mercia gave extensive exemptions to a monastery including that from 'pastus regis et principum' two ealdormen (*ealdorman* is the normal Old English equivalent of *princeps*) were compensated, one with land, the other with gold.[27] In 848, when Beortwulf of Mercia granted liberties to Breedon, Humberht, *princeps*, agreed that it should be free from 'omnibus causis . . . quae mihi aut principibus Tonsetorum unquam ante ea pertinebant'. (The Tomsaetan, whether truly a people or rather an administrative district is for discussion, extended from Leicestershire to near Birmingham.[28]) One must wonder whether Friduricus could not have appeared in other sources, if we had them, as *subregulus* or even *rex*, and whether the coordinate rights of king and ealdorman revealed in the ninth-century documents derive from delegation, or from subordination. And what were the *principes Tonsetorum*? There is a wide range of possibilities, from their having once been an independent dynasty, to their having been a series of Mercian functionaries.

In such musings it is essential to take note of that astonishing document, the 'Tribal Hidage'. Of unknown, but not improbably seventh or eighth century date, this assigns hidages to the 'Heptarchic' kingdoms south of the Humber, but also to to a remarkable number of what historians call 'peoples' with assessments varying from 300 to 7,000 hides. A recent study of the 'Hidage' by Dr Davies has suggested that sixth-century England was ruled by kings only in part, the remainder being inhabited by kingless 'peoples'; and that the only truly

[24] H. M. Chadwick, *Studies on Anglo-Saxon Institutions* (Cambridge, 1905), pp. 282–90 (p. 286 for the quotation). See also P. H. Sawyer. *From Roman Britain to Norman England* (1978), pp. 45–49, for an important account of this and related matters.
[25] *OH*, i, p. 243.
[26] B. 841, 842 (S. 1803, 1805).
[27] B. 416 (S. 190).
[28] B. 454 (S. 197); Stenton, *Preparatory to Anglo-Saxon England*, op. cit. p. 184 n. 3.

independent dynasties there are likely to have been (South of the Humber) are those of the 'Heptarchy', other *reges, subreguli* etc., known or suspected, being subordinates appointed by Mercian rulers to administer 'peoples', or groups thereof who fell under their control from the seventh century.[29]

Among the many merits of Dr Davies's work courage is not the least; to say that her hypotheses are questionable is to say little more than that they are an attempt to make sense of the 'Tribal Hidage'. But questionable they are. While it is likely that our sources are good enough to permit reasonable certainty as to which were the major dynasties in the seventh century, it does not follow that these alone were important earlier. How lost to us is the history of nearly two centuries after the *Adventus* is illustrated by the *Chronicle's* annal for 597: 'Ceolwulf began to reign . . . and he continually contended against the English, or the Britons, or the Picts, or the Scots'.[30] That is all we know of Ceolwulf's extensive contentions. To argue against there having been independent, even important, dynasties in Lindsey, Middle Anglia or elsewhere on the ground that we have no record of such importance is to argue, not from the silence of sources, but from their absence. The dynasties prominent in the seventh century may have often elbowed their way to greatness in recent generations; *damnatio memoriae* may well have been the fate of those they displaced. An instructive, though not completely parallel, instance is that of Elmet. Were we dependent on sources of English origin we should have no idea that a British dynasty survived there into the seventh century. If the *Elmed saetna* of the Hidage had once had kings of their own, why should not others of its 'peoples' have done so? It could have been that in the invasion period, and for long afterwards, many Anglo-Saxons lived outside the authority of any dynasty whom a Latin author would have called *reges* or *principes*. Certainly the governmental arrangements of the Old Saxons as reported by Bede do not include royal rule. In any case we know so little about Anglo-Saxon society in Germany or in England that many possibilities must be admitted. But even if *reges* did not control the whole of early England it is likely that there had once been more dynasties than survived to be heard of in the seventh century; and possible that at the head of many of the 'peoples' of the 'Tribal Hidage' were subordinated *subreguli* or *principes* whose ancestors had known more independence.

The rulers of the England Bede described may be roughly divided into three groups, which are not, however, completely separable from one another, but merge into a continuum. First great overlords such as the seven whom he lists in Book II, chapter ix, with others such as

---

[29] W. Davies and H. Vierck, 'The Contexts of the Tribal Hidage: Social Aggregates and Settlement Patterns', *Frühmittelalterliche Studien* 8 (1974), pp. 224–93, esp. 236–41.
[30] *Two Chronicles*, i, p. 20.

Penda, Wulfhere and Aethelbald. These had many rulers subordinated to them, including some whom Bede had no doubt about calling *reges*. Second, *reges* of major kingdoms. Third a class, probably a large class, of lesser potentates for whom it is not easy to find a single or unambiguous term, because contemporaries could not find one. Bede's hesitation on whether to call Peada *rex* or *princeps* and his use of such an ambiguous expression as *duces regii* are characteristic of contemporary difficulties in finding a word for such men. It would have been possible in the eighth century for the same man to have been described by different writers and in different contexts as *rex, subregulus, princeps, dux, praefectus* and *comes*.[31] In Old English he would probably have generally been called *ealdorman*, a term commonly taken to imply a functionary, but one whose poetic use suggests that in this period it was also associated with kingship; alternatively he might sometimes have been called *cyning*.[32] What these men had in common was an authority over an at least fairly extensive area, subordination or inferiority to greater *reges*, and something about their status and functions which made them in some ways similar to *reges* and ensured that it was impossible to draw a clear distinction between them and *reges*. They were probably of diverse origins. Some were in the position of Peada, close relatives of a major king who had been given an area to rule. There may have been little difference between such and some of those who shared kingdoms such as Kent and Essex where division of the kingdom sometimes took place, if, as is likely, one of the beneficiaries of such a division generally had a position superior to the others. Some may have been the descendants of cadets established as Peada was. Some may have been the heirs of formerly independent dynasties. Some may have been noblemen rewarded by territorial authority. The importance of their areas of authority varied greatly; from the 7,000 hides of that of the *reges* or *subreguli* of the Hwicce to the 600 of the *principes* of the South Gyrvii. (Though it is worth remembering that Bede could write of a *rex* of Wight, which is only assessed at 600 hides in the Tribal Hidage; had his information on Tonberct come from a different source we might have heard of him as *rex*.) It is a question how much of England was divided up among such men. It is likely that Wessex was and that there were far more *principes* or *subreguli* in Mercia than we hear of. Perhaps each of the 'peoples' of the 'Tribal Hidage' had such a potentate over it.

This was a world in which there were hierarchies of kings and relativities of kingliness and in this may have been not too unlike that of contemporary Ireland. Those higher up the scale were concerned to depress the status of those lower down. A great *rex* such as Wulfhere

---

[31] Chadwick, *Studies on Anglo-Saxon Institutions*, op. cit. pp. 282–90.
[32] *Ibid*, pp. 286, 280.

had other *reges* subordinated to him, and they in turn could have men of something like royal status subordinated to them. Thus Wulfhere had authority over Ethelwalh of Sussex, and if, when he gave Ethelwalh the *provincia* of Wight, it had a *rex*, as a few years later it did, then a triple hierarchy of *reges* was established.[33] Greater kings were concerned to emphasise the inferior status of those below them. A ruler of the Hwicce might be *rex* or *subregulus* of his own people; to his Mercian overlord he was *meus subregulus*, or *comes*, or *minister*.[34] Offa was concerned to reduce other kings south of the Humber to the status of *subreguli*, men whose charters had to be confirmed.[35] At a lower level on the scale the rulers both of Mercia and of Wessex were in the eighth century probably trying to ensure that their *subreguli*, *principes*, or *ealdormen* became more like functionaries and less like subordinated rulers. A successful ruler had to gather and hold the allegiance of as many *reges*, *subreguli*, *principes*, *duces regii* as he could. He might be well advised to share his gains by granting something like royal status and power to members of his family. But he also had to ensure that potentates subordinated to him had as little of the *rex* and as much of the *comes* about them as possible. In such a world it was not easy to draw clear distinctions. Bede's ambivalences in the use of *rex* and related words probably reflect his feeling that while there was a distinction between *reges* and their immediate inferiors, it was not easy to see where to draw it.

Many kings and princes rose and fell in the struggle for power in the England Bede described. In considering the determinants of that struggle it is helpful to set beside what Bede tells us other sources and in the hope that they may give to details and episodes in his story significance which is less apparent when they are seen in the context of Bede's vision of the past, one partly dominated and so in a measure distorted by his purposes. *Beowulf* is such a source. One cannot be certain of its date; it may be considerably later than the eighth century which the balance of supposition has generally favoured.[36] Still, it may take us nearer to the thoughts and motives of men in power than do works written for religious purposes.

In the political world of the poem four things stand out. The importance of the king's noble retinue, whose origins may lie in kingdoms other than his own; an indissoluble connection between gold and success; the store set by good weapons which are regarded as treasure; the endless insecurity associated with feud. A king lives

---

[33] *OH*, i, pp. 230, 237.

[34] A. H. Smith, 'The *Hwicce*', in *Medieval and Linguistic Studies in Honour of F. P. Magoun* (1965), p. 58.

[35] F. M. Stenton, *Anglo-Saxon England* (3rd ed. Oxford, 1970), pp. 206–12.

[36] E.g. E. John 'Beowulf and the Margins of Literacy', *Bulletin of the John Rylands Library*, 56 (1974), pp. 389–91, and see p. 48 above.

surrounded by noble warriors who feast with him, sleep in his hall by night, fight for him and are ready (or anyway were most sincerely hoped to be ready) to die for him. Their number and loyalty were crucial for royal power. As king Hrothgar prospered, so did the number of his young retainers increase. A king's followers could come from kingdoms other than his own, as Beowulf came from Geatland to Denmark. Adventure or the hope of profit bring some; the harsher compulsions of exile others. To secure followers and power, treasure is essential. Kingship and treasure-giving go hand in hand. Kings are 'treasure-guardians', 'ring-givers', 'gold friends'. A good king gives: Hrothgar was 'the best of earthly kings . . . the best of those who bestowed gold'.[37] A bad king 'begins to hoard his treasures, never parts with gold rings'.[38] Treasure rewards service, creates the expectation of loyalty, and is the outward sign of honour. The gift of a splendid sword ensures that the recipient 'was honoured on the mead-bench that much the more'.[39] The social and emotional significance of gold-giving and gold-wearing is complex and deep; and it was not for nothing that Beowulf died to win a treasure hoard. With the poet's interest in treasure goes a similar interest in weapons. They are described in detail and with love. Gifts of armour and of pattern-welded swords are treated on the same footing as treasures. All the kings and kingdoms mentioned in the poem ultimately come to grief and the poet is at pains to remind his audience of this. In short this world is one in which it is all-important for a king to give treasure, which includes arms. If he has treasure and is successful in war (these things feed one another) he can attract followers from other kingdoms, because noblemen are often on the move through hunger for reward or the necessities of exile. To keep giving he has to keep taking, and so adds feud to feud. No kingdom or king can hope for long success. When a great king grows ill or old or mean there are always enemies waiting at home and abroad. They seize their advantage and other kings rise, gaining the treasure, the men, and the glory.

This picture is a construct; from a work of fiction. But its elements were important in Bede's England. A retinue of noble warriors was necessary to a king and could be recruited from kingdoms other than his own. Oswine of Deira was, Bede says, so handsome, so jovial, so civil and (last, but doubtless not least) so generous that noblemen came to his service from almost every *provincia*.[40] When adequate land was not available to reward young Northumbrian noblemen they went to serve overseas. It was probably common, or normal, for a nobleman to

[37] Ed. F. Klaebur (3rd ed. Boston, 1950) lines 1684–6. The transition here and below is that of K. Crossley-Holland (Cambridge, 1968).

[38] Lines 1749–51.

[39] Lines 1900–1903.

[40] *OH*, i, pp. 155–6.

go to fight for a king or his own hand. Our best example is that of Guthlac. When he was about fifteen 'a noble love of command began to glow . . . he gave himself up to arms . . . laid waste the towns and dwellings, the villages and fortresses of his enemies . . . brought together comrades *diversarum gentium* and collected vast booty'.[41] It is important that his retinue was of diverse peoples and that (as we are told elsewhere) he was for some time in exile among the Britons.[42] Exiles are omnipresent in this period. Many kings spent part of their lives as exiles: for example, Edwin, Eanfrith, Oswald, Oswy and Aldfrith of Northumbria; Sigbert of East Anglia; Cenwalh and Caedwalla of Wessex; Aethelbald of Mercia. Naturally we hear most of those exiles who ultimately came to power. There were others. Some occur in Eddius's life of Wilfrid's 'nobiles quidam exules cum exercitu causa iniuriae suae spoliantes' burned down the monastery of Oundle.[43] Exile was inevitably important in a society to which feud was intrinsic. It is of feuds in and between royal houses of which most is known and it may be that the openness of successions to kingdoms made royal exiles particularly common. It is significant that some of these, for example Caedwalla of Wessex and Aethelbald of Mercia, were not closely related to the kings whom ultimately they succeeded. Many kings must have had the exiled enemies of other kings in their service; and a king's enemies must often have been his relations.

Treasures performed much the same social role in early England that they did in *Beowulf*. Thanks above all to Sutton Hoo we know what the treasures of the day were like and it is the easier to understand how men could live and die for them. Hrothgar settled a feud by giving many valuable old treasures; Oswy sought to buy off Penda by offering *ornamenta regia*.[44] A passage in one manuscript of the Penitential of Theodore deals with a man who has entered the church and to whom a king has given some rich thing; if the king is alive, the man must return it.[45] This reflects a feeling, almost a system, apparent in *Beowulf*. If you have a sword or a treasure your lord gave you, that binds you to him. The weapons surviving from early England enable us to see why the best of them should have been treated as treasures. Armour survives very rarely; pattern-welded swords, which were superior to others, are by no means common. Such equipment was probably confined to the great and their beneficiaries and may well have sufficed to give great advantages in battle. If there were strong social distinctions in military

[41] *Felix's Life of Guthlac*, ed. B. Colgrave (Cambridge, 1956), p. 80.
[42] *Ibid*, p. 110.
[43] Eddius Stephanus, *Het Leven van Sint Wilfrid*, ed. H. Moonen ('S-Hertogenbosch, 1946), p. 210 (cap. 67).
[44] *OH*, i, p. 177.
[45] *Councils and Ecclesiastical Documents*, ed. A. W. Haddan and W. Stubbs, iii (Oxford, 1871), p. 203 n. 15. (This canon does not necessarily derive from England.)

usefulness then the significance of the movement of armed noblemen from one king's service to another's was enhanced.

If in many violent ways Bede's kings and kingdoms were divided, many strands linked them together. Naturally the most important of these was marriage. Kings commonly married wives from other royal houses. Queens were very important for good or ill. A queen brought to her new home a household from her old and maintained contact with her family. When Wilfrid first sought to go to Rome. Eanfled, queen of Northumbria, helped him by sending to her relative Eorconberht, king of Kent.[46] Later he was less successful with queens. The hostility of Iormenburh, Egfrith of Northumbria's queen, was important in driving him into exile. He later fled to Mercia, but there the queen was Egfrith's sister, and had him driven out. Next he went to Wessex, but, bad luck, its queen was Iormenburgh's sister and out he was driven again.[47] His adventures show how royal families were linked to one another by blood as well as divided by feud. There were other connections. Kings sent emissaries to one another; the West Saxon ambassador who sought to murder Edwin must have had an atypical purpose.[48] A ninth-century Mercian charter makes regular provision for emissaries coming from Wessex, Northumbria or overseas.[49] Many kings must, as exiles, have experienced kingdoms other than their own. Lesser rulers visited the courts of greater and served in their armies. Bede's account of Sigbert of Essex '. . . amicus eiusdem Osuiu regis, qui, cum frequenter ad eum in provinciam Nordanhymbrorum veniret . . .' is a reminder that kings could be friends.[50]. The great men of England were involved with one another not only by war but also by peaceful connections. Their society and customs, in more peaceful as well as in more violent aspects, were such as naturally to multiply contacts not only between English rulers, but also theirs with others, elsewhere in the island, in Gaul, and in Ireland. It was this which did much to determine the nature and success of the conversion to Christianity.

Underlying the shifting hierarchy of *reges* and *principes*, their wars and their peaces, lay systems for the exploitation and government of lands and men. The early laws of Kent and Wessex appear to show, so far as laws can, effective royal power and considerable complexity in its exercise. Recent work has emphasised and extended the evidence for comparable regularities in the division and organisation of land. The essence of the argument is that the system of lordship and local government over much, possibly all of early England resembled, and at

[46] Eddius, op. cit. pp. 66–68 (cap. 3).

[47] *Ibid.* pp. 108, pp. 140–42 (caps. 24, 40).

[48] *OH*, i, pp. 98–99.

[49] B. 454 (S. 197). The authenticity of this charter has been disputed. It is hard to imagine a motive for forgery of the passage in question.

[50] *OH*, i, p. 171.

least in wide areas, was connected with that of early Wales. The main unit in such a system was an area of varying but substantial size (say, not less than a hundred square miles) centred on a royal vill. To this vill the settlements within its area owed dues and services of some complexity, including those intended to provide for the ruler and his court on his regular tours, and to maintain his men, horses and dogs on other occasions. The area centred on the royal vill would often or always have common grazing. The subordinate settlements could vary in the nature of their obligations. There is no doubt that such a system prevailed in early Kent and in much of Northumbria. Elsewhere the evidence is less strong, but in many areas highly suggestive. Setting on one side questions of origin, it is reasonably certain that in much at least of early England the organisation of dues and services for the ruler was systematic, on schemes which methodically integrated settlements to their respective royal vills.[51] The evidence of charters from the late seventh century on supports such a conclusion; for they strongly suggest that every settlement had an assessment in hides, and it looks as if these hidages related to round sum assessments for larger units centred on royal vills.

Bede is not concerned with such matters. But to bear them in mind is to attach a significance to some of what he says which might otherwise be missed. For example, he tells how Oswy, in gratitude for victory, gave 'XII possessiunculi terrarum', six in Bernicia and six in Deira. The diminutive has been suggested to imply disparagement. It is far more likely that *posessiunculi* means component settlements, in distinction from *villae* or *vici* meaning estate centres, generally royal; and that Bede means that Oswy gave away twelve such settlements.[52] Or consider the memorable incident of Oswine's giving Aidan a horse, which the saint handed on to a beggar. It was *equum regium* and royally caparisoned. Oswine was cross; he had, he said, many other horses, *viliores* and so more suited for charitable purposes.[53] This glimpse of the royal stables is a reminder of the importance of horses in society and for the exercise of power. The great distances at which campaigns were fought suggest that armies rode to battle. Bishops rode round their dioceses; Chad was made to do so; and we meet John of Hexham's entourage racing one another on horses.[54] In some of the rare early charters which provide details of services owed from estates, the duty of maintaining horses is

[51] W. Rees. 'Survivals of Ancient Celtic Custom in Medieval England', in J. R. R. Tolkein and others, *Angles and Saxons* (Cardiff, 1963), pp. 148–68; G. W. S. Barrow, *The Kingdom of the Scots* (1973), pp. 9–17; G. R. J. Jones, 'Multiple Estates and Early Settlement', in *English Medieval Settlement*, ed. P. H. Sawyer (1979),m pp. 9–34.
[52] J. Campbell, 'Bede's Words for Places', below, Chapter 6.
[53] *OH*, i, p. 156.
[54] *OH*, i, pp. 206, 289–91.

mentioned.[55] Here is a point at which the long distance raids Bede mentions and the fluid violent world of *Beowulf* meet the investigations of those who concern themselves with renders and grazing rights. The great needed horses; that horses needed to be fed was one of the reasons why land was coveted as much as gold. A similarly suggestive passage in Eddius is that in which he describes Egfrith of Northumbria, with his queen, going round what sounds like the whole kingdom, or a large part of it, *gaundentes et epulantes*, rejoicing and feasting.[56] The medieval Welsh system included *gwestfa*, the obligation to entertain the king and his court when they came round twice a year.[57] Egfrith may well have been exercising such a right. It is likely that it is that which is sometimes mentioned in charters as *pastum regis* or *convivium regis*. That at least in the West Midlands it corresponded to *gwestfa* is indicated by a charter in which Offa let the beneficiary off *pastiones* for three years, and added, 'id est vi convivia'.[58] References in the early sources to kings dining with subjects may relate not to socialising, but to the exercise of rights. If there was much which was chaotic in early England there was also much which was orderly. The absorption of one kingdom by another, the collection of tribute, the regulation of subordinated powers, would all have been simplified if all or most of the lands for control or supremacy over which *reges* struggled were organised on similar, and orderly, systems.

These struggles early led to the dominance of a handful of dynasties and in the end to that of one. One of the problems which faced those which were rising and successful was that of defining their status in such a way as to mark it off from that of the, probably numerous, lesser rulers who had something royal about them. It was a world in which one of the questions which most needed answering was, 'What is a king?'. Bede's history was teaching by examples the answer to a different, if related question, 'What is a Christian king?'. But he gives not so much one answer as two, offering two types of Christian kingship. One is that of Oswald, *christianissimus*, instrumental in the conversion of his people, *victoriosissimus*, rewarded by God with great conquests, *miranda sanctitatis*, though defeated and slain, triumphant in miracles.[59] This almost implies the view that kingship is a divinely appointed office; and Bede does indeed say, in the preface to the Ecclesiastical History, that kings are appointed by God to rule. But that is the only place where he says it, though as the author of a commentary

[55] B. 370, 443, 450, 454 (S. 186, 1271, 198, 197). The first of these relates to Kent; the others to Mercia. The authenticity of the last two has been questioned. All are ninth century; but it is probable that what comes to light here has prevailed earlier.
[56] Eddius, op. cit. p. 138 (cap. 39).
[57] Rees, op. cit. p. 153.
[58] B. 241 (S. 1257).
[59] *OH*, i, pp. 139, 89, 127, 144, 153.

on Samuel he had the opportunity to do so elsewhere.[60] His work may have come to play a part in the development of the ideology of Carolingian kingship, but he was not the Alcuin of the Northumberland dynasty. The other model he presents is not that of a king appointed by God to rule, but of a king abandoning rule for God, as several kings of his generation did. When he describes how one of these, Coenred of Mercia, abdicated to become a monk at Rome, Bede says that he reigned most nobly, but much more nobly abandoned the sceptre of rule.[61] This is of course a cliché of hagiography. Still, commonplaces often express the deepest convictions. Bede was clearly aware of the archetypal Christian dilemma about secular powers, whether they should be regarded as divinely appointed for divine purposes, or rather as parts, if necessary parts, of an essentially sinful world which Christians should flee. I suspect that, if Bede, in thinking about great good kings long dead could feel about kingship rather as Alcuin and Aquinas were to do, he was led nearer to an Augustinian position in considering the kings of his own day. He knew too much about them.

---

[60] Vollrath-Reichelt, op. cit. pp. 21–29.
[61] *OH*, i, p. 321.

Additional Bibliographical Note

Significant contributions to themes touched on in this paper and which have appeared since it was written are: W. Davies, 'Die angelsachsischen Konigreiche in England' in *Sachsen und Angelsachsen*, ed. C. Ahrens (catalogue of an exhibition held in the Helms-Museum, Hamburg, Hamburg, 1978), pp. 85–96; P. Wormald, 'Bede, the *Bretwaldas* and the origins of the *Gens Auglorum*' in *Ideal and Reality in Frankish and Anglo-Saxon Society* (see p. 48 above), pp. 99–129; Clare Stancliffe, 'Kings who Opted Out', *Ibid.*, pp. 154–76; B. A. E. Yorke, 'The Vocabulary of Anglo-Saxon Lordship', *Anglo-Saxon Studies in Archaeology and History*, ii (B.A.R. British Series 92, 1981), pp. 171–200 and A. T. Thacker, 'Some Terms for Noblemen in Anglo-Saxon England', *Ibid.* pp. 201–236.

6

Bede's Words for Places

It is possible that something can be found out about settlements in early England by considering the words used by contemporaries to indicate them. The obvious man with whom to begin is Bede. What follows is based on an analysis of words he uses for places in the *Ecclesiastical History*, *Lives of the Abbots* and prose *Life of Cuthbert*.[1] Passages in which he is known to have been using the words of another have been excluded.

The words which Bede uses most frequently for important places are *civitas* and *urbs*. Granted that there are four places for which he employs both words it could be deduced that, like Isidore of Seville or Gregory of Tours, he regarded them as representing different aspects of the same thing, or as largely synonymous (Lindsay ed. 1911, xv, i; xv, ii, esp. 1; Dalton 1927, p. 159). Closer examination shows that this was not so. Bede refers to eighteen places in Britain as *civitates*. (For details see the Appendix.) It is his normal term for Canterbury and London (each called *civitas* far more frequently than *urbs*) and the only one he uses for Cambridge, Carlisle, Chester, Dorchester, Lincoln, Richborough, Rochester, *Verulamium*, York and Winchester (except that Cambridge is once *civitatula*). These were all places of at least modest consequence under the Romans. His remaining eight *civitates* are a mixed bag. Four are places at which a monastery was founded and which had vernacular names terminating in *caestir: Ythancaestir, Kaelcacaestir, Tiouulfingcaestir* and *Tunnacaestir*. The first of these was the Saxon Shore fort of *Othona*, the second the Roman *Calcaria*; the other two are unidentified. Of the remaining places *Dommoc* is hard to characterise, because it is unidentified. It may have been a place of some Roman importance and/or have had a name in *caestir*.[2] It is likely that Bede used *civitas* for Tilbury only because he was led into so doing by the construction of the sentence in which he refers to it.[3] Thus there are only two places

---

[1] Full references to all works cited can be found at the end of the article. General statements below apply to these works only. Plummer ed. 1896, I is hereafter abbreviated as *OH*. Extensive use has been made of Jones 1929. Unreferenced statements below about Bede's use of words are based on this concordance.

[2] The Old English Bede in calling the place *Dommucceastre* (Miller ed. 1890, I, p. 142) may simply be translating Bede's *civitas* by the suffix, but cf. Bede's treatment of Dorchester which he once calls *Dorcic* and once *Doriccaestrae* (*OH*, pp. 139, 254).

[3] '. . . maxima in civitate quae lingua Saxonum Ythancaestir appellatur sed in illa quae Tilaburg cognominatur' (*OH*, p. 173).

99

which he advisedly calls *civitas* and which are known neither to have been places of Roman significance nor to have had names in *caestir*: *Alcluith* and Bamburgh. These two he more often calls *urbs* (pp. 116-17 below).

The British places which Bede calls *urbes* number eight. They may be placed in three categories. Two were British: *Alcluith* (almost certainly Dumbarton) and *Giudi Urbs* (possibly Stirling, Jackson 1963, p. 57). Five were Anglo-Saxon places which had names terminating in *burg*: Bamburgh, Canterbury, *Cnobheresburg*, Malmesbury and *Colodaesburg*. London, called *urbs* on one occasion, is in a category of its own, though Canterbury resembles it in being more generally termed *civitas*. The other places named above are invariably called *urbs*, with the exceptions of *Alcluith* and Bamburgh.

It is important to observe how numerous are the places which Bede does not call either *civitas* or *urbs*. He does not call a place *civitas* simply because it was the seat of a bishop. Lindisfarne, Hexham, Lichfield and Selsey are not so termed. Lichfield, for example, is simply *locus* OH, p. 207) and *locus* seems to be for Bede an exclusive term to the extent that he does not use it for *civitates* or *urbes*. Although he names a considerable number of places at which monasteries were founded he never describes them as either *civitas* or *urbs* unless their vernacular names terminated in *caestir* or *burg* respectively.

It seems clear that the distinction between *civitates* and *urbes* in Bede's usage was closely connected with the distinction, whatever it may have been, in contemporary vernacular usage between *caestir* and *burg*. A high proportion of the English places which he calls *civitas* had vernacular names in *caestir*;[4] a high proportion of those which he calls *urbs* had names in *burg*. The meaning of *caestir* and *burg* has attracted considerable attention from students of place-names. Professor A. H. Smith concludes that in literary sources *caestir* means 'a large town, a city' with higher status than a *burg*; that in place-names it was 'clearly used to describe important Roman towns and cities' but also, particularly in the North 'used of any ancient fortification or remains of them whether Roman or British'. So in his view the main senses of *caestir* in place-names are 'a (Roman) city or town or the remains of an ancient fortification (or what was thought to be such)'. *Burg* has as its primary meaning 'fortification, fortified place'; and is used in place-names to denote 'ancient earthworks, Roman stations or camps, Anglo-Saxon fortifications, fortified towns and (later) towns' (Smith 1956, 1, pp. 58–62, 85–87).

It is tempting to simplify, indeed curtail, discussion by assuming that

---

[4] That the Old English translator of the *Ecclesiastical History* almost always calls York and London *Eorforwicceastre* and *Lundenceastre* even when Bede does not use *civitas* suggests that these towns are among them.

Bede's use of *civitas* and *urbs* was largely determined by whether the vernacular name for the place concerned terminated in *caestir* or *burg* and that the vernacular connotations of these terminations were sufficiently overlapping greatly to reduce the meaningfulness of Bede's apparent distinction. It is true that Bede may generally have worked on the principal that *civitas* was the Latin for *caestir* and *urbs* the Latin for *burg* and have rendered the names of places accordingly and mechanically, as he does, for example, when he writes 'Cnobheresburg id est urbs Cnobheri' (*OH*, p. 164; contrast Eddius's usage p. 104 below). But in at least one important instance he did not act in this way, for he almost always calls Canterbury, with a name in *burg*, *civitas* (though the town may just possibly have an alternative name in *caestir*[5]). Furthermore the question remains as to whether in the vernacular usage of his day there was a sharper distinction between *caestir* and *burg* than appears when the place-name usage of many later centuries is added to complicate and blur the picture. That is to say, it is likely that Bede, rather than using two partly synonymous Latin words to translate two partly synonymous Anglo-Saxon words, was distinguising carefully between *caestir* and *burg* because they had distinct meanings for him?

All the identifiable places which Bede calls, or usually calls, *civitas* had a significant Roman past. This is true not only of the places with vernacular names in *caestir* but also of Canterbury, Carlisle and Lincoln which probably did not have such names. None of the identifiable places which Bede calls, or usually calls, *urbs* is known to have had a significant Roman past. There is one inconsiderable exception: there was probably a Roman signal station at Bamburgh. If it is true that *Cnobheresburg* was the Saxon Shore fort at Burgh Castle, Suffolk, there is a major one also. But this identification, though almost universally accepted, seems to rest on nothing earlier or more substantial than a guess of Camden's.[6] That Bamburgh, *Alcluith and Giudi Urbs* are *urbes* and that the primary force of *burg* has to do with fortification strongly

---

[5] The name as recorded from the mid-eighth century is *Cantawarburg* or the like (Ekwall 1960, *s.v.*). There is one exception. In a twelfth-century interpolation, translating a passage of Bede's, into the E version of the Anglo-Saxon Chronicle Canterbury appears as *Dorwit ceastre* (Earle and Plummer ed. 1892, 1896, I, p. 20). Whether this form (obviously connected with *Doruvernis*) is ancient I cannot judge. It was certainly possible for an Anglo-Saxon place to have alternative and very different names, as Bath did (*ibid.*, I, p. 118; II, p. 168).

[6] The place is described as *castrum*. (*OH*, p. 164.) This word is not part of Bede's ordinary vocabulary for places (below p. 104) and is here taken from *Vita Prima Fursei* (Krusch, ed 1902, p. 437). It is sometimes taken to mean 'Roman camp' (e.g. Cramp 1976, p. 212) but it is a large assumption that the usage of the author of the *Vita* was so specific. On the arguments above the name *Cnobheresburg* suggests a non-Roman site. Saxon, possibly monastic, remains have been found at Burgh Castle (*ibid.*, pp. 212–15). They do not suffice to prove the identification with *Cnobheresburg*; and could as well serve to claim for Burgh Castle a place in the East Anglian game of musical *sedes episopales*. There is a Flixton conveniently to hand.

suggests that what distinguished a place whose name ended in *burg* or which Bede called *urbs* was that it was fortified. It seems that there was a significant difference between *civitas* and *urbs* for Bede. One was a Roman place (?significant, ?fortified), the other a fortified place, not of Roman origin. It is true that he was probably often dependent on what a vernacular name told him about the nature of a place. But it appears likely that he was right in taking it that the vernacular distinction between *caestir* and *burg* was not one without a difference.

If so, some explanation must be offered for the awkward fact that Bede sometimes used *urbs* for a place he normally called *civitas* and sometimes *civitas* for a place he normally called *urbs*. In the first category are two references to Canterbury and one to London. In the Canterbury instances *urbs* is used in a fairly general sense and not in conjunction with the name of the place ('in urbe regis sedem episcopatus acceperit', 'ventus . . . urbi incendia sparserat', *OH*, pp. 46, 94). In the second instance *urbs* could have slipped in from a letter from such an informant as Albinus, but the first comes in a chapter heading. The reference to London as *urbs* comes in close conjuction with the place-name (*urbis Lundoniae . . . episcopo*, *OH*, p. 226). This could have come from a letter to Bede (*OH*, p. 6). It is just possible that Bede's use of *urbs* for Canterbury and London but for no other former Roman towns in England reflects their importance. They are the only places which he calls *metropolis*. While his normal word for a Roman town on the Continent is *civitas*, he generally uses *urbs* for Rome, Constantinople and Jerusalem, but only for them.[7] Thus in the one instance where *urbs* is almost certainly his own choice of word for a place he normally calls *civitas* he may be thinking of the *metropolis* of Canterbury as an *urbs regia* in the sense in which Constantinople was such and Cologne say, was not.

Rather more difficult is his use of *civitas* for Bamburgh and *Alcluith*. There is small justification for supposing that his choice of words here is other than his own. However, on both the occasions he uses *civitas* for Bamburgh he calls it *regia civitas* with no other identification. So it looks as if he is using *civitas* here for a particular important kind of *urbs*, the main royal fortress. The same could well apply to *Alcluith*. To the extent that Bede's aberrant uses of *urbs* and *civitas* are not to be explained by his using the words of another the repellently paradoxical suggestion that an *urbs* is a capital *civitas* and a *civitas* a capital *urbs* is therefore offered. However such divergencies from the normal pattern of Bede's usage are to be explained there is no doubt that there is such a pattern and that he does not use *civitas* and *urbs* indifferently.

It is of some interest to compare Bede's usage with that of the Old

---

[7] *OH*, pp. 86, 88, 100, 104, 240, 327 (Rome); 75, twice as *urbs regia* (Constantinople); 317 (Jerusalem); 34, 48, 141, 194, 301 (other towns as *civitates*).

English translation of the *Ecclesiastical History* made in the last decade of the ninth century. In this *ceastre* is the almost invariable translation of *civitas*. It is commonly put at the end of the name, e.g. *in civitate Lundoniae* is rendered *in Lundenceastre*. *Urbs* is translated *burg*. Exceptions are few. On the sole occasion on which Bede calls London *urbs* the translator (who is not, however, here following the Latin closely) calls the city *Lundenceastre* (Miller ed. 1890, 1, p. 294). The translator's most interesting difficulties are in regard to Canterbury. He sometimes translates, e.g. *in civitate Doruuernensi* as *Cantwara byrig* (ibid., pp. 60, 478) but he also uses *ceaster Cantwara burge* for *civitas Doruuernenesis* (ibid., pp. 118, 310). On occasion when Bede is referring to the city of Canterbury but not by name the translator uses *ceastre* (ibid., p. 90) but elsewhere *byrg* (ibid., pp. 60, 90). That such variations occur only in relation to the one place with a vernacular name in *burg* which Bede habitually calls *civitas* is highly suggestive of that name's falling outside a normal pattern.

Metropolis occurs only three times in Bede's notices of British places, twice for Canterbury and once for London. It is important because he clearly uses it to mean 'capital', saying of one 'imperii sui totius erat metropolis' and of the other 'Orientalium Saxonum . . . quorum metropolis Lundonia civitas est' (*OH*, pp. 46, 85). The ninth-century translation's equivalent is *ealdorburg, aldorburg* (Miller ed. 1890, I, pp. 60, 104).

Perhaps the most striking thing about Bede's urban vocabulary is the number of words for towns which he could have used, but did not. Thus, for example, Isidore uses *oppidum* as almost synonymous with *civitas* and *urbs*; *castellum* and *castrum* are other words which Bede could have used. In fact it can be shown that when Bede uses one of these words he is certainly or almost certainly following a written source. Consider his use of *oppidum*. It occurs three times in the *Ecclesiastical History* in contexts in which it is not plainly copied in with the rest of a passage from e.g. Orosius. Bede's first apparently independent use of it comes in his description of Osric's rashly besieging Cadwallon in *oppido municipio* (*OH*, p. 128).[8] This passage is the only one in which he uses *municipium*. The second instance comes in his list of the types of place which Chad visited: *oppida, rura, casa, vicos, castella* (*OH*, p. 195). This passage also contains one of his only two uses of *casa* (the other is in the life of Cuthbert, Colgrave ed. 1940, p. 252), and one of his two uses of *castellum* when he is not following a written source. The third superficially independent use of *oppidum* is in his description of Utrecht

[8] The common identification with York seems simply a guess. It is more likely that *oppidum municipium* is a Latin version of the *Cair Mincip* (Mencipit) which occurs in the Nennian list of twenty-eight *civitates* (Jackson 1938, pp. 46–49, maintaining that *Mincip* derives from *municipium*). If so, the place is not York, which appears elsewhere on the list as *Ebrauc* (Hebrauc). I am obliged to Dr D. Dumville for transcripts of the Nennian list.

(*OH*, p. 303). In this description he also uses *castellum*, his only apparently independent use of the word to set beside that in the list of places visited by Chad. Thus on the three occasions of his using *oppidum* where he is not following a known written source it appears once with *municipium*, twice with *castellum*. On both the occasions he uses *castellum* it appears with *oppidum*. On the only occasion he uses *municipium* it appears with *oppidum*. On one of the only two occasions he uses *casa* it appears with *oppidum* and *castellum*. This marked clustering of words for places which he does not generally use except when following a written source strongly suggests that in the passages where they occur he is in fact following written sources now lost, very possibly letters. *Castrum* he uses only once (*OH*, p. 16, to mean, probably, something like 'fortified camp') except where following a written source known to us. That Bede deliberately limited his vocabulary in describing towns and the like and eschewed the full and confusing range of words available to him must be of some significance. It strengthens the case for his having a conscious purpose in his use of *urbs* and *civitas*. If, notwithstanding what is contended above, it is supposed that he used these words almost at random, then it has to be explained why he did not take the opportunity open to him to employ a vocabulary with much more possibility of elegant variation.

A preliminary examination of some other writers using Latin in England before *c.*800 does a little to illuminate Bede's use of *urbs* and *civitas*. Eddius's usage is not dissimilar. London and York are *civitates* (Moonen ed. 1946, pp. 148, 78, 86, 92, 152, 168). Three *urbes* are mentioned, Bamburgh, Dunbar and the unidentified *Inbroninis* (ibid., pp. 196, 134, 138). All are described as royal and the context makes it clear that all are fortresses. Lichfield is simply *locus* (ibid., p. 92). Eddius gives the vernacular names for *Colodaesburg* and Bamburgh, as Bede does not, but calls only the latter *urbs*, not the former (ibid., pp. 140, 196). Strasbourg (*Streitbyrg*) is for him *civitas* (ibid., p. 114). So far as the limited number of examples goes it seems that for him *civitas* is a former Roman town (cf. ibid., pp. 110, 184) and an *urbs* is a fortress, all his *urbes* being Northumbrian and royal. His usage is less affected by vernacular forms than is Bede's. Other early hagiographers have less to offer. The anonymous biographer of Cuthbert calls Carlisle a *civitas*, as does Bede (Colgrave ed. 1940, pp. 117, 123, 125). Felix calls Cambridge *castellum*, so using a word which Bede avoids (Colgrave ed. 1956, p. 86).

Charters and other documents are more helpful.[9] Sometimes the

---

[9] What follows is based on an examination of the charters earlier than 800. Those agreed to be spurious have been excluded. In deciding which to include I have relied considerably on the comments reported by Sawyer 1965. The roughness of this procedure does not, I believe, affect the main conclusions below, which derive from the consensus of the documents.

usage corresponds to Bede's. Worcester is almost always *Weorgana civitas*, *Wegernensis civitas*, *Weogornacaestre* or the like, with variations of spelling (Birch, nos. 223, 183, 256, cf. 137, 164, 220, 269, 283). Once it is *castrum Uueogernensis* (no. 156). There is one possibly early charter which refers to Winchester and one for Hereford: these places appear as *civitas* and *locus* respectively (nos. 180, 295). A striking correspondence with Bede's usage appears in a document from the Council of *Clovesho* (803) (no. 312).[10] Of thirteen bishops who attest eight do so in the form *Legorensis civitatis episcopus*: those of Canterbury, Leicester, Worcester, Winchester, London, Rochester, *Syddensis civitas* and *Dummucae civitas*. The other five use the form *ecclesiae Liccedfeldensis episcopus*: those of Lichfield, Hereford, Sherborne, Elmham and Selsey. Thus Bede's distinction between places in *caestir* (with Canterbury) and other places is observed and (setting on one side the two unidentified places) it is also a distinction between places which had been of some Roman importance and those which had not.

Canterbury is often called *civitas* in charters (Birch, nos. 67, 90, 190, 191, 195). But it significantly appears as *urbs* also (nos. 159, 192, 265). That the use of *urbs* here is due at least in part to the pull of the vernacular name is strongly suggested by Birch no. 265, which first says *in urbe Dorobernia* then *in urbe Canteuuariorum*. (It also mentions *Lundoniam civitatem*.) Apart from its use for Canterbury, *urbs* seems to be employed in the pre-800 charters only to denote a fortification (nos. 230, 232, in both cases the fortification has a name in *burg* and in one is certainly a hill-fort).

Rochester is sometimes *civitas* (Campbell ed. 1974, nos. 5, 13) but also *castellum* (ibid., nos. 7, 12) and *castrum* (ibid., no. 14). The use of *castellum* and *castrum* here is interesting because while they do not appear to be used in charters for other towns (for one exception see above) they do appear in the first two documents to mention Rochester. The record of the council of Paris of 614 calls the bishop of Rochester 'Ex civitate Castro ultra mare Iustus episcopus' and that of the council of Hertford (672) calls him 'episcopus castelli Cantuariorum quod dicitur Hrofescæstir' (Maassen ed. 1883, I, p. 192; *OH*, p. 215). It seems therefore that the use of *castrum* or *castellum* for Rochester in charters was not casual, but had a long history. The area associated with Rochester appears to have been known as *regio Caestruuara*; *Burgwara* appears in connexion with the area associated with Canterbury (Chadwick 1905, pp. 250, 252). Perhaps in early Kent Canterbury was known simply as the *burg* and Rochester as the *caestre*.

London does appear as a *civitas* (Birch, no. 265) but more frequently as *portus* (nos. 34, 149, 152) and once as 'loco cuius vocabulum est Lundenwic' (no. 189). Bede only once calls a place *portus* when he is not

---

[10] Miss C. Colyer pointed out to me the interest of this document.

using the words of another, Quentovic (*Quentauic*) and Eddius also only uses *portus* once, of Sandwich (*portum Sandwicae*) (*OH*, p. 203; ed. Moonen 1946, p. 88). It looks very much as if *portus* was the Latin equivalent of *wic*, so that *portus Londoniae* was *Lundenwic* put into Latin. It is not certain however, that *Lundenwic* and London were quite the same thing. It may be that the former was a port area beside the latter. Three of the charters which use *portus* of London refer to customs dues and the fourth (Birch no. 34) refers to land given 'iuxta portum Lundoniae ubi naves applicant super idem flumen in meridiana parte iuxta viam publicam'. This could mean that the *portus* was on the south bank or that it was a separate area e.g. downstream of the bridge.

In one case only do charters use *civitas* for a place where Bede does not. This is Reculver which he mentions simply as 'monasterio . . . Raculfe nuncupatur' (*OH*, p. 295). It appears in charters in forms similar to this (Birch, nos. 199, 173) but also as *Raculfcestre* and *civitate Recuulf* (nos. 243, 45). It is significant that Reculver had an important Roman past.

In short there is some general correspondance between Bede's usage in regard to *urbs* and *civitas* and that prevailing among other early English writers in Latin. In the other sources referred to above *civitas* seems nowhere to be used for a place not of Roman significance and for only two without a name in *caestir*: Carlisle and Canterbury. An *urbs* is a fortress, not at a place of Roman significance. The only exception is Canterbury with its name in *burg*. Unlike Bede other writers occasionally use *castrum* and *castellum* and in particular for Rochester, where the employment of these words may reflect something special about the place and its early name. Consideration of other sources adds *portus* to the list of significant terms for places and suggests that it is the equivalent of *wic*.

The examination of the use made by Bede and others of *urbs, civitas* and similar terms does permit a few general conclusions and suggestions about places in early England. It seems that there was a real distinction drawn between Roman and non-Roman places. This is reflected not only in the evidence cited above but in the fact that names in *burg* were very rarely given to Roman places of significance, notwithstanding their fortifications. Of between ninety and a hundred places in Roman Britain with some claim to be called a town (not all were fortified) no more than six ended with names containing *burg*.[11] These were Canterbury, Richborough, Littleborough, Wanborough, Aldborough and Brough. Of these Canterbury may possibly have had an early name in *caestir* (p. 36 n. 5 above), Richborough certainly did (*OH*, p. 9) and the other four have names which first appear in the late

---

[11] This figure is derived from the lists of towns or likely towns in *Map of Roman Britain* 1956 and Rodwell and Rowley 1975.

eleventh century and need not reflect early usage. That Canterbury was a special case is indicated by the way in which, for this town alone, the charters fluctuate between *urbs* and *civitas* and the Old English translation of Bede between *burg* and *ceastre*. It was a place with a name in *burg* but of a kind which would normally have been called *civitas, ceastre*. With the sole exception of Bede's one reference to London as *urbs* I have found no instance of a British place which is normally called *civitas* being called *urbs*, Canterbury apart. While it would be unreasonable to assert that there was an absolute distinction in vernacular usage between *burg* and *caestir* it is reasonable to deduce that there was a real and general distinction. This tells one a little about the views taken of the Roman past; for example it clearly mattered to someone in 803 to distinguish between bishops whose *sedes* were *civitates* and the others (though his interest could have been philologicial rather than historical). The distinction between the names of Roman places and of others certainly affords clues in the search for the location of, for example, *Cnobheresburg* or *Sidnacaester;* the one probably was not a Roman place, the latter probably was.

Urbes deserve more attention than they have received. Eddius is suggestive about them. Those he mentions (above p. 104) were significant places; each of the two (apart from Bamburgh) in his book was suitable for the safe-keeping of an important prisoner and in the charge of a *praefectus*. *Praefectus* is commonly translated 'reeve', but it was a word with a range of meanings and could denote men of the highest rank of the kind who elsewhere could be termed *principes, duces* or *ealdormen* (Chadwick 1905, pp. 228, 251, 259–60, 282–84). Another *praefectus* whom Eddius mentions was the king of Mercia's nephew (Moonen ed. 1946, p. 142). His Northumbrian *praefecti* may have exercised authority over wide areas from their *urbes*.[12] Eddius does not extend *urbs* to cover such places as *Colodaesburg*. This is a likely indication of the way in which Bede's habit of translating vernacular names into Latin could lead him to apply the same word to places of different kinds. Nevertheless it is not without significance that some monasteries had names in *burg* translated *urbs*. Granted that it is by no means certain that all monasteries had a defensive *vallum* (Cramp, 1976, pp. 204–6, 209) the names afford some means of detecting those associated with a fortification, though not of determining its age. *Urbs* and *burg* continued to be used to describe fortified monasteries in later centuries. William of Malmesbury saw a stone which had been taken from an old wall at Shaftesbury and which bore the inscription 'Anno Dominicae incarnationis Elfridus rex fecit hanc urbem DCCC octogesimo regni sui viii' (Hamilton ed. 1870, p.

---

[12] Edwin's *praefectus* at Lincoln may have been in a similar position. The *gerefa* of the Anglo-Saxon translation has tended to drag down in historians' eyes one who *may* have been more like a 'sub-king' than a 'reeve', *OH*, p. 117; Miller ed. 1890, I, p. 145.

186). A passage (probably twelfth century) interpolated into the Anglo-Saxon Chronicle, E version, explains that after a wall was built round the monastery of Medeshamstead in about 1000 it was called *Burch* (Earle and Plummer ed. 1892, I, p. 177). A fortress may have contained a good deal of ground and many men have lived in and around it, especially if it was a centre of royal power. A fortified monastery may have had many buildings and a considerable population and have been not unlike a royal fortress. The early uses of *urbs* and *burg* may indicate not so much the undue inclusiveness of these terms as the undue divisiveness of ours: town, fortress, monastery.

In considering the hierarchy of places it is significant that Bede uses *metropolis* to mean 'capital'. A charter of 718 ×745 provides another *metropolis* to set beside his London and Canterbury: Worcester, *metropolim Huicciorum* (Birch, no. 166). A letter of Alcuin's gives a similar role to York: *caput totius regni* (Duemmler ed. 1895, p. 43). The way in which Bamburgh is treated in early sources indicates the possibility that it had a similar position in Bernicia (above p. 00). That the Old English translation of Bede renders *metropolis* as *ealdorburg* suggests that a *burg* could be something like a capital. Notwithstanding the extent to which early kings perambulated round their vills, early kingdoms were not necessarily multifocal but could have a *civitas* or an *urbs* which was the chief one of all.

Bede's most frequently used terms for less important places as *vicus* and *villa*. They are used in a fairly general sense to mean something like 'village' and synonymously. There is no apparent difference between *villa* in e.g. 'veniente in villam clerico vel presbytero, cuncti ad eius imperium verbum audituri confluerunt' and *vicus* in e.g. 'siquis sacerdotum in vicum forte devineret mox congregati in unum vicani verbum vitae ad illo expetere curabant' (*OH*, 269, 191). *Vicus* and *villa* are similarly used synonymously with a qualification such as *regis* or *regia* to denote a royal vill e.g. *Ad Murum* is called both *vicus regis* and *villa regia* (*OH* pp. 170, 172). There may be just a shade of difference between them in this context in so far as Bede twice refers to a *villa regia* as being *at* a place. (*OH*, p. 115). No use of *vicus* quite like this occurs; and so it looks as if *villa* rather than *vicus* was the word which came to him when he was thinking of the buildings and establishment of a royal vill. Bede uses the diminutive *viculus* fairly frequently. That he could employ *vicus* and *viculus* in successive sentences to denote the same place (Colgrave ed. 1940, p. 200) makes it plain that he did not distinguish sharply between the two, though it is likely that quite often he used the diminutive advisedly (see p. 111 below). A more remarkable usage is that of *possessio* for a place. The most unambiguous instance of this comes in the life of Cuthbert, where the saint is described as going to a *possessio* of the monastery of Whitby to see the abbess Aelfflaed and to dedicate a church (Colgrave ed. 1940, p. 262 and p. 112 below).

So far it might seem that there is not a great deal to be learned by considering Bede's words for minor places. But some of his usages seem more significant if looked at in relation to what is becoming increasingly clear about the organisation of lordship and local government in large areas of early England. It appears, largely thanks to the remarkable way in which Professors Jones and Barrow have built on the foundations laid long ago by Robertson, Maitland and Jolliffe that common, possibly omnipresent, elements were units of government and exploitation of the type of the Northumbrian small shire and the Kentish lathe, centred on a royal vill, and in close, probably elaborate, relationship with 'extensive estates' with scattered members owing dues and services to some central place (Jones 1976, Barrow 1973). One thing in Bede's usage which fits with the nature of such an early system is his use of *vicus* and *villa* synonymously. No investigation of the distinction and relations between the two such as has been undertaken for early Gaul (e.g. Latouche 1956, pp. 76–85) could possibly be based on his work.[13] This is probably because the property and rights of the great were not concentrated in *villa* estates in the Continental sense, but were focused on central places which were often also centres of population. An English *villa regia* was not a great estate in the sense of a discrete block of land owned and exploited in special ways. Rather was it the centre of a fairly wide area all or most of whose people owed something to it. If, as may well have been, there were lands within such an area which were particularly bound to and exploited from it, they probably formed a kind of archipelago. There would have been no point in trying to decide whether the central place of such a complex was more appropriately termed *villa* or *vicus*.

It is probable that many of the *villae* and *vici* to which Bede refers were not just villages, but central places of this kind. Of those which he names or provides some information about in the *Ecclesiastical History* eight were royal and one belonged to a *comes*.[14] Of three which are named in the anonymous life of Cuthbert one was not improbably royal;[15] we know nothing of the others. It is likely that the *vici* and *villae* of which we read in the accounts of the lives of holy bishops were often royal even when we are not told so. Paulinus seems to have worked from royal vills (*OH*, pp. 114–15). Aidan also based himself 'in aliis villis regis' apart from that at which he died (*OH*, pp. 159–60). Although we have no such specific information about Cuthbert and

[13] By the eighth century *vicus* and *villa* may have been drawing closer together in Gaul.

[14] *Ad Murum, Campodonum*, Rendlesham, Yeavering, *Maelmin* and Catterick (not explicitly stated as royal), for all of which see the appendix, with the vills by the Derwent and near Bamburgh (*OH*, pp. 99, 159). For the *villa . . . comitis, OH*, p. 286.

[15] *Medilwong* (Colgrave ed. 1940, p. 119), because a Northumbrian king was killed by his *familia* there in 759 (Arnold ed. 1882, II, pp. 41, 376).

Wilfrid it is likely that they, similarly, based themselves on royal vills. If so it was probably at such that they wrought their wonders. So, on occasion *villa* or *vicus* in the hagiographical sources may have a more specific meaning that is immediately clear from the context.

Even though Bede sometimes uses *villa* and *vicus* in fairly wide or vague senses there may have been contexts in which it seemed to him inappropriate to do so. One way of approaching this possibility is to set it beside the odd fact that although *villa* and *vicus* are common words in the narrative sources they are not so in the charters. I have found seventeen references to gifts of rural *villae* and *vici* in charters of before 800. Of these only three are in texts which appear sufficiently authentic for significance to be attached to their wording.[16] The shortage of references to *villae* and *vici* suggests that, in charters, these are not words applied to the common run of settlements but rather to royal vills which were not often given away. The commonest word for a settlement in early charters is simply *terra*, in formulae such as '. . . terram juris nostri quinque aratrorum quae appellatur Littelburne' (no. 90) or '. . . terram VIII manentium quae nominatur æt Bæccessor . . .' (no. 163). These names, like many of those given to *terrae* in early charters, survive as those of modern places (Cox 1975/76, passim). It seems likely that a *terra* with an assessment at about the level of that of these two places was a single settlement with its land. Sometimes a *terra* has a much larger assessment. It then generally has component settlements which have names and often assessments of their own, as for example in grants of Caedwalla's ('. . . terram . . . confero cuius vocabulum est Farnham in cassatos LX . . . quorum X in Bintumgom, II in Cert . . .'),[17] Frithuwold's ('. . . sunt tamen diversa nomina de . . . terra supradicta, scilicet . . .') and Offa's ('. . . dabo terram septies quinos tributariorum jugera continentem . . . Est autem rus praefatus in IIIIᵒʳ villulis separatum hoc est Teottingtun . . . v manentium . . . viculus qui nominatur æt Uuassanburnam . . . x cassatorum . . . tertius viculus est . . . æt Codesuuallan aeque x mansionum et quartus viculus hoc est Nordtun x manentium') (Birch, nos. 72, 34, 236). Such grants reveal a system whereby substantial areas were assessed at considerable round numbers of hides which were apportioned among the component villages. It is likely that such areas (which sometimes have names of their own stated, sometimes not) were often those centred on royal vills,

---

[16] Birch nos. 202/3, 209/10, 246. The spurious or more doubtful charters are Birch nos. 6, 27, 64, 66, 82, 130, 169, 204, 226, 231, 235, 240, 244, 252 (82 and 169 have attracted some favourable opinions; the *villa* in the former has an *-ingaham* name, cf. p. 48 below; the reference in the latter is general . . . *in vilis et in vicis* . . .). I have excluded e.g. nos. 185 and 219 because they refer to lands which *ad villam* . . . *subjacent, pertinet ad villam*. 192 and 248 relate to a *villa* and a *vicus* in Canterbury.

[17] The list of names in this charter gives the impression of having been abbreviated by a copyist.

which may therefore, in such charters, be what are being given away, though no trustworthy early charter seems to say so. One which is probably spurious does and is worth quoting even if it does no more than show how an eleventh-century monk of Worcester believed land tenure to have been organised three hundred years before. It is attributed to Offa. 'Dabo . . . regalem vicum Cropponþorn . . . cum omnibus membris per loca varia fundatis et nominibus segregatis ad vicum eundem pertinentibus. Ad Croppeþorn VII manentes, ad Noeþeretune I, æt Elmlege II, æt Criddesho I, æt Ceorletune XIIII, æt Heantune XV, æt Bencinwyrede I. Quae in unum collectae sunt L manentes' (ibid., no. 235; Ker 1948, pp. 54, 68). The charters granting estates containing several settlements are those which provide the most helpful clues to the relationship between the system of assessment and the system of organisation described by Jones and Barrow. Such large grants often give the appearance of being of a single block of land. It is likely that some at least of the 'multiple' estates which later appear as archipelagos dependent on a particular centre represent what was left of such a block after numerous gifts of single settlements of the kind familiar in the charters had been made. Such grants of single places or of groups less than the whole set depending on a royal vill are those most frequently met with.

It is argued above that the apparent reluctance of the early charters to use *villa* or *vicus* for settlements is because those words denoted royal vills. Although Bede uses them more freely it is likely that to him also they carried with them the implication that a royal vill was, or might, be intended. (He describes Catterick, which was almost certainly a royal vill, as *vicus* without qualification (*OH*, pp. 115, 155). It is likely, therefore, that his employment of other words for settlements is on occasion due to a wish to avoid *villa* or *vicus* in contexts where juxtaposition with a royal vill or possible ambiguity made it seem desirable or natural to avoid the possible implication that such a vill or vills was intended. Thus, when he writes of Paulinus baptising at Yeavering and of 'confluentem eo de cunctis viculis et locis plebem' he probably avoids *villa* or *vicus* because Yeavering had just been mentioned as *villam regiam* as he does not mean that people were flocking to it from *villae* in the sense that it was a *villa* (*OH*, p. 155). A similar instance is the account of Penda's assault on Bamburgh 'discissisque viculis, quos in vicinia urbis invenit' (*OH*, p. 159). The only royal vill in the vicinity of Bamburgh was probably that at which Aidan died; and so a different word was appropriate for the settlements round about. Bede does not use *terra* by itself to indicate a place, except perhaps in the *Lives of the Abbots* where he writes of 'terram octo familiarum . . . terram viginti familiarum . . . in loco qui incolarum lingua ad Villam Sambuce vocatur . . . terram decem familiarum . . . in loco villae quae Daltun nuncupatur' (*OH*, p. 380). These descriptions of lands acquired by his abbey use language recalling that of charters,

and may indeed be derived from such. (It is likely but not certain that
what was given in the last two instances was not the places named but
others dependent on them.) Ordinarily Bede's nearest equivalent to the
terra of the charters is *possessio*. The plainest instance of his using
possessio to mean a place is in his account of Cuthbert's coming 'ad
possessionem monasterii ipsius (cf. Whitby)' on purpose to dedicate a
church, which makes it reasonably certain that the *possessio* was a
settlement (Colgrave ed. 1940, p. 262). It may be that Bede's use of the
somewhat unusual *possessio* here is the counterpart to the unusual
parrochia used by his source, the anonymous life, in its account of the
same miracle '. . . in parrochia eius quae dicitur Osingaeun . . .' (ibid.,
p. 126). Just what the latter meant by *parrochia* is not easy to know, but I
would suggest that Bede took it to mean something like 'the area
dependent on Ovington'; that is to say assumed that the miracle took
place not *at* Ovington but at some component settlement of the
Ovington estate and that this suggested *possessio* as the appropriate
word. Similarly in his account of a miracle at Selsey '. . . neque aliquis
de hoc monasterio sive adiacentibus ei possessiunculis hac clade ultra
moriturus est.' he probably means by *possessiuncula* the settlements
which were component parts of the Selsey estate (*OH*, p. 234). Again in
the life of Cuthbert, when he refers to 'magnis quondam refertisque
habittaoribus villis et possessionibus' he is probably thinking of *villae*,
estate centres, and *possessiones*, subordinate settlements (Colgrave ed.
1940, p. 258). In the account of the Selsey incident as in his description
of Oswy's gift of *XII possessiunculis terrarum* in gratitude for victory he
uses not *possessio*, but the diminutive (*OH*, p. 178). The implication
cannot be pejorative, for he uses the diminutive in contexts in which
there can be no question of such an intention (*OH*, pp. 28, 234). It
might derive from a polite formula in a charter (cf. Birch, no. 229). In
any case there can be no sharp distinction between *possessio* and its
diminutive, for the estates Oswy gave are also described as *possessiones*
(*OH*, p. 178). It is possible that there was a degree of ambiguity in
possessio (as there was in *terra* in charters), because it could be used either
to denote a settlement or a wider area containing several settlements,
for example in Bede's reference to Caedwalla's gift of a *possessio terrae* of
three-hundred hides (*OH*, p. 237). Thus there may have been an
inclination to use *possessiunculum* when a single settlement was in mind.
In any case what Bede almost certainly means in his description of
Oswy's gift is that he gave twelve villages, not *villae regales*, but
important components of twelve such.

In a grant of Caedwalla's, Farnham, which has become the name of a
single place, is that of a large estate, with named components (Birch,
no. 72). It is likely that in early usage the same name could be applied
both to a place and to an area; e.g., as the author of the Cropthorne
charter supposed, both to the actual place at which a royal vill was

situated, and to the area dependent on that vill (above, p. 109). It looks as if sometimes, as at Farnham, the name of a place was extended to an area; but also as if, sometimes, the name of an area became attached to its central place. The latter is suggested by the English place-names which seem to have originated as area names, for example, Leeds, Lyminge, Ely, and some of these when they appear in early sources are explicitly applied to a *regio*: for example, Cuningham, Dent, Yeading (for all these names see Cox 1975/76, pp. 39–42, *s.v.*). A comparable instance appears in Bede. Eddius says that Wilfrid had a monastery 'qui in Undolum positum est', 'coenobum in Undolum', (Moonen ed. 1946, pp. 204, 210). Bede, in a passage in which he is probably following Eddius says that Wilfrid died 'in provincia quae vocatur Inundalum', and 'in monasterio suo quod habebat in provincia Undalum' (*OH*, pp. 322, 330). Thus he goes out of his way to indicate that Oundle was not so much a place as an area, indeed a wide area, for *provincia* is his normal term for a kingdom or sub-kingdom and he elsewhere applies it to nothing of less importance than the *provinciae* of the Meanuari, the Hwicce, and the South Gyrvii (Jones 1929, *s.v.*). Thus Oundle is a clear example of an area name which later became a place-name. It is likely that all the names of English places which Bede gives in such a form as *In Getlingum, Ingyruum* were of the same kind, related to his *In Brige*, which is now Faremoûtier-en-Brie. The relationship between names for places and names for areas raises questions about those in *ingas* and *ingaham*. Perhaps such as Barking, Woking, Lastingham and *Hruringaham* gained their names because they were central places for areas or peoples (for these names see Cox 1975/ 76). That is to say that they may have been royal vills. It is important to avoid the preconception that there must necessarily be something primitive or 'tribal' about such names. There may be; but the Anglo-Saxons gave 'people' names to areas and governmental divisions to which later centuries would have given 'area' names. What sounds like a tribe may have been only an administrative district.[18]

Some of the difficulties in which Bede found himself in selecting words for lesser places are echoed and to a degree illuminated by the vernacular sources. The Old English translation of Bede rightly draws no distinction between his *villa* and his *vicus*; both are usually translated *tun*, and, if royal, as *cynelican tun*.[19] *Tun* as an element in place-names

---

[18] Ekwall 1960, p. xiii. The early forms of Dorset and Somerset are particularly suggestive, for they are 'people' names derived from administrative centres, and when they first appear denote not tribes, but shires.

[19] The most significant exceptions are the use of *cyninges alderbold* and *cyninges bold* in translating Bede's references to Edwin's vills by the Derwent and at *Campodonum* respectively (Miller ed. 1890, I. pp. 122, 140). *Alderbold* means head or chief *bold* which suggests that the translator may have had independent information about the vill in question. The common meaning of *bold* is 'dwelling-place' but it appears in poetry in

continued

has been considerably discussed. Professor Smith concluded that its original meaning was 'enclosure' but that in the course of time its meaning became extended to include, for example 'village', 'estate' (Smith 1956, 11, pp. 188–97). In giving the derivations of place-names experts seem generally to render it as 'farm'. It may deserve further consideration. It is not a common element in names which occur in early sources. Dr Cox found six instances in his examination of sources earlier than *c.* 730 and could have added a seventh from Bede's *Lives of the Abbots, Daltun* (Cox 1975/76, esp. pp. 51, 53, 63; *OH*, p. 380). Of these, three are the names of places of three or four hides (Acton, Wilmington (*Pleghelmstun*), *Herotunum*), one of a place of twenty hides (Wootton), one of a *vicus* at which Ethelred of Mercia made a grant (*Tomtun*), one of a *villa* (*Daltun*) and one of a place in Scotland (*Penneltun*). It could be that in these cases the element always, as Dr Cox suggests, means 'an enclosure, farmstead'. Some doubt as to this arises if one adds to the list places named in the Anglo-Saxon Chronicle before 800 with names in *tun*. They are Bensington (taken by Cuthwulf in 571 and by Offa in 779 (Earle and Plummer ed. 1892, 1897, I, pp. 19, 51, cf. p. 50 below), *Meretun* where Cynewulf met his death while visiting his mistress in 757 (ibid., pp. 46, 47), Taunton, which Ine built and Aethelburh destroyed (ibid., pp. 42, 43), Somerton which Aethelbald occupied in 733, *villa regia* (ibid., pp. 44, 45; Campbell ed. 1962, p. 21) and *Seletun* where a Northumbrian ealdorman was burned to death (Earle and Plummer ed. 1892, 1897, I, p. 50). Certainly in most cases, probably in all, these are royal vills. It could be that, at least by 800, *tun* was already so common a place-name element that, by statistical necessity, it was found in the names of places of many kinds. Thus the places met in *tun* in the Chronicle could be royal vills, not so much because royal vills were particularly likely to have names in *tun* as because the Chronicle was particularly likely to give the names of royal vills; events tended to happen at such places and the Chronicle is concerned with events. It is true that while the early *tuns* in the Chronicle are significant places, most of those whose gift is recorded in charters are not.

The argument that the apparent connexion between names in *tun* and

continued
contexts which suggests 'a superior hall, a castle, a mansion' (Smith 1956, I, pp. 41, 43–44). It seems that the poetic meaning here appears in prose. The words occurs once in the laws, in a law of Alfred's, in a compound *boldgetale* (Attenborough 1922, p. 81). *Boldgetale*, elsewhere used to translate *provincia*, probably means 'shire' here, though possibly some smaller unit. It has been suggested that its derivation in this context is from a collection of dwellings (e.g. Smith 1956, I, p. 44) but it could be that the collection is not of dwellings but of people, e.g. those dependent on a royal vill. That this law of Alfred uses *bold* as other laws do not, and that the word was used in the formation of place-names in the North and Midlands but not in Wessex suggests the possibility of derivation from Offa's code.

royal vills is substantially coincidental is seductive but involves difficulties. A famous annal in the Chronicle, that for 571, uses *tunas* for four places which Cuthwulf captured from the Britons: Limbury, Aylesbury, Bensington and Eynsham (Earle and Plummer ed. 1892, 1899, I, pp. 18, 19 'iiii tunas genom'). It seems unlikely that this annal is singling out homesteads or farms for special mention. These must be places of significance, and the most recent translation of the Chronicle recognises this by translating *tunas* here as 'towns', though elsewhere the word is rendered 'village' (Whitelock, Douglas and Tucker 1965, p. 13 and p. 14 (*s.a.* 584). These places were probably not towns in any usual sense, though, but royal vills. Bensington was a place which later had four and a half hundreds associated with it and Aylesbury had eight and so we can reasonably guess that they were centres of authority at an early date (Cam 1944, p. 106). Had Bede been writing of the events of 571 probably he would have said that Cuthwulf took four *villas* or *vicos regales*, just as if he had been describing Ceawlin's capture of three *ceastre* in 577 he would probably have used *civitates*. Of course, the Chronicle's choice of words is not strictly evidence for what they were taken to mean before the late ninth century.[20] But it is very hard to believe that its use of *tun* for a significant place, likely to have been a royal vill, simply reflects late ninth-century idiom. It is much more likely that, from an early date, one of the meanings of *tun* was 'royal vill' and, for example, that the *Tomtun* where Ethelred of Mercia had a *vicus* and made a grant 'in cubiculo proprii vici qui nominatur Tomtun' was not, as Dr Cox implies, a place by the Teme, which took its name from a farm, subsequently keeping that name when a royal vill was built there, but rather was called *Tomtun* because it was a royal vill by the Teme. Such an early meaning for *tun* would help to explain the much later translation of *tun* by *pagus*, if the term were extended from a royal vill to the area dependent on it (Wright and Wülcker 1884, I, p. 177; Smith 1956, II, p. 190). I do not seek to maintain that *tun* does not, in place-names, mean all the things which experts say it means. But it does look as if an important meaning, and an early meaning, was 'royal vill'. Place-name studies seem in the past to have proceeded on a tacit assumption that the early history of England is largely one of the progress of settlement and have not always given attention to the possible relations between the names of places and their functions within structures of authority.

[20] The origin of such early annals is an unsolved problem. That they so often refer to warfare between Britons and Saxons and almost never to warfare between Saxons (which must have been common) suggests an ultimate British and so Latin origin as a possibility. The names given in the 571 annal can hardly be contemporaneous with the date attributed, unless there were already Anglo-Saxon names (or Germanizations of British names) for places in British hands. If the interpretation of *tunas* suggested above is accepted then there is an implication of a possible transfer not only of places, but also of organized areas of government, from Britons to Saxons.

The largely late evidence used by Jones and Barrow, the early charters, and Bede's choice of words all tell the same tale, that there were such structures and that fundamental to them was the organisation of administration and exploitation round royal vills on systems to which assesssment in hides and the like was intrinsic. In exploring the in some ways oddly orderly world of early England the identification of places with special functions is of particular importance. The study of vocabulary has at least this to contribute to the much-to-be-hoped for historical gazeteer of early England. It permits the formulation of questions which go with the grain of sources. 'What and where were the metropolises, *civitates*, *urbes*, *villae/vici regales* and *portus?*' are not questions which hold forth the hope of complete or unambiguous answers. But they are in large measure answerable.[21]

[21] This paper derives from one circulated at a conference on early towns organized by the Council for British Archaeology at Birmingham in June 1976.

APPENDIX

Words used for places in Britain by Bede in his *Ecclesiastical History*, *Lives of the Abbots* and prose *Life of Cuthbert*.

Name (The modern name is given when the identification is sure)	Times called *metropolis*	Times called *civitas*	Times called *urbs*	Times called *vicus*	Times called *villa*
Ad Murum				1[1]	1[2]
Alcluith		1[3]	2[4]		
Bamburgh		2[5]	10[6]		
Cambridge		1[7]			
Campodonum					1[8]
Canterbury	2[9]	10[10]	2[11]		
Carlisle		3[12]			
Catterick				2[13]	
Chester		1[14]			

[1] p. 170
[2] p. 172.
[3] p. 13.
[4] p. 26 (twice).
[5] p. 152; Colgrave ed. 1940, p. 245.
[6] pp. 138, 158 (twice), 159 (seven times).
[7] p. 245 (*civitatula*, p. 244).
[8] p. 115.

[9] pp. 46, 47.
[10] pp. 46 (twice), 47, 70 (twice), 85, 93, 94 (twice), 350.
[11] pp. 46, 94.
[12] p. 274; Colgrave ed. 1940, p. 243 (twice).
[13] pp. 115, 155.
[14] p. 84.

Name (The modern name is given when the identification is sure)	Times called *metropolis*	Times called *civitas*	Times called *urbs*	Times called *vicus*	Times called *villa*
Cnobheresburg			1[15]		
Coludi urbs			4[16]		
Daltun					1[17]
Dommoc		1[18]			
Dorchester		2[19]			
Giudi urbs			1[20]		
Lincoln		1[21]			
London	1[22]	7[23]	1[24]		
Maelmin					1[25]
Malmesbury			1[26]		
Rendlesham				1[27]	
Richborough		1[28]			
Rochester		7[29]			
Ad villam Sambuce					1[30]
Tadcaster (*Calcaria*)		1[31]			
Tilbury		1[32]			
Tiouulfingcaestir		1[33]			
Tunnacaestir		1[34]			
Verulamium		1[35]			
Winchester		6[36]			
York		3[37]			
Ythancaestir		1[38]			
Yeavering					1[39]

[15] p. 164.
[16] pp. 243, 262 (twice); Colgrave ed. 1940, p. 189.
[17] p. 380.
[18] p. 117.
[19] pp. 139, 140.
[20] p. 25.
[21] p. 117.
[22] p. 85.
[23] pp. 85 (twice), 141, 218, 225, 327, 350.
[24] p. 226.
[25] p. 115.
[26] p. 320.
[27] p. 174.

[28] p. 9.
[29] pp. 85, 93, 154, 206, 228 (twice), 354.
[30] p. 380.
[31] p. 253.
[32] p. 173.
[33] p. 117.
[34] p. 250.
[35] p. 21.
[36] pp. 140 (twice), 236, 321, 350 (twice).
[37] pp. 154, 229, 354.
[38] p. 172.
[39] p. 115.

BIBLIOGRAPHY

Arnold, T. ed. 1882: *Symeonis Monachi Opera Omnia*. Rolls Series. 2 vols. London

Attenborough F. L. 1922: *The Laws of the Earliest English Kings*, Cambridge

Barrow, G. W. S. 1973: Pre-feudal Scotland: shires and thanes. *The Kingdom of the Scots*. London

Birch, W. de G. ed: *Cartularium Saxonicum*. 3 vols, 1885–93. London

Cam, H. M. 1944: *Liberties and Communities in Medieval England*. Cambridge

Campbell, A. ed. 1961: *The Chronicle of Æthelweard*. London

—— 1973: *Charters of Rochester* (Anglo-Saxon Charters I). London

Chadwick, H. M. 1905: *Studies on Anglo-Saxon Institutions*. Cambridge

Colgrave, B. ed. 1940: *Two Lives of St Cuthbert*. Cambridge

—— 1956: *Felix's Life of Guthlac*. Cambridge

Cox, B. 1975/76: The Place-names of the earliest English records. *English Place-Name Society Journal*, VIII, 12–66

Cramp, R. J. 1976: Monastic sites. *The Archaeology of Anglo-Saxon England*, ed. D. M. Wilson. London

Duemmler, Ed. ed. 1895. *Epistolae Karolini Aevi*, II. MGH. Berlin

Dalton, O. M. 1927: *The History of the Franks by Gergory of Tours*. 2 vols. Oxford

Earle, J. and Plummer, C. ed. 1892, 1897: *Two of the Anglo-Saxons Chronicles Parallel*. 2 vols. Oxford

Ekwall, E. 1960: *The Concise Oxford Dictionary of English Place-Names*. Fourth edition. Oxford

Hamilton, N. E.S.A. ed. 1870: *Willelmi Malmesbiriensis Monachi de Gestis Pontificum Anglorum*. Rolls Series, London, etc.

Jackson, K. 1938: Nennius and the twenty-eight cities of Britain. *Antiquity*, XII, 44–55

—— *et al.* 1963: Celt and Saxon. Cambridge

Jones, G. R. J. 1976: Multiple estates and early settlement. *Medieval Settlement. Continuity and Change*. ed. P. H. Sawyer, 15–40. London

Jones, P. F. 1929: *A Concordance to the Historia Ecclesiastica of Bede*. Cambridge, Massachussetts

Ker, N. R. 1948: Hemming's Cartulary. *Studies in Medieval History presented to F. M. Powicke*, 49–75. Oxford

Lindsay, W. M. ed. 1911: *Isidori . . . Etymologicarum . . . Libri XX*. 2 vols. Oxford

Krusch, B. ed. 1902: *Vita Fursei, Scriptores Rerum Merovingicarum*, IV, 423–49. MGH. Hanover and Leipzig

Latouche, R. 1956: *Les origines de l'économie occidentale*. Paris

Maassen, F. ed. 1883: *Concilia Aevi Merovingici. Concilia*, I. MGH. Hanover

Map of Roman Britian 1956. Ordnance Survey. Third edition. Chessington

Miller, T. ed. 1890, 1898: *The Old English Version of Bede's Ecclesiastical History*. Early English Text Society XCV, XCVI, CX, CXI. London

Moonen, H. ed. 1946: Eddius Stephanus. *Het Leven van Sint Wilfrid*. 'S-Hertogen-bosch'

Plummer, C. ed. 1896: *Baedae Opera Historica*. 2 vols. Oxford

Rodwell, W. and Rowley, T. 1975: *Small Towns of Roman Britain* (British Archaeological Reports 15). Oxford

Sawyer, P. H. 1968: *Anglo-Saxon Charters: an Annotated List and Bibliography*. London

Smith, A. H. 1956: *English Place-Name Elements*. EPNS, xxv–xxvi. 2 vols. London

Whitelock, D., Douglas, D. C. and Tucker, S. I. 1965: *The Anglo-Saxon Chronicle: a Revised Translation*. Second edition. London

Wright, T. and Wülcker, R. P. 1884: *Anglo-Saxon and Old English Vocabularies*. 2 vols. London

Additional Bibliographical Note

It has now been demonstrated that the supposed monastic remains at Burgh Castle (p. 101 n.6) above, were almost certainly not such: S. Johnson, *Burgh Castle: Excavations by Charles Green, 1958–61 (East Anglian Archaeology,* xx (1983)). Professor G. R. J. Jones has made a strong case for identifying *Inbroninis* (p. 104 above) as Fenwick, or a centre very near Fenwick, in Northumberland: 'Historical Geography and our Landed Heritage', *The University of Leeds Review* xix (1976), pp. 53–78.

3. The excavations under York Minster. The column is one of those of the basilica of the headquarters building of the legionary fortress. There is evidence that this and adjacent buildings remained standing and in good repair until at least the ninth century. Edwin's first church at York may have stood in one of the courtyards here. Ultimately the Roman buildings did not fall but were demolished. *(National Monuments Record)*

7

The Age of Arthur*

So difficult, diverse and inadequate are the sources that to seek to write a history of the British Isles from the fourth century to the seventh must be to abandon some of the usual principles of historiography. To permute the innumerable possibilities is to impose more on ordinary prose than it can bear and to carry reasoning to the point of agnostic chaos. Only a learned and imaginative man could, and only an imprudent one would, attempt a comprehensive survey. Mr Morris fills the bill. His imprudence is marked. He uses to excess the ancient historian's black arts for making objects resembling bricks with odd stalks of what may or may not be straw. Supposition is repeatedly presented as fact. But, however easy experts may find it to use his book for target practice, it is of great importance. It is brave, comprehensive and imaginative. These qualities outweigh the flaws which are inevitable when a powerful and sensitive historical imagination is inadequately controlled and waxes dogmatic, and over-specific on particulars.

For example, it is mere meiosis to say that Mr Morris's account of Palladius and Patrick (or indeed of Irish history generally) will fail to command universal assent. He relies on so doubtful an inference as that a son of Vortigern married a daughter of Loegaire. He is inclined to bully his sources as in implying that Prosper must, rather than may, have regarded Palladius's mission as directed largely against British Pelagianism. Still, as the first historian to treat of Irish and British history simultaneously he sees more clearly than most of his predecessors that the missions to Ireland may belong to a context in which not only British Pelagianism but also the (hypothetical) policies of Vortigern towards Irish invasions of Britain were very important. His habit of using unconditional expressions when the difficulties cry out for conditional does not diminish the value of his suggestions.

Similarly with his forays into the luxuriant jungle of Welsh, Cornish and Breton hagiology. Most historians look at it, shudder, and pass on, occasionally muttering something about St Samson of Dol. Not Mr Morris, who sets to work to see what he can make of it. For example, a king or kings called Tewdrig are mentioned in late hagiographies relating to South Wales, to Cornwall and to Brittany. From them Mr Morris has worked out the interesting, the all too interesting, careers of

*Review of John Morris, *The Age of Arthur* (London, 1973).

Theodoric, a Goth in the service of King Arthur, and of another man of the same name, probably a son or grandson of the first. His passion for the unjustifiably specific creates the urge to defenestrate his book. Nevertheless it is unlikely that the Tewdrigs appearing in unrelated sources referring to the same period are all different men. What is said about them or him cannot be pure fable, if only because of Gregory of Tours' account of a Breton Theudericus (which also strengthens the case for the name's being the Germanic one suggested).[1] It is not unlikely that there were Goths on the loose at the right time. In short, here and elsewhere, Mr Morris makes a reasonable case for supposing that not all that glitters in the late hagiology is fools' gold. It may be harder to extract the pure metal than he alleges, but his predecessors have hardly tried at all.

Even when it is almost certainly wrong he draws attention to neglected sources and possibilities. For example, he ingeniously tries to make out that dedications to St Winwaloe (a Breton saint of the sixth century) in Norfolk and Hertfordshire derive from visits by the saint or a pupil. His arguments on two of them (Cokenach and Wereham) are to refute the obvious explanation: that both churches were so dedicated because they belonged to the abbey of Montreuil, whose patron Winwaloe was. They are weak. Contrary to what he alleges there is nothing very extraordinary in English churches being given to a Picard abbey in the twelfth century. His contention that an early cult in Hertfordshire is indicated by the description of the Icknield way, five miles from Cokenach, as *Wynewalestrete* (*c.* 1470) depends on the unsupported assumption that this name did not, in fact, apply to some thoroughfare nearer St Winwaloe's chapel.[2] What he takes to be a reference to monks already there when the church was given to Montreuil is almost certainly to the monks of Montreuil.[3]

It is possible that the cult of Winwaloe in the far west went back to near the saint's own time. Much of the evidence for interest in the saint in other parts of England almost certainly derives from Breton exiles of the tenth century, among whom refugees from Winwaloe's monastery of Landévennec were important.[4] After the translation of his relics to Montreuil in the tenth century the cult of Winwaloe was to a large extent a Picard one. Commercial and other relations with Picardy were

---

[1] The case for its being specifically Gothic is not overwhelming. See e.g., G. T. Gillespie, *A Catalogue of Persons Named in German Heroic Literature* (Oxford 1973), 30.

[2] J. E. B. Gover, Allen Mawer and F. M. Stenton, *The Place-Names of Hertfordshire* (Engl. Place-Name Soc., 1958) 175.

[3] Dugdale, *Monasticon*, edd. Caley, Ellis and Bandinel, iv. 151 no. 15.

[4] G. H. Doble, *The Saints of Cornwall* ii (Chatham 1962) 59–65, 93–4, 101. The dedication to Melor at Amesbury which Mr Morris regards as similarly deriving from a very early period probably also comes from the Breton immigration of the tenth century, R. B. Pugh, in *Victoria County History of Wiltshire* iii (1956) 242–3.

probably responsible for its occurence in eastern England in the Middle Ages.[5] If, however, Mr Morris is wrong in what he deduces about the early period he nevertheless draws attention to interesting and unused evidence for the extremely complex relations between Britain and the area between the mouth of the Loire and that of the Rhine in later centuries.

On the earlier history of these relations he is particularly valuable. He pays due attention to the evidence for Saxon invasions of Gaul in the fifth century and provides the fullest account so far available of the Saxon re-migration to the Continent in the sixth. There is a great deal more to be found out, for example, from place-names, where such a suggestion as that of the late C. T. Chevallier that continental place-names cast light on the conquest of Sussex is worth more attention that it has received.[6] The mystery remains that while the other evidence for Saxon settlement in the Boulonnais and the Bessin suggest sixth century settlement these are the only areas where the Gallic part of the *Notitia* uses the expression *in litore Saxonum*.[7] The more these subjects are considered the more it seems that much of the history of England in the Anglo-Saxon period makes sense only if it is regarded as part of, as it were, Channel history. Mr Morris has taken a long stride in the right direction.

To establish the sequence of events he has reconsidered both the archaeological and the written evidence. He takes Nennius more seriously than do many of his predecessors, especially on the date of the *Adventus*. He takes up Liebermann's suggestion that late sources contain a trace of early record on the history of East Anglia. There may be a little of this kind still to find. Bede's inclusion of the Huns and the Rugini among the peoples *a quibus Angli vel Saxones genus et originem duxisse*

[5] The only dedication to Winwaloe in E. England apart from those mentioned above was at Norwich. There is no evidence that this church was early. It is not, as Doble (op. cit., 101) alleges, mentioned in the Carrow foundation charter (*Regesta regum Anglo-Normannorum*) iii, edd. Cronne and Davis, no. 615) and its site is rather against an early date. If, as is possible, the church is pre-Conquest in origin its dedication probably reflects Flemish or Picard influence in the tenth or eleventh century; cf. the pre-Conquest church in Norwich dedicated to St Vaast and St Amand (St Vedast). For Winwaloe's being regarded as a Picard saint see Doble, op. cit., 62; for a little further evidence for his medieval cult in East Anglia S. C. Cockerell, *The Gorleston Psalter* (London 1907) 11; and for commercial connections between Norwich and Picardy in the 13th century, W. Hudson and J. C. Tingey, *The Records of the City of Norwich* ii (Norwich 1910) 209–12. The only evidence for the cult of Winwaloe in England outside the far West before the tenth century is the inclusion of his feast in a kalendar of the mid-ninth century in Bodleian MS. Digby 63 and the French and Flemish company he keeps there suggests that he appears as an import rather than a survival, H. A. Wilson, *The Missal of Robert of Jumièges* (Henry Bradshaw Society, 1896) xxxi.

[6] 'The Frankish Origin of the Hastings Tribe', *Sussex Arch. Coll.* civ (1966) 56 ff.

[7] D. A. White, *Litus Saxonicum* (Madison 1961) 68–72.

noscuntur[8] suggests the possibility that an early source lies behind what he says, for these names belong to a fifth rather than an eighth century context. Huns sound odd; it is equally odd that Priscus heard of a boast by Attila that he had authority over the islands in the ocean.[9] The Rugii appear a people who might have gone anywhere and done anything.[10]

Mr Morris's treatment of the archaeological evidence is extremely characteristic. He presents what is in many ways a more methodical synthesis of the evidence than any archaeologist has produced so far, and makes a more general attempt to relate the dates of cemeteries to the course of events. Here, as generally, he has had so much to do which others have left undone that his work is rough. How rough may be seen by, for example, comparing his survey of the East Anglian evidence with the gazeteer compiled by Miss Green and Mr Clough.[11]

The course of events as he sees it is this. Britain continued to be essentially Roman for more than a generation after 410. Even Hadrian's Wall continued to be defended. Hengist and Horsa were brought in as federates *c.* 428 and German forces were settled in many threatened areas. In the 440s they rebelled, seized control of large parts of Britain and destroyed much of civilised life. Nevertheless between *c.* 460 and *c.* 515 Ambrosius and Arthur re-established British power and restricted Saxon independence to limited areas, notably Kent and East Anglia. Arthur was the last Roman emperor of Britain. After his death power was divided among many British rulers, some of whom were of military origin. In about the middle of the sixth century came the 'second Saxon rebellion'. Within two generations most of modern England was overrun and before the end of the seventh century almost the whole.

If Mr Morris's reconstruction of this sequence is often questionable in large and small particulars it carries conviction as an account of the kind of thing which probably happened. His wise decision to treat the period 350–650 as a whole enables him to establish a better chronological perspective than his predecessors', avoiding that foreshortening which can make a generation in the sixth century seem much shorter than one in the twentieth. The subjection of modern England (outside Cornwall) to Saxon dynasties took a period as long as that from the accession of George III to the present day. During nearly all that time some areas were

---

[8] *Hist. Eccles.* V, ix. The question Haverfield raised long ago ('Some Place-Names in Bede', *Engl. Hist. Rev.* x (1895) 710–11) of how Bede came to know Latin names for places in Kent and Yorkshire which do not appear in written sources known to have been available to him remains unanswered.

[9] C. E. Stevens, *Engl. Hist. Rev.* lvi (1941) 363, n. 7.

[10]10 E. Schwarz, *Germanische Stammeskunde* (Heidelberg 1956) 80–83. (For another view of the passage in question see Morris, p. 270).

[11] J. N. L. Myres and B. Green, *The Anglo-Saxon Cemeteries of Caistor-by-Norwich and Markshall* (London 1973) 258–62.

under British control and it is likely that until well into the sixth century these included considerable parts of the south and the east. In some areas Saxon power may have come late. In yet others early Saxon success was probably followed by British recovery and the later re-establishment of Saxon power. The relationships between Celts and Saxons must have been very varied, both in different areas at the same time and at different times in the same area. Mr Morris rightly contends that the Brito-Saxon period is too long to be regarded merely as a destructive interlude. For some two centuries Britons and Saxons both ruled in England in varied and changing relationships. Those centuries, he argues, did not so much clear the ground as lay the foundations for later developments.

It is therefore surprising that he has relatively little to say about institutional and social continuity. He believes that Kent was taken over by the invaders as 'an intact Roman society' and thus that the characteristic Kentish institutions are of pre-Saxon origin. He argues for a Roman origin for important elements in the early institutions of Wales and much of northern England, indicating possible traces of similar survival elsewhere. But his discussion of Celtic and Anglo-Saxon institutions in general leaves them apart. This is a pity, for the course of events and the kind of development he describes create a plausible context for a closer relationship.

The evidence for such a relationship is becoming strong. Some of the early medieval institutions of lordship and local government in northern England bear such strong resemblances to those of Wales, extending to matters of detail and vocabulary that the most reasonable conclusion is that the areas in which the serjeant of the peace rather than frankpledge prevailed saw substantial continuity through the invasion period.[12] Furthermore, there are strong resemblances between what appear to have been the early institutions of 'agrarian and political lordship' over much of Britain. Professor Davis showed that the basic institutions of West Suffolk, as revealed in Abbot Samson's *Kalendar*, were almost certainly of pre-ninth century origin and bore important resemblances to those of Kent.[13] Professor Barrow in a brilliant study (which came too late for Mr Morris) has gone much further, arguing powerfully that 'from Kent to Northumbria, without a break, some system of "extensive" royal lordship known variously as lathe, soke, shire or *manerium cum appendiciis* had survived long enough for its main features to be traceable in records of the eleventh and twelfth centuries'. This system was one whereby goods and services were 'rendered at, and

---

[12] W. Rees in J. R. R. Tolkien and others, *Angles and Britons* (O'Donnell Lectures, Cardiff 1963) 148 ff; G. W. S. Barrow, 'Northern English Society in the early Middle Ages', *Northern History* iv (1969) 1 ff.

[13] R. H. C. Davis, *The Kalendar of Abbot Samson* (Camden Soc., 3rd Ser. lxxxiv, 1954) xxxii–xlvii.

directed from, particular centres often at some distance from their dependencies'. The similarities between the services owed in different areas and, e.g. in grazing rights, are such as to suggest that the apparent uniformity of the system is not attributable to the coincidental repetition of similar *ad hoc* responses to similar circumstances.[14] Important studies by Dr G. R. J. Jones, on a somewhat different basis, led to similar conclusions, at least for some areas.[15]

If it is granted that the renders and services associated with 'extensive lordship' in the north bespeak a Celtic origin, what is to be made of the south, where specific evidence of the same kind is lacking, but what appears to have been essentially the same system was common? It is not easy to avoid the conclusion that either these institutions are Celtic, or else the organisation of Anglo-Saxon lordship at the level in question bore strong resemblances to what prevailed among the Britons.

The problems which arise in such connections as this are of major importance for the history of Britain, and indeed of Europe. The basic organisation of the countryside outside the great estates of great men is largely unknown for the Roman period. For example, discussion of the origins of the institutions of medieval Kent is bedevilled by lack of knowledge of those of Roman Kent.[16] Even in medieval times the structure of rural society and of the means by which it was governed and exploited comes to light only episodically. The true nature of the soke organisation of West Suffolk is plain only because an abbot of singular energy took the trouble to record it; otherwise not even the exceptional record of Domesday Book would reveal it adequately.

Nevertheless a great deal did come to be recorded about the systems on which the peoples of north western Europe were or had been organised. In the chaos of information recorded at various dates all kinds of resemblances between different areas occur; for example, in the present context, between those of Kent and those of the middle Rhine and between those of East Anglia and those of Frisia.[17] It is not difficult to

---

[14] G. W. S. Barrow, *The Kingdom of the Scots* (London 1973) 1–68. It is important that he has been able to show that the system of 'shires' and 'thanages' in Scotland is almost certainly older and very possibly much older than the ninth century. His demonstration of a likely relationship between the 'shires' of N. England and of Scotland and place names with the element 'eccles' is a powerful reinforcement of the case of the antiquity of the system.

[15] For references to Dr Jones's numerous articles see *The Agrarian History of England and Wales* i, pt. ii, ed. H. P. R. Finberg (Cambridge 1972) 265 n. 1. C. Taylor in *Anglo-Saxon Settlement and Landscape* (ed. T. Rowley, Oxford 1974) 5–15 surveys recent and relevant discoveries on the continuity of settlement patterns and of boundaries.

[16] For what there is, S. Applebaum in *The Agrarian History of England and Wales*, op. cit., 97, 261–2.

[17] J. E. A. Jolliffe, *Pre-Feudal England: the Jutes* (Oxford 1933); G. C. Homans, 'The Frisians in East Anglia', *Econ. Hist. Rev.* 2nd Ser. x (1957–58) 189 ff.

find strands linking different areas which may be of coincidence or of connection: for example, is it significant that indications of a conventional valuation of the hide at 10d. can be found in England, that the *gafol* rate was often 1d. on the hide and that taxation in Merovingian Gaul was sometimes said to be levied by *decimatores*?[18]

Some of what is revealed in late sources may go back to a very distant period indeed. It is easy (not quite so easy in Ireland) to forget that institutions which first come to sight in the Dark Ages or later must often have had centuries or millenia of history behind them, and that similarities between them may reflect a common and distant ancestry. A paradigm case of the antiquity of institutions and of their connections could be that of the hide as Mr Charles-Edwards describes it. His is a powerful case for regarding it as a very ancient institution and part of a schematized system or view of society; the 'five hide system' having its origin in a particular conventionalisation of the family. He maintains that the Irish evidence shows important resemblances to the Anglo-Saxon system here, which indicate the survival of a common Indo-European inheritance.[19]

Jesting Pilate is the patron saint of these studies. At one extreme the institutions of 'extensive lordship' in England sketched above could, in principle, just, bespeak an immemorial continuity little affected by Roman, let alone Saxon, conquest.[20] At another they could for the most part simply indicate that German and Celtic peoples had a considerable inheritance in common and tended to organise themselves in similar ways. Nevertheless it is very important that it does seem likely that over much of England there was continuity in certain basic institutions through the Brito-Saxon period and/or that at the level in question

---

[18] E. W. Robertson, *Historical Essays* (Edinburgh 1872) 102–4. Robertson's work seems to have been almost entirely forgotten, except by Professor Barrow. His essays on 'The Land Gavel' and 'The Shire' in part anticipate and to a considerable degree supplement the works referred to above (p. 125–6, n. 12, 13, 14). Compare his remarks on land gavel (loc. cit.) with those of Davis (op. cit. xxxvii–xxxviii) and his references to early charter evidence from Kent and the W. Midlands suggesting parallels to *gwestfa* (p. 109) with Professor Rees's paper. His remains the best survey of Continental parallels to systems found in Britain. A particularly important feature of his work is his interested in mensuration. Customary measures of length and area, the latter often related closely to systems of social organisation and assessment, provide an important corpus of material for the study of the early history of Europe which could well throw light on the problems of 'continuity' and of the relationships between recorded history and its prehistoric past. It is presumably the extreme difficulty of such studies which has led to their relative neglect in England since Frederick Seebohm, whose work, e.g., on 'The Old British Mile' (*Customary Acres and their Historical Importance* (London 1914) 79–94) points to many potentially fruitful lines of inquiry.

[19] *Past and Present* no. 56 (1972) 3–33.

[20] For some salutary remarks on the dangers of carrying 'continuity' too far, G. W. S. Barrow, *Scott. Hist. Rev.* lii (1973) 196.

Anglo-Saxon institutions much resembled those of the Britons. It is sometimes overlooked how similar the Saxons and the Britons were in other respects. The economic organisation of Roman Britain was very different from that of Anglo-Saxon England. But the mastery of basic tools and techniques was not dissimilar. As carpenter, smith, shipwright or ploughman, the intruding pagan had little to learn from the native *paganus*, not least because Roman tools and techniques were widely diffused beyond the imperial frontiers in the preceding centuries.[21]

To consider the organisation of the native peoples of northern Europe as they emerge into the light of documents, beginning with the Irish laws, is to discover integrated systems, or the fragments thereof. German and Celtic peoples were not organised on the basis of a rough and transient pragmatism. On the contrary, the distribution, measurement and assessment of land, the graduations of society and the institutions of government seem to have been, or at least seem once to have been, related together in elaborately regular ways.[21] Into such a context the regularities which Professor Barrow discerns fit easily. So it could be that early Anglo-Saxon and Celtic government was more elaborately organised and had larger possibilities than is commonly, often tacitly, assumed.

If so, important questions arise about, for example, the Tribal Hidage. Mr Morris is not among those who push that baffling document to one side. True to form, first he dates it (with implausible precision) to *c.* 661 and then faces it head on. He concludes (unsurprisingly) that it is a tribute list and (more dashingly) that each hundred hides represents a territorial hundred in the full late Anglo-Saxon sense. It is very unlikely that the hundred as a unit of jurisdiction is so early. That the hidage is based on territorial 'hundreds' of assessment was first suggested by W. J. Corbett. His case depended largely on the important observation that the numbers of hundreds in the Domesday counties strongly suggest that the hundred had once had a primary role in assessment which was much diminished, except in East Anglia, by 1086. He did not claim that this (? tenth century) assessment was in general that of the Tribal Hidage , but rather that its having existed increases the likelihood of an earlier and comparable system. The interest, though not perhaps the *a priori* plausibility of his contentions, was increased by weighty arguments to show that the total of hides in the hidage for areas outside Wessex was

[21] For an example of regularity in a Celtic system of assessment etc. see Dr J. Bannerman's discussion of *Senchus Fer nAlban* for whose early (? seventh century) date he makes a powerful case (*Studies in the History of Dalriada* (Edinburgh 1974) 132–56.) (I am obliged to Dr R. A. Fletcher for drawing my attention to this.) For an example of early Saxon systematisation consider the most detailed account we have of how a king sought to deal with conquered Britons, the laws of Ine, which demonstrate an intention to dovetail them into West Saxon society on an orderly plan.

144,000 and that the assessment was systematized in multiples and simple fractions of a unit of 12,000 hides. If he was right, then in the seventh or eighth century not only were there distinct territorial units each assessed at a hundred hides, but also these reflected an overall assessment imposed by an authority having power over most of the kingdoms.[22]

It seems too much to believe. It may indeed *be* too much to believe. But even before so extreme a case one should hesitate. What seems the saving power of common sense may be no more than an *ignis fatuus*, a simple prejudice against believing that such things could have been at so early a date. Certainly Anglo-Saxon government and assessment were very elaborate and orderly by the eleventh century. Much in what then existed went back to the ninth and tenth centuries, when innovation was probably extensive and Carolingian example powerful. Nevertheless much of what is revealed in Domesday Book and in later evidence antedates Alfred. This must be true of large parts of the systems of lordship and rural organisation discussed above. It is known to be true of the hidage assessments of certain estates. Such an early system as Professor Barrow describes would be consonant with one of territorial units of assessment such as Mr Morris and Corbett suggest. It could be that common views of the Anglo-Saxon polity are too much determined by assumptions that development must have been from the chaotic to the orderly, from the *ad hoc* to the schematized and from weaker rule to stronger.

Such assumptions may be true, but they are not imposed by the evidence. A different hypothesis is as plausible. This would emphasise the great capacity for order (though not in the sense of 'law and . . .') of the Celts and the Germans and the strong similarities between them, owing something to a common Indo-European inheritance, something to a long Continental relationship. During the Brito-Saxon period (*c.* 425-*c.* 650) amid much violence there were slower and more complex processes of assimilation between Iron Age peoples at what was in many important respects a similar stage of development. One may suppose British, Brito-Saxon and Anglo-Saxon kingdoms to have had basically similar structures at the level described by Professor Barrow. These would have formed the foundation for the exercise of royal power on an

---

[22] Corbett revised his account of the Hidage in *Trans. Roy. Hist. Soc.* NS xiv (1900) 187 ff. in *Cambridge Medieval History* ii, 550–51. The most recent work on the Hidage is C. J. Hart, *Trans. Roy. Hist. Soc.* 5th Ser. xxi (1971) 133 ff. He strengthens the case for Corbett's 144,000 hides as against J. Brownbill, *Engl. Hist. Rev.* xxvii (1912) 625 ff. He makes the interesting, indeed plausible, suggestion that Bede had access to a tribute list compiled for a seventh century Northumbrian *Bretwalda* and including at least some non-Anglo-Saxon parts of Britain. It is likely that seventh century rulers did not draw so sharp a distinction between German and Celt as historians have done, since Bede.

orderly and extensive basis in ways such as are implied by the laws of Ine. (This is not incompatible with the bloody tale of the narrative sources for early Anglo-Saxon history; the history of almost any state can show how foreign wars and civil disorder can coexist with elaborate and durable institutions). The institutional foundations of Offa's empire may not have been essentially very different from those of its Carolingian neighbour. Late Anglo-Saxon government would appear as the result of a long development which did not begin with mere chaos in the fifth and sixth centuries but rather rested on a resilient sub-structure of institutions, geared to the production of renders and hospitality for rulers, and partly derived from and partly resembling those which had been there in Roman times, between and beyond the towns and beneath the military and bureaucratic superstructure of imperial rule. To suggest so much is little more than to suggest a particular application of a truism: that much of the nature and power of Dark Age and early medieval states must have derived from institutions and habits of mind whose origins were prehistoric, and in particular from systems for the provision of services and renders which had become nearly as integral to society as those for the conduct of feud.

Mr Morris's work is a great encouragement to speculate, that is to say think again, about his period. He is surely right in maintaining that many of the *idées reçues* about it are themselves no more than speculations, swaddled in the prudent language of cautious men and hallowed by repetition. As a text-book or a work of reference his work is a failure. He is not the Good King Wenceslas in whose footsteps the neophyte may safely plod. But the energy and sense of his general approach and the wonderful fertility of his mind give *The Age of Arthur* lasting value. All future work on the period will, or should, be indebted to it.

Additional Bibliographical Note

The study of this period has progressed considerably since the publication of John Morris's book. An excellent account of the more recent literature is to be found in Peter Salway, *Roman Britain* (Oxford, 1981). Colin Smith, 'Romano-British Place-Names in Bede', *Anglo-Saxon Studies in Archaeology and History*, i (1979), pp. 1–20 meets the need mentioned (n. 8) above. W. Davies and H. Vierck, 'The Contexts of the Tribal Hidage: Social Aggregates and Settlement Patterns', *Frühmittelalterliche Studien* viii (1974), pp. 224–93 is important for the Tribal Hidage.

8

Early Anglo-Saxon Society
According to Written Sources

Our first sources for social history are the early laws. Three sets survive from seventh century Kent, one from seventh century Wessex. Thereafter there is nothing until Alfred's code (871–99) which ostensibly drew not only on the earlier Kentish and West Saxon laws but also on a lost code of Offa, king of Mercia (757–96). The laws are not easy to interpret. They are cryptic in expression, may include archaic elements, and by no means deal with all social and legal relationships. One thing they do make obvious: complexity.

Consider the multiplicity of social ranks and the diversity of relationships in early Kentish society. Freemen are divided into at least two grades (perhaps into more, for there are four grades of free widow); below them are three grades of *læts*; and at the bottom are slaves, at least the women among these also being divided into three grades. Two words are used for unfree men, *theow* and *esne*, with overlapping but not necessarily synonymous meanings. Other words expressing dependent relationships appear: we read of the king's *fedesl* and the ceorl's *hlafæta*; but the meaning of these words is uncertain. In addition there are references to the king's reeves, smith and messengers, and to resident foreigners.

The West Saxon code of Ine gives a yet more complicated picture. From one point of view free society is divided into three: men with wergelds of 1,200, 600 and 200 shillings. But other distinctions appear. Among the higher classes we find: i) *ealdormen* each at the head of a territorial division, a *scir*; ii) 'other distinguished councillors'; iii) *scirmen*; iv) 'other judges'; v) king's *geneats*; vi) the *geneats* of other men; vii) *gesiths* apparently with some local authority; viii) king's thegns who are in some way superior to ix) *gesithcund* men holding land, who in turn count for more than x) *gesithcund* men not holding land; and lastly, xi) *hlafords* with authority over *gesithcundmen*. These descriptions are not mutually exclusive. But, once the hierarchy derived from royal authority, from lordship and from landholding is taken into account the nobility are divided, at a minimum, into *ealdormen*, men less than they but exceeding in status ordinary *gesiths* holding land, *gesiths* holding land and *gesiths* not holding land.

At the lower level of free West Saxon society the predominant figure seems to be the *ceorl*, who is presumably the same as the man with a wergeld of 200 shillings. Apparently in this category are *geburs* and *gafolgeldas*, words which are not synonymous, though they may denote the same men. Furthermore there are five grades of free Britons in Wessex, besides slaves, traders, smiths, foreigners and the reeves both of kings and noblemen.

That the laws are difficult to interpret derives in part from their dealing with rather elaborately divided societies whose relationships were complicated and possibly being transformed by economic developments, by lordship and perhaps above all by royal lordship.

The most important men in an early kingdom were those at the head of a major territorial sub-division. Their status varied with time, place and circumstances but was part of a continuum between kingship and nobility. The seventh century kings of Northumbria sometimes put a relative at the head of the formerly independent kingdom of Deira, and he was called *rex*. When Penda of Mercia put a son at the head of a recently conquered area (*c.*652) Bede was uncertain whether to call him *rex* or *princeps*. Eighth century Mercia included areas where dynasties which had once been independent survived in subordination. Their heads may have regarded themselves as *reges* but their Mercian lords regarded them as *subreguli, duces* or *comites*. It is often unclear whether the *principes* who were at the head of some important sub-division of Mercia were the head of subordinated dynasties or important royal agents: they may often have occupied a middle ground between the two. In seventh century Wessex there seem at times to have been several *reges* or *reguli* simultaneously; these were probably members of the royal family with authority over large areas of the kingdom. It is likely that over much of England the dominions of the more important kings were largely divided among subordinate rulers, whose status varied, but which often had something royal about it. The complications of this situation are reflected in the extensive Latin vocabularly used to describe such men. *Rex, regulus, subregulus, princeps, dux,* and *comes* are among the terms which could be employed to describe men in substantially the same position. *Ealdorman* is the commonest English term used. The emphasis in Ine's laws on the *ealdormen* being the king's *ealdormen*, and removable functionaries, may represent a West Saxon parallel to Mercian efforts clearly to subordinate such men who may well have all been of royal blood and what others might have called *reges* or *subreguli*. In considering such men, in Wessex and elsewhere, it is important to bear in mind how open royal successions were. Kings could be succeeded by very remote cousins and it seems that, at least in Mercia and Wessex, a small share of royal blood could justify a nobleman in 'striving for the kingdom' and in holding it, if he could seize it.

The *Vita* of St Guthlac (who died in 714) gives an account of the early life of a nobleman with royal blood which sheds light on important aspects of the life of the nobility. As a child Guthlac was, we are told, good, even holy. But in adolescence his disposition was changed. He gave himself up to warfare, gathered round himself 'comrades from diverse races', revenged himself on his enemies, plundered widely, and for nine years led a successfully violent life. He then became devout and gave up such excitements. It seems to have been common for young men of high birth to spend their early adult years as Guthlac did. He led a retinue of his own, whether he went with it in the service of greater men is not clear. Others certainly entered the service of kings, not necessarily their own kings. Just as Guthlac recruited comrades of diverse races so did Oswine (king of Deira 642 or 644–651) gather in his retinue noblemen 'from almost every kingdom'. Young noblemen were sometimes prepared to go overseas to take service. What they probably sought above all was a successful and rich lord, who would give them gifts. It was a world in which the gift of treasures, and of weapons, which counted as treasures, was of great importance as the sign of honour and success and the bond of service. An indication of this is given in the *Penitential* of Theodore (*c.* 700) when it states that if someone who has been converted from the world has a royal *specie* (probably meaning treaure here) from a living king, it should be at the king's disposal. There are indications that in his twenties a nobleman would expect to be given land by his lord, would marry, and, although remaining bound to military service when required, would no longer serve in the continuous company of his lord.

To say even so much is to run into the danger of that spurious precision which comes from over-generalisation with selected details. The safest course is to delineate not knowledge, but ignorance. Our lack of knowledge comes under three main heads: the size and graduations of the noble class; the importance or otherwise of office-holding; the nature of noble land-tenure.

No one has any precise idea of what proportion of the population was in some sense noble. That there were distinctions between noblemen may readily be seen, for example, from what is said above about the laws of Ine. How extensive our ignorance is may be realised from the dispute about whether St Cuthbert was noble or not: some saying he cannot have been noble because he looked after his father's sheep when he was young; others that he must have been noble because he had a horse and a spear. We know that there were many graduations within the nobility; but how great the social and economic gap was between, for example in Wessex, an *ealdorman* and a *gesithcund* man not holding land was we do not know, though we may guess it to have been very substantial.

The problem of office-holding is equally intractable. Certainly there were, even in the seventh century, offices to be held in royal households. Oswald of Northumbria (634–42) had a *minister* whose duty it was to relieve the poor. Aethelthryth, queen of East Anglia had a *primus ministrorum et princeps domus*. The courts of such potentates as

Ine, Aethelbald and Offa must have had officers for various functions, but we know little of them. Our sources mention royal officers of one kind and another: reeves, *judices*, *exactores* and the like but we know little that is precise about these nor whether they were noble. The essence of the difficulty is that the nature of the government of the English kingdoms in the seventh and eighth centuries is not understood. If, as is possible, English government differed from Carolingian in the eighth century chiefly in the extent to which its records have not survived, then in considering noble careers we may have to think more of administrative functions than is usual.

The most acute difficulties of all arise in relation to noble tenure of land. The main problem can be simply outlined. No source tells us whether noblemen could hold land by hereditary right without a charter. All that we know is that by *c*. 730 Northumbrian noblemen were setting up bogus monasteries in order to get chartered rights to land and that from the reign of Offa some noblemen received rights of *ius perpetuum* by charter. Inevitably there are two schools of thought. One maintains that early noble land tenure was entirely precarious, or anyway only for life, until noblemen, by fair means or foul, began to gain perpetual rights by charter. The other maintains that it is contrary to all probability that noble families should not have had hereditary lands from an early date and that while some lands may have been held precariously from kings, others must have been transmitted within families. Faced by meagre sources, wide possibilities, and the likelihood that the tenurial arrangements of the period were highly complex, it is hard to do more than to reserve judgment. It is plain, however, that some members of the class of *principes* at least claimed perpetual tenure, for they claimed to be able to confer it. That attitudes towards land were different from what they were able to become in later centuries is plain from the laws of Ine envisaging circumstances in which a nobleman would leave his land.

If our knowledge of the nobility is scanty and confused, that of the peasantry is derisory and worse confounded. It naturally follows that learned controversy has been extensive and sustained with an assertiveness which owes more to the passions of battle than to the possibilities of the evidence. One extreme point of view is that the basis of early Anglo-Saxon society was the free *ceorl* with a holding which may have been as much as a hide (up to 120 acres); those at the opposite pole maintain that the peasantry were for the most part unfree, or much subordinated. The contemporary evidence is sparse in the extreme. In Kent the *ceorl* has a wergeld one-third of that of the *eorl*. Many of the laws made no differentiation between *eorl* and *ceorl*; and both classes have a direct connection with the king in that he receives a fine if any freeman is killed. The *ceorl* has a fine to protect his peace, it is anticipated that he may have slaves and dependants. We are told nothing about his agricultural activities. If the *ceorl* is the ordinary Kentish peasant, then the impression given by these laws is that he probably was of considerable status. But then we have to consider the *læts*, of whom we know nothing except what had to be paid for killing them; and the unfree. The laws afford no means of telling whether Kent was a kingdom largely in the hands of free *ceorls* or on the contrary, whether it was for the most part divided into great estates cultivated by *læts* and/or by slaves and *esnes*.

The laws of Ine give rather different, but still no more conclusive, glimpses of the *ceorl*. He has the peace of his house protected. He owes military service to the king, of how important a kind we do not know. He can be under a lord who is responsible for his good conduct or who can tell him to work at any time. He may share a common meadow with other *ceorls* and hire a yoke of oxen in return for fodder. He may hire land from a lord, who may seek services as well as rent from him, but is only entitled to them if he provides a dwelling as well. That is nearly all that these laws tell us about the West Saxon *ceorl*. They give a general impression that he was more subordinated and had a lower status than his Kentish counter-part. They show that *ceorls could* be strongly under the authority of a lord (not necessarily that all or most were). They are interesting in showing them involved in contractual relationships. They cannot tell us how proportionately numerous *ceorls* were, how much land they held or to what extent they were cultivating the land of their lords.

If the contemporary evidence for the agrarian arrangements of society is so scanty, can later evidence help? Once extensive evidence is available, that is to say from the time of Domesday Book (1086) onwards, the wide variety and many regional variations of agrarian organisation are apparent. At the very least the contemplation of so much complexity and diversity reminds one how complex the society from which all this had ultimately developed may have been and how vain the effort must be to seek to reconstruct the agrarian world of early England from twenty sentences, often ambiguous, in the early laws. Very important in the evidence from the eleventh century onwards is that which suggests that important elements in institutions of agrarian lordship in much of northern England were of pre-Saxon origin, and that similar institutions, whether of such origin or not were to be found elsewhere in early England. There is no space here to provide more than a concise summary. It appears that the basic unit of government and exploitation was quite often an area, roughly of the order of a hundred square miles, but varying with the nature of the country, centred on a royal vill. All free inhabitants owed some services and dues to that vill, the services being of a non-servile kind, and the dues partaking of the nature of a uniform rent. The area concerned could be an agrarian unit in so far as it had common grazing. Within it there were sometimes or generally particular villages which were more strictly bound to the lord and owed heavier services. It is thought that linked with this system were the so-called multiple estates, those consisting not of one contiguous tract of land, but rather of a main centre with subordinated parts scattered often at a considerable distance. If there is much which is not entirely demonstrable in these suggestions there is much that is plausible, however surprising, in the attempt to link what is described in Domesday Book and later sources with what existed at a very early date. They are at the very least a warning against seeking to oversimplify as we imagine early Anglo-Saxon arrangements and against assuming that all the institutions of early English society were imposed or developed by the Saxons in Britain rather than adopted there. And it is helpful to be reminded, for example, that close agricultural subordination may be characteristic, not so much of whole classes scattered over the country as of particular villages within a complexly organised estate.

If our texts tell us little about peasants they reveal less about those who undertook non-agricultural tasks. A crucial question here is: what did slaves do? *Inter alia*, household tasks for the great, doubtless. The preparation of food for numbers such as could have been accommodated in the great halls found at Yeavering with kitchen equipment such as that found at Sutton Hoo would have required large domestic staffs, presumably unfree. The references to grinding-slaves in the Kentish laws are a reminder of how costly in labour milling must have been until mechanical mills were introduced. (We do not know when that was but it may be significant that two of the earliest examples known are at royal centres, Tamworth and Bamburgh.) What else did slaves do? Above all were they artisans? The laws reveal a little about smiths: that they were valued and that a lord had his smith almost as a matter of course; but not whether they were free or not. We know even less of other artisans. It could have been that many were slaves and that the production and distribution of manufactured goods was a function of lordship. When Bede tells us of Wilfrid's manumitting 250 *servos et ancillas* at Selsey, *c.* 678, it is imprudent to assume, as some have done, that these were largely engaged in agriculture rather than forming the domestic and artisan staff of a large estate centre. It is easy to find other important questions about the non-agricultural employment. For example, what was the status of men who boiled the salt of Worcestershire or mined the lead of Derbyshire? As so often, for precise answers there has to be substituted a general suggestion: that the non-agricultural elements in the economy may have been particularly important to the great and powerful and particularly dependent on slave-labour.

At all levels of society there were strong elements of instability. In the case of the noble class this is most strongly seen in the prevalance of exile. The openness of royal successions and the prevalence of feud ensured that exile was a common incident in the life of a man of high blood. A very high proportion of the kings of the period of whose lives we have any detailed knowledge were at some time in exile: for example, Edwin, Oswald, Oswy and Aldfrith of Northumbria, Caedwalla of Wessex; Sigbert of East Anglia, Aethelbald of Mercia. These exiles ultimately became kings; many others must have been less successful. Guthlac was in exile in Wales for a time. Exiles are come across in the sources in such contexts as an attack on the monastery of Oundle by a body of exiles 'ravaging because of some harm done to them'. When a great man went into exile he might take his *comitatus* with him.

It is likely that many men, from various ranks of society, were on the loose and driven to live as best as they could. We learn of 'poor men' who crowded round the court of Oswald in Northumbria, awaiting his charity. This suggests the possibility of there having been elements in society unprovided with land. Even for those who had land it might not suffice. Bede describes a famine in Sussex in the 670s which was so severe that men joined hands in groups of thirty and forty and jumped off the cliffs rather than starve any longer. The prevalence of feud and the very heavy penalties laid down by the laws probably drove many into exile. Wanderers presumably often lived by crime. Certain areas were regarded as haunts of robbers. The laws of Ine are conspicuous in their efforts to check marauders. When Cuthbert lay dying he was anxious that he should not be buried at Lindisfarne. He knew this would lead to its becoming a sanctuary and he was afraid of the effect on the monastery of the numerous bad characters who would congregate. Other men may have moved about England not through necessity but from choice. Some may have followed their lords when they took service in kingdoms other than their own. How far the wars and conquests of the early period were accompanied by large-scale movements it is not easy to tell. It is likely that migration on at least a moderate scale accompanied the wide extension of the areas under English control in the seventh century but such movements leave no trace in the written sources unless in the form of place-names: for example Conderton in Worcestershire means 'settlement of Kentish men', though we do not know when it gained the name. For further light on internal movements we must look to archaeology. What the written record does suggest is that there may have been much movement over long distances in short periods and that the archaeological record should be as much one of men being attracted towards centres of power as of their moving out from them.

Slavery must have been a powerful source of insecurity in early Anglo-Saxon society. We do not know how many slaves there were, but there is good reason to suppose that enslavement was an ever-present risk. In war, though noble captives were probably killed, non-nobles were enslaved, as were women. At least in the sixth and seventh centuries such captives were often sold abroad, though the church made efforts to stop this. When Bede described a vision of hell the image which came to his mind was that of captives being led off into slavery, the crowd mocking round them. When Aidan was a missionary in Northumbria he bought some of his first converts. There are frequent references in the laws to penal slaves, (literally fine-slaves). It is likely that men got into this position by being unable to pay a fine or other composition. The penalties laid down by the laws appear to be in general high. Even a 200 shilling *ceorl's* wergeld or a 60 shilling fine for cutting down a big tree or for theft was very heavy when 100 shillings was, for wergeld purposes, counted as a slave, a coat of mail and a sword. A slave was counted as at least notionally worth 60 shillings and there are indications that a 60 shilling fine could be counted as alternative to or even synonymous with enslavement. In such circumstances a man must often have been dependent on his kin if he was to avoid enslavement (they could indeed ransom him after he had become a slave). It appears that there were circumstances in which men might sell their children into slavery, or sell themselves, for a period of years or perhaps permanently. It was a society full of risks at all levels.

It was also a society full of changes. It is these which the scattered and imperfect nature of our sources make it hard to deal with. We can, for example, be certain that the spread of Christianity in the seventh century brought with it extensive changes, not least those which derived from the foundation before the end of the century of numerous monasteries. These may have included even changes in the economy; for it is a question how far the church was responsible for the introduction of new techniques, as for example, we find Wilfrid introducing improved methods of fishing in Sussex in the 670s. That the period saw extensive transformations of the economy is highly probable; in particular the use of silver coin in some areas from the late seventh century onwards may have been of great importance, in the development both of society and of government. In the laws of Ine a smith is a man who in some way belongs to a lord. In those of Alfred two hundred years later he is a business man dealing with his clients. This apparent change may be characteristic of many which took place as money and markets grew in importance. The written sources are not such, by no means such, as to enable us to discern neat patterns of development, or even to construct firm outlines. They give a certain amount of light, sometimes a bright flash, more frequently a dim flicker, in a darkness which for long periods and large areas is all but complete. The safest impressions to take from them are of great complexity and fairly rapid changes.

9

The Church in Anglo-Saxon Towns

To begin, as is natural, by considering the *sedes episcopales* of early England is to realise how little we know of its significant places – even to use the word 'town' is to beg a question. It is certain that some *sedes* were established at major centres of authority. Bede used *metropolis* to describe London and Canterbury and by that he meant the capital of a kingdom.[1] Gregory the Great was probably wise in selecting London as the seat of an archbishop, an intention in which he seems to have persisted even after he was informed of English conditions.[2] Not only was it the capital of a kingdom but it had geographical advantages which Canterbury could not rival. Even though Canterbury was established as the archbishops' *sedes* there are indications that already from the seventh century they were using London as a meeting place, and perhaps as a dwelling place, at least on occasion.[3] No major council of the early English church was held at or near Canterbury.[4] York's position in the north probably resembled that of London in the south. Our view of it has been transformed by Phillips's excavations, which have shown that the great headquarters building of the legionary fortress was maintained and used, at least in part, until well after the conversion period.[5] This discovery is a reminder of how much *Romanitas* may have remained and fits with what used to seem odd, that according to Bede Paulinus was able to start building a fine stone church at York (as also at Lincoln), which implies he found masons.[6] Other excavations, those of Biddle, have done much to illuminate one further *sedes*, Winchester, which appears to have survived as a centre of authority, but not of population

---

[1] [Ed C. Plummer,] *Opera Historica*, 2 vols (Oxford 1896) I pp. 46, 85.

[2] D. Whitelock, *Some Anglo-Saxon Bishops of London* (London 1974) p. 4 n 3.

[3] *ibid* p. 9 n 4 for archbishops of Canterbury consecrating bishops at London in 676 and 838–9 and for ninth-century councils there. Some eighth century councils were held at Chelsea, nearby. Boniface thought Augustine had held a synod at London, *Die Briefe des Heiligen Bonifatius and Lullus*, ed M. Tangl (Berlin 1955) p. 84. However suspect Eddius's account of Theodore's summoning Wilfrid and Eorconweald to him it is significant that it is to London he says they were summoned, *Eddius [Stephanus. Het Leven van Sint Wilfrid*, ed H. Moonen] ('S-Hertogenbosch 1946) cap 43 p. 148.

[4] Unless some unidentified meeting place or places was in that area.

[5] This derives from a paper read by Mr Phillips to an Anglo-German archaeological colloquium at York in September 1977.

[6] *Opera Historica* 1 pp. 114, 117. The Lincoln church is now thought to have been discovered. *The Times* (26 July 1978) pp. 1, 2.

(though the presence of something in the nature of a palace there in the early period remains to be demonstrated).[7] It is likely that others of the fifteen *sedes* of before 900 which have been definitely located were similarly centres of authority for wide areas. Worcester was described in the eighth century as the *metropolis* of the *Hwicce*[8]; such a place as Leicester may have had the same kind of significance.

But the location of *sedes* was not necessarily at major centres with a Roman past. Bede gives a clue to why this was so when he complains that kings have given so much land away that *non facile locus vacans ubi sedes episcopalis nova fieri debeat inveniri valeat.*[9] It seems that to him a *sedes episcopalis* meant something like an estate sufficient to sustain a bishop. This agrees with Eddius's account of how Lichfield came to be the *sedes* of the Mercian bishopric in 669. It was, he said, a *locus* which Wulfhere had given to Wilfrid to be a *sedes* for himself or someone else and which Wilfrid gave to Chad.[10] What made Lichfield suitable may be guessed from Domesday Book which shows it as the centre of a vast multiple estate.[11] Similarly with Selsey, which was a royal vill to which eighty-seven hides were attached.[12] Such *sedes* as Sherborne and Hexham were not improbably of the same type.

Recent research has emphasised the importance in early England not so much of towns as of centres of authority for units of government of the 'small shire' or lathe type for multiple estates.[13] It is becoming increasingly clear that all or most of England had a network of such places. They were not towns but significant places. Their relationship to the church is important; for it was at such places that minsters tended to be built. For example Miss Deanesly showed the relationship between the minsters and the lathes of early Kent, and a relationship with governmental arrangements (sometimes very old) is apparent in the minster system as it appears in partial decline in Domesday Book.[14] Bede mentions the construction of a major church at a local centre of royal

[7] M. Biddle, 'Felix Urbs Winthonia', *Tenth Century Studies*, [ed D. Parsons] (London/Chichester 1975) pp. 125–7.

[8] W. de Gray Birch, *Cartularium Saxonicum*, 3 vols. and index (1885–89), i no. 166. Hereafter CS.

[9] *Opera Historica* I p. 413 (Letter to Egbert).

[10] Eddius cap 15 p. 92.

[11] *VCH Staffordshire* 4 pp. 8–10 (though the estate may have been enlarged after the eighth century).

[12] Eddius cap 41 p. 144.

[13] G. R. J. Jones, 'Multiple Estates and Early Settlement', *Medieval Settlement, Continuity and Change*, ed P. H. Sawyer (London 1976) pp. 15–40; G. W.S. Barrow, *The Kingdom of the Scots* (London 1973) pp. 7–27.

[14] M. Deanesly, 'Early English and Gallic Minsters', *TRHS* 4 ser 23 (1941) pp. 15–40; [W.] Page ['Some Remarks on the Churches of the Domesday Survey'], *Archaeologia* 66 (London 1914–5) pp. 61–102; [F.] Barlow, [*The English Church 1000–1066*] (London 1966) p. 184.

authority as early as the time of Edwin when at his *villa regia* of
Campodonum the king built a *basilica*.[15] The late ninth-century
translator of Bede rendered his description of Aidan's journeyings *per
cuncta et urbana et rustica loca* as *þurh mynsterstowe ge þurh folcstowe*.[16] He is
indicating the distinction which seemed important to him, not so much
one between town and country, as between important local centres of the
kind where minsters were built and ordinary places. His distinction is
important in the history of the early church in England. It could not be an
urban church but, as it developed under the aegis of kings, so its pattern
of authority echoed theirs and where the *villa regis*, the royal *tun*, was,
there, more often than not, the minster was; and there often enough, in
later centuries a real town grew up.

It is a question how far in the early period the church helped to create
towns. It may have been that in a sense some of the communities most
resembling towns were major monasteries. When Ceolfrith left
Monkwearmouth-Jarrow in 716 there were over six hundred *milites
Christi* there apart from those he took with him.[17] For many centuries a
population of three hundred would have been enough for a small town
and no secular settlements in the early period can be proved to have
been so populous (though doubtless at least a handful were so). A
monastery such as Whitby, with its numerous buildings, its crafts and
its maritime contacts must have been considerably more like a town
than were most places.[18]

An important meeting-place for the urban and the ecclesiastical
historian is the graveside of the great. The importance attached to burial
in particular places throughout the Anglo-Saxon period enables us both
to identify centres and to see means whereby piety could attract
population to them. The Anglo-Saxon Chronicle shows a steady
interest in places of burial, and that bodies were often take a long way.
Thus after the fight between Cynewulf and Cyneheard in 757 the
former was taken to Winchester for burial, the latter to Axminster.[19] In
871 the body of a ealdorman who was killed at Reading was transported
to Derby to be buried.[20] The gilds of the late period provided for the
transport of deceased members' bodies to their chosen burial places; at
Abbotsbury there was a distance limit, sixty miles.[21] It was customary

[15] *Opera Historica* I p. 115.
[16] *The Old English Version of Bede's Ecclesiastical History*, ed T. Miller, pt I, *EETS* 95 (1895) p. 161.
[17] *Opera Historica* I pp. 400–1 (anonymous life of Ceolfrith).
[18] R. J. Cramp, 'Monastic Sites', *The Archaeology of Anglo-Saxon England*, [ed D. M. Wilson] (London 1976) pp. 223–9, 453–7, 459–62.
[19] *Two of the Saxon Chronicles Parallel*, ed J. Earle and C. Plummer, 2 vols (Oxford 1899) I p. 48.
[20] *The Chronicle of Aethelweard*, ed A. Campbell (London 1962) p. 37.
[21] *Diplomatarium* [*Anglicum Aevi Saxonici*, ed B. Thorpe] (London 1865) pp. 607, 611.

to make a substantial legacy to one's burial-place. With this often went provision for the poor. The earliest evidence is a grant by the ealdorman Oswulf to Christ Church, Canterbury, *c.* 810. He provides for 1,120 loaves to be distributed annually on the anniversary of his death 'as is done on the anniversaries of lords'.[22] About twenty years later a priest called Waher mentioned similar provision for the anniversary of archbishop Wulfred's death. One thousand two hundred poor men were to be fed, each was to be given bread with cheese or bacon and a penny.[23] Such practices continued in the later period. For example, in 1015 Athelstan provided for a hundred poor men to be fed at Ely on St Ethelreda's day.[24] If, as is likely, there were many such benefactions a great religious centre must have had considerable power to attract population, perhaps especially the poor such as we find crowding round Oswald, or huddled at a monastery door.[25] The prestige of a sanctuary could attract the less deserving. Cuthbert feared that his burial at Lindisfarne would lead to *incursionem profugorum vel noxiorum.*[26]

Provision for the distribution of pennies to twelve hundred men is an important indication of the early circulation of coin and of the extent to which the economy developed before 850. Much greater development took place in the next two centuries. It is strikingly demonstrated in the extensive growth of towns. By 1066 possibly about a tenth of the population lived in towns. The major provincial towns were of the same order of size as in the later middle ages. Urban manufactures flourished in an economy in which silver coin circulated abundantly. The last Anglo-Saxon centuries may have seen economic changes on a scale not paralleled till the eighteenth.[27]

The transformation of the church in the towns in the late Anglo-Saxon period was as notable as the economic changes which accompanied and influenced it. The impact on towns of reformed monasticism was various but often of a second order kind. At Winchester not only did the West Saxon kings create a real and

---

[22] *Select English Historical Documents of the Ninth and Tenth Centuries*, ed F. E. Harmer (Cambridge 1914) pp. 1–2, 39–40; cheese or something of the sort was to go with the loaves.

[23] CS 1 no 402.

[24] D. Whitelock, *Anglo-Saxon Wills* (Cambridge 1930) no xx.

[25] Bede, *Opera Historica* I p. 138; Aethelwulf, *De Abbatibus*, ed A. Campbell (Oxford 1967) p. 38.

[26] *Two Lives of Saint Cuthbert*, ed B. Colgrave (Cambridge 1940) p. 278.

[27] M. Biddle, 'Towns', *The Archaeology of Anglo-Saxon England*, pp. 120–41; H. R. Loyn, 'Towns in Late Anglo-Saxon England', *England before the Conquest: Studies in Primary Sources presented to Dorothy Whitelock*, ed P. Clemoes and K. Hughes (Cambridge 1971) pp. 115–28; [J.] Campbell, 'Norwich', [*The Atlas of Historic Towns*, ed M. D. Lobel] 2 (London 1975) pp. 5, 7–8; J. C. Russell, *British Medieval Population* (Albuquerque 1948) p. 305.

prosperous town where previously there may have been only a centre of government, they also created a holy city within it, where the New Minster stood just beside the Old Minster, the one grandly built, the other grandly rebuilt, with a west work probably over a hundred feet high; immediately opposite stood a royal nunnery.[28] Canterbury remained what it had been, a church town, and one to which kings went but rarely. It must have depended very largely on the wealth of its two great monasteries; and by the end of the Anglo-Saxon period that was great indeed, together their landed incomes were of the order of a quarter of that of the crown.[29] Bury Saint Edmund's was by 1086 certainly a considerable, perhaps a major, town; a major addition had been made to it since 1065 by abbot Baldwin.[30] Winchester, Canterbury and Bury were extreme cases. Worcester and Gloucester were the only other towns of much note which had Benedictine abbeys at the Conquest. Some other abbeys, notably Saint Alban's, had attempted to stimulate urban growth beside the abbey but without Bury's success.[31] The chief connection between urban growth and monastic reform was probably this, that reformed monasteries were very expensive. They required rich patronage. That it was available probably owed much to a prosperity in which towns played a large part. It may be significant that much of what Ethelwold received seems not to have been land, but rather gold and silver with which he bought land.[32]

The important religious communities in most towns were not Benedictine monasteries, but minsters of secular priests. Though important, they are not well-documented. The surviving sources generally amount to a handful of enigmas, separated by large empty spaces. The evidence for Saint Frideswide's at Oxford is unusually rich: two charcoal burials (probably ninth century), a reference in an early eleventh-century tract, a charter of Ethelred II indicating fairly extensive land-holdings round Oxford, mention of the canons in Domesday and a cock-and-bull origin story from William of Malmesbury which may retain a faint residue of fact.[33] That is all, until Saint Frideswide's was made over to Augustinian canons under Henry I. Yet, as Stenton argued, the community may indeed have had a very long history and considerable importance; its tithe claims suggest a

---

[28] Biddle, 'Felix Urbs Winthonia', *Tenth Century Studies* pp. 127–38.

[29] D. Knowles, *The Monastic Order in England,* (2nd ed Cambridge 1966), pp. 702–3; F. Barlow, *Edward the Confessor* (London 1970) pp. 153–4.

[30] [M. D.] Lobel, [*Bury St Edmunds*] (Oxford 1935) pp. 4–13, 12.

[31] *VCH Hertfordshire* 4 p. 67.

[32] *Liber Eliensis,* [ed E. O. Blake] Camden Soc. 3 ser 92 (1962) pp. 75, 80, 82, 84, 89, 91. 91.

[33] F. M. Stenton, 'St Frideswide and her Times', *Oxoniensia* I (Oxford 1936) pp. 103–12; T. G. Hassall, *Oxoniensia* 28 (1973) pp. 270–4.

connection with the big royal manor at Headington nearby.[34] In considering the growth and development of Oxford in the tenth century it is impossible to tell whether or when Saint Frideswide's was a focus or on the contrary a backwater. More characteristic, because less well-evidenced, is Cirencester. A major and very ancient demesne centre, one would expect there to have been an important minster there. There is no mention of any such thing in any pre-Conquest source. Yet there was one; it has been found under the remains of the Norman church and was a hundred and seventy nine feet long.[35] Often our first reference to a minster comes in Domesday. It is, however, nearly demonstrable that minster communities could be omitted from the survey.[36] This makes Hill's argument that Saint Mary's Lincoln, was a major minster with extensive rights in the late Saxon period the more plausible;[37] and imposes a certain caution in deducing too much from Domesday's failure to mention a minster community at, for example, Norwich. As often in Anglo-Saxon history we know enough to realise there was more than we know.

Still, we do know that urban minsters were numerous. Some, as was probably the case with Saint Frideswide's, were old and ante-dated the town with which they were associated. Others were new. The most obvious example was the New Minster at Winchester, though there the canons were not allowed many generations in which to enjoy their comforts. Saint Oswald's, Gloucester, was probably founded early in the tenth century by Ethelred and Aethelflaed, who moved the body of Saint Oswald to it from Bardney.[38] It is not certain how far the burh building of Alfred and Edward was accompanied by the foundation of new minsters. In Ethelred II's reign the fortification and occupation of South Cadbury for no more than ten years was accompanied by preparation for the erection of what may have been intended to be an impressive church.[39] The appearance of minsters in such a Danelaw town as Derby suggests foundation or refoundation in the tenth century, though the discovery of a splendid ninth century coffin at one of them, Saint Alkmund's, indicates at least continuity of site.[40] A

[34] The authenticity of the clause in the charter of 1004 relating to tithe is questioned: D. Whitelock, *English Historical Documents* I p. 546.

[35] [H. M.] Taylor, *Anglo-Saxon Architecture*, 3 (Cambridge 1978) p. 751.

[36] Domesday Book does not mention canons at, for example, Great Paxton or Worksop but there is evidence for them somewhat later: C. A. R. Radford, 'Pre-Conquest Minster Churches', *Arch[aeological] J[ournal]* 130 (London 1973) p. 133; C. Brown, 'Foundation Charter of Worksop Priory', *Thoroton Society* 9 (Nottingham 1905) p. 85.

[37] [J. W. F.] Hill, *Medieval Lincoln* (Cambridge 1965) pp. 64–73.

[38] *VCH Gloucestershire* 2 p. 84.

[39] L. Alcock, 'By South Cadbury is that Camelot . . .' (London 1972) pp. 198–200.

[40] *VCH Derbyshire* I pp 87–8; R. A. Hall, 'The Pre-Conquest Burh at Derby', *D[erbyshire] A[rchaeological] J[ournal]* 94 (Kendal 1974) p. 18.

considerable number of northern and Midland churches later claimed a tenth-century founder.[41] There are instances of towns with more minsters than one: for example Derby, Shrewsbury, Chester, Gloucester (where besides Saint Oswald's there was Saint Peter's, which was not monastic until the eleventh century); Hereford, beside the cathedral minster of Saint Ethelbert, had another, Saint Guthlac's.

The urban minsters of late Anglo-Saxon England were numerous and diverse. Many had formed part of fairly orderly systems of ecclesiastical authority corresponding to those of secular government. Some retained some of what this had given them (Saint Mary's Derby is a case in point)[42] but many must have lost much of what they once held. Some were small and poor, others large, rich and nobly built. For example recent work indicates that Saint Oswald's at Gloucester had very considerable buildings.[43] It would have been very much a shrine to West Saxon success. That no source earlier than Wendover even professes to record where Offa was buried is an indication of Mercian failure and of how that failure must have carried minsters down with it.[44] Wherever Offa actually was buried it must have been in what was at the time a powerful minster. Many minsters may have had residual rights and residual memories from regimes long toppled.[45] Others were new; and that they continued to be founded is a warning against accepting too easily that they were institutions without a future. It is true that they were threatened in various ways. Monastic reformers cast pious and greedy eyes on lax ways and substantial estates. Minster property was coming to be exploited to maintain great royal servants. In the towns, even more than in the country, the proliferation of parishes threatened the substance of 'old minster' rights. Still, relatively few were monasticised. A number survived the middle ages with the select status of royal free chapels.[46] Some survived as ordinary secular colleges. A considerable number were made over into houses of Augustinian canons in the twelfth century. In Edward the Confessor's England communities of priests, doubtless often married and often hereditary, were very important in some towns. The thirteen *canonici prebendarii*, alias *presbyteri de burgo* of Saint Mary's Stafford must, if

[41] [A.] Hamilton Thompson ['Notes on Secular Colleges of Canons in England, *ArchJ* 74 (1917) p. 142].

[42] *VCH Derbyshire* I p. 310; *The Cartulary of Darley Abbey*, ed R. R. Darlington, Derbyshire Archaeological and Natural History Society (Derby 1945) I p. liv; A. Saltman, 'The History of the Foundation of Dale Abbey', *DAJ* 87 (1967) p. 25.

[43] Taylor, *Anglo-Saxon Architecture*, 3 p. 1073.

[44] R. Vaughan, *Mathew Paris* (Cambridge 1958) p. 191.

[45] Blythburgh in Suffolk could be a case in point if there was substance in the twelfth-century contention that Anna king of the East Angles was buried and still venerated there, *Liber Eliensis* p. 18.

[46] J. H. Denton, *English Royal Free Chapels* (Manchester 1970).

resident (and certainly they had been intended to be, for Domesday shows them with a messuage each) have formed a conspicuous element in a small town.[47] In very many towns such bodies if they did not weigh as once they had must still have counted for something.

The most remarkable thing in the church in towns before the Conquest is the multiplication of parishes. This growth was recent, probably reaching its peak in the eleventh century, and ceasing in the twelfth; and it was on the largest scale.[48] Norwich, the only major town for which Domesday provides a comprehensive figure had a minimum of forty nine churches and chapels by 1086.[49] London must have had more and some other major towns cannot have been far, if at all, behind. It is certain that many of these urban churches were, or had originated as, private chapels and that many, but not all, were very small.[50] Why was it that in the towns, and in particular (though by no means only) in the great eastern towns, of England there was a church on every corner?

First, as Brooke points out, this is the urban aspect of something more general. The proliferation of churches in East Anglian countryside was as marked. It is unlikely that there was any rural area in medieval Europe where parishes were so small as in parts of Norfolk. By the time of Domesday East Anglian village churches were very numerous; some villages had more than one.[51] It is interesting that the contemporary Adam of Bremen describes something similar in Denmark: there were, he says, three hundred wooden churches in Scania alone.[52] One simple explanation for the proliferation of churches is important. People needed space to go to church in. The smallest urban churches were tiny: one at Winchester was thirteen feet by sixteen and the average size cannot have been great.[53] Even fifty

---

[47] *VCH Staffordshire* 4 pp. 22–3. The recorded population of the town was a hundred and sixty six. If this figure was accurate one household in thirteen was that of a canon.

[48] [C. N. L.] Brooke, ['The Church in the Towns, 1000–1250'], *Studies in Church History* 6 (1970) pp. 59–83; [C. N. L.] Brooke and [G.] Keir, (*London 800–1216: the Shaping of a City*] (London 1975) pp. 128–48; [A.] Rogers, ['Parish Boundaries and Urban History'], *Journal of the British Archaeological Association*, 3 ser 35 (London 1972) pp. 46–64 are the most important recent studies.

[49] D[omesday] B[ook seu Liber Censualis Willelmi Primi Regis Angliae, ed A. Farley], 2 vols (London 1783) pp. 117–18; Campbell, 'Norwich' pp 3, 23–4.

[50] [M.] Biddle and [D. J.] Keene, ['Winchester in the Eleventh and Twelfth Centuries', *Winchester in the Early Middle Ages: an Edition and Discussion of the Winston Domesday*, ed F. Barlow, M. Biddle, O. von Feilitzen and D. J. Keene] (Oxford 1976) pp. 329–35, 498–9.

[51] Page pp. 85–6.

[52] L. Musset, *Les Peuples Scandinaves au Moyen Age* (Paris 1951) p. 144.

[53] Biddle and Keene p. 334; *Medieval Archaeology* 18 (London 1974) for a church in York little larger; T. G. Hassall, *Oxoniensia* 39 (1974) for a church in Oxford converted from a domestic building. In a Suffolk village the construction of a chapel beside the cemetery of the mother church was explained on the ground that the latter could not

churches may have been hardly enough for such a place as Norwich, where more, perhaps many more, than five thousand people lived. As, again. Brooke, to whom I owe much, points out, the founding of new churches was the fruit not only of an impulse from below but a failure of authority above in that one church can be created only at the expense of another.[54] Brooke suggests that the failure was to some extent personal, by the default of absent or negligent bishops, and to some extent institutional. One cannot be totally happy about the hypothesis that Stigand's deficiencies extended to a neglect of his own interests; as the proprietor of two churches in Norwich he must have been well-acquainted with the problems.[55] That there were institutional reasons is probable. The institutions which had most to lose by the proliferation of new parishes were the head minsters. It is probable that the most likely explanation for the dearth of early charters from East Anglia will serve also to explain in part the abundance of late churches there; that the minsters had been destroyed or weakened by the Danish invasions.[56] Thus, that Domesday shows much fainter traces of an orderly minster system in the east as against the west would indicate as much the cause as the consequence of extensive church foundation. There were, of course, very numerous churches in some western towns. But at least in Winchester they seem generally to have lacked rights of burial and sometimes even of baptism.[57] Third, Brooke emphasises simple devotion and the extent to which pious groups of craftsmen clubbed together to build themselves a neighbourhood church. One has only to look at the surviving gild regulations to see how devout late Anglo-Saxons could be. Some of the Winchester churches were associated with gilds and gild halls. Attempts to stop eating and drinking in churches suggest that the churches themselves may sometimes have fulfilled the functions of halls, perhaps in particular for funeral feasts.[58]

They had other public functions also. Certain kinds of ordeal were held in churches; and a post-Conquest tract says that a man accused of theft was to be kept in a church from the Tuesday before the Sunday when he took the ordeal.[59] It is a question how far churches were used as

hold the whole parish, *DB 2*, p. 281.

[54] Brooke pp. 76–7.

[55] *DB* 2 p. 116. Stigand may possibly have been a Norwich man, Barlow p. 78 n 1.

[56] Though there are indications in Norwich that Edgar's law on the division of tithe between an old minster and a new church may have been applied, Barlow p. 195; Campbell, 'Norwich' p. 4 n 12.

[57] Biddle and Keene p. 332.

[58] *Ancient Laws [and Institutes,* ed B. Thorpe] (London 1840) p. 397; *Die Hirtenbriefe Ælfrics,* ed B. Fehr (Hamburg 1914) pp. 24–5.

[59] M. Deanesly, *The Pre-Conquest Church in England* (London 1961) pp. 332–3; [F. Liebermann, *Die] Gesetze [der Angelsachsen],* 3 vols (Halle 1898–1916) I p. 417 (dated by him to 1066–c1150).

courts and meeting-places. There is abundant evidence for their being so used in the medieval period. Earlier it is harder to find. Eadmer says that the south porch of Canterbury cathedral was used as a court 'where pleas were settled which could get no solution in hundred or shire or the royal court'.[60] A reference in the *Leges Edwardi* to *proprinquiorem ecclesiam ubi iudicium regis erit* is suggestive of a connection between churches and justice.[61] Certainly in the early twelfth century the joint county court of Norfolk and Suffolk sometimes met in one of the churches of the French borough.[62]

Churches had a part to play at the point where commercial transactions met the law. Bishops were supposed to have a responsibility for weights and measures.[63] It is understandable that manumissions of the unfree should take place in church 'on the altar' but when slaves are sold 'at the church door' that is another matter and probably indicates a connection between the church and proper legal form.[64] A connection between priests, churches, trade and public order appears particularly clear in a passage in the *Leges Edwardi* relating what is to happen when anyone claims to have found cattle or property. He is to bring it before the church and then to summon the priest and the reeve.[65] This was a society in which the priest is a natural link between authority and his flock. The priest who was summoned to come with the reeve and six men from each vill to give evidence in the Domesday inquiry was fulfilling one of his normal roles.[66] There may have been much work for him to do in towns.

But he had, of course, his living to make. Some urban priests received tithes and it was at least hoped that 'shipmen' would pay a tithe on their gains.[67] Others had livings which were virtually unendowed. One manuscript of the taxation of 1254 lists not only 29 churches in Norwich which were taxed but adds that there are other churches in Norwich not taxed *propter beneficiorum exilitatem* and goes on to list twenty-eight of them.[68] Many priests, if their church had burial rights, must have depended heavily on funeral dues. The image of ravens swooping on a

---

[60] R. W. Southern, *Saint Anselm and his Biographer* (Cambridge 1963) p. 242.
[61] *Gesetze* I p. 633 (earlier twelfth century but probably often reflecting pre-Conquest law).
[62] *Saint Benet of Holme*, ed J. R. West, Norfolk Record Society (Norwich 1932) nos 120, 178, 217.
[63] *Ancient Laws* pp 426–7.
[64] *Diplomatarium* pp. 642–9, 628.
[65] *Gesetze* I p. 649.
[66] W. Stubbs, *Select Charters* (9 ed Oxford 1951) p. 101.
[67] Brooke and Keir pp. 126–7; Rogers p. 50 n I; *Ancient Laws* p. 484 (an Old English version of the *Capitula* of Theodulf of Orleans).
[68] W. Hudson, 'The Norwich Taxation of 1254', *Norfolk Archaeology* 17 (Norwich 1910) p. 106.

corpse was one which twice occurred to Aelfric in this connection.[69] Wulfstan of Worcester's biography tells of those who would not christen a child without payment.[70] We do not know how far being a parish priest was normally a full-time job. They were forbidden to act as traders or reeves, which suggests that they did.[71] This was a society which would probably have seen nothing remarkable in a priest undertaking ordinary work; for the compatibility of orders and marriage may have ensured not only that most clergy were married but that some men were clergy who had no intention of being ministers. There almost certainly were far more clerics than there were benefices. In Bury St. Edmunds in 1086 thirty priests, deacons and clerks were among the inhabitants of the three hundred and forty-two new houses in the recently built extension to the town.[72]

Most town churches, like most other churches, were property which could be bought and sold.[73] Churches seemed quite often to have been owned by priests and they may often have been in the nature of family businesses. One extremely interesting passage in the Domesday account of Lincoln shows an intention, perhaps a system, for keeping ownership within the community. A Lincoln man had given the church of All Saints to the abbey of Peterborough on becoming a monk there. All the burgesses of Lincoln declared that such a grant could not be made outside the city or the family without royal consent.[74]

This concern to exclude outsiders contrasts with the appearance of a marked tendency in the latest Anglo-Saxon period towards the use of churches as sources of profit not simply by landowners but by distant pluralists. In a degree there was nothing new about this; great religious houses had long owned far-off churches and minsters. What may well be new is the appearance of such a figure as Regenbald, whom Round called 'the first great pluralist'. Regenbald is well enough known, not least because of the controversy as to whether he was the Confessor's chancellor. He was in any case a very important clerk in Edward's service, so important that he was granted some of the status of a bishop. He swiftly attached himself to the Conqueror, receiving writs in 1067 which secured his property and gained him more. We know the extent of what he was given before and after the Conquest chiefly because Henry I used his possessions to endow a house of Augustinian

[69] *Ancient Laws* p. 462; K. Jost, *Die 'Institutes of Polity Civil and Ecclesiastical'* (Berne 1959) pp. 97–9.
[70] *The Vita Wulfstani of William of Malmesbury*, ed R. R. Darlington, Camden Soc. 3 ser 40 (1928) pp. 12–3.
[71] *Ancient Laws* p. 462.
[72] Lobel p. 12.
[73] For example p. 150, n. 80 below.
[74] Barlow p. 193.

canons at Cirencester in 1133.[75] A high proportion consisted of churches. Regenbald held nineteen churches, all, like the rest of his property, in the south and west. Twelve of these were sufficiently important to have one or more subordinate chapels. Several were at places of note: Cirencester itself (where he was almost certainly head of the college of secular canons),[76] the market towns of Frome and Milborne Port in Somerset, both important demesne centres, and Cookham and Bray, similarly important centres. At two of the places where he held benefices, Cookham and Cirencester, Domesday says there was a new market.[77] At Cirencester there was a college of canons; Cookham and Cheltenham had at one time been the seat of monastic houses of some kind and so possibly had Frome.[78] In short, what the prospering Regenbald had been given was to a large extent churches associated with the royal demesne, often minsters, and naturally often at centres of local importance. Other royal clerks were similarly endowed, though none apparently on quite the scale of Regenbald.[79] Such clerks were prominent at court from the middle generations of the eleventh century as they never seem to have been before. Probably they were the men who ran Edward's administration, and their rewards were commensurate with its not inconsiderable virtues. The active nature of their interest in ecclesiastical property is brought home in the Domesday entry which shows a royal chamberlain buying the church at Huntingdon from two of the king's priests and then selling it again.[80] Thus in the Confessor's England among the currents in the distribution and creation of ecclesiastical property there were two which were in a degree opposite. While old churches at centres of royal authority (often places which, if they were not towns were not ordinary villages either) were passing into the hands of distant pluralists, the new churches which were being created in major towns, especially in the east, seem chiefly to have been held by local men.

Such currents could frequently change their directions. Minster

---

[75] [C.] Ross, [The] *Cartulary [of Cirencester Abbey]*, (Oxford 1964) prints (no 28/1) the foundation charter and refers (pp. xix, xxi-xxii, xxv-xxv-xxviii) to the literature on Regenbald. J. H. Round, 'Regenbald the Chancellor', *Feudal England* (London 1909) pp. 421-30 is fundamental.

[76] Ross, *Cartulary* no 575 and Round's article on him in *DNB*.

[77] *The Domesday Geography of South West England*, ed. H. C. Darby and R. Welldon Finn (Cambridge 1967) pp. 200-1, 204, 209; *The Domesday Geography of South East England*, ed H. C. Darby and E. M. J. Campbell (Cambridge 1962) p. 281; *The Domesday Geography of Midland England*, ed H. C. Darby and I. B. Terrett (Cambridge 1954) pp. 20, 49.

[78] D. Knowles and R. N. Hadcock, Medieval Religious Houses in England and Wales, (2nd edn., Cambridge 1971) pp. 470, 471, 473.

[79] Barlow pp. 129-37; J. H. Round, 'Ingelric the Priest and Albert of Lotharingia', *The Commune of London and other Studies* (London 1889) pp. 28-38.

[80] Barlow pp. 192-3.

communities probably found Edward the Confessor's and William I's new clerks as much of a threat as Edgar's new abbots had been. One might have supposed that such institutions as Cirencester (in which Roger of Salisbury had an interest after Regenbald), Christchurch (Twyneham) and Saint Martin's, Dover (in both of which Flambard had his claws) would have faded away. In fact all three were transformed into Augustinian houses.[81] So too were a number of other secular communities, not least in towns. The urban parishes, whose extensive creation had been an indication of burgess independence, also went in a new direction from the early twelfth century. To a large extent they passed into ecclesiastical ownership: for example, by 1200, the bishops of Lincoln and of Norwich held a high proportion of the churches which once had belonged to the priests and burgesses of those cities.[82]

In the Confessor's time there had been no bishop in either Norwich or Lincoln. It is an important question why so many of the Anglo-Saxon *sedes* remained in minor places. Only one of their pre-Conquest moves was to an important town: that from Crediton to Exeter.[83] A partial explanation for so many sees remaining in places which by 1066 were relatively unimportant was that the urban growth which made major towns very different from lesser had often been fairly recent. Norwich may well have been much more like North Elmham in 950 than it had become by 1050. Another is that it was not necessarily inconvenient for a bishop to live in the country: at their country manors was precisely where many medieval bishops spent most of their time. Perhaps above all, a move of the kind which was made to Norwich or Lincoln could not have been accomplished without powerful royal support expressed in ways which might have seemed difficult or inconceivable to an Anglo-Saxon king. To construct the equivalent of a continental *cité episcopale* at Norwich Herbert Losinga had to clear a substantial part of the town. To support a cathedral monastery on the scale he envisaged endowments exceeding those of the see of Elmham were essential.[84] Similarly the new see and cathedral of Lincoln were extensively endowed by means which involved the gift of a good deal

---

[81] *DB* I fols 1–2, H. H. E. Craster, 'A Contemporary Record of the Pontificate of Ranulf Flambard', *Archaeologia Aeliana*, 4 ser 7 (Newcastle-upon-Tyne 1930) p. 47, *MRHEW* pp. 154, 470, *VCH Hampshire* I, p. 152. For valuable remarks on the conversion of minster communities to Augustinian, [M.] Brett, [*The English Church under Henry I*] (Oxford 1975) pp. 138–40.

[82] Hill, *Medieval Lincoln* pp. 141–5; F. Blomefield and C. Parkin, *An Essay towards Topographical History of the County of Norfolk*, II vols (London 1805–11) 2 pp. 75, 91, 105, 116, 118, 126, 137, 145, 238, 255, 272, 299, 353, 367, 423, 429, 438, 439, 443, 466, 475 (2), 484.

[83] Barlow pp. 208–31 gives a most thorough acount of the sees and their moves.

[84] Campbell, 'Norwich' pp. 8–9 and the works there cited.

of ecclesiastical property and a willingness to treat burgesses high-handedly.[85] Particularly interesting is Henry I's gift to bishop Robert of all the, apparently numerous, churches which the burgesses held of the king.[86] Such moves of *sedes* as these were not just a matter of deciding to take a sensible practical step. They involved heavy expenditure, royal support, and the transformation of the cathedral establishment.

They also involved the building of enormous new churches. The problem of how far these were needed, apart from being thought appropriate, raises other questions about the relationship in Anglo-Saxon times between bishops and towns, and between mother churches and their dioceses. The first lively glimpse we get of life in Norwich comes from the life of Saint William of Norwich and relates to Stephen's reign. It mentions two events in 1144 relating to the connection between the cathedral and the diocese. One is a diocesan synod, treated as if it were a matter of course.[87] The medieval diocese of Norwich contained more than one thousand three hundred parishes. It is a fair guess that a very high proportion of them were there by 1100. If Æthelmer, the last Saxon bishop of Elmham, had thought fit to hold a diocesan synod (as some of his contemporaries did), and all his clergy had come, where could he have put them? The other regular diocesan event mentioned in 1144 is Absolution Sunday when 'the penitents of the whole diocese were accustomed to assemble in crowds in the mother church'. The streets were said to have been packed with them.[88] This event may well have been a Norman innovation.[89] It is a question how far the religious life of men living at some distance was involved with their cathedral church in the Anglo-Saxon period. There are indications at Exeter that it could be. The records of the Devonshire village gilds associated with the cathedral are of 1072–1103, but they may very well describe pre-Conquest institutions. As far away as Bideford men had been adopted into association by the bishop and canons, were making small annual payments to them and were rewarded by the canons 'performing such service as they ought to perform'.[90] (It may be significant that this was a cathedral which had been moved to a major town and whose chapter had been reformed before the Conquest.) Those looking to a cathedral in such a way are

[85] For example, *VCH Bedfordshire* I pp. 196–7; *VCH Buckinghamshire* I pp. 223–4, 281; *VCH Derbyshire* 2 pp. 87–8; Hamilton Thompson, op. cit., pp. 155–6; C. W. Foster and K. Major, *The Registrum Antiquissimum of the Cathedral Church of Lincoln*, i (Horncastle, 1931) nos. 10, 19, 33–36.

[86] Hill, *Medieval Lincoln* pp. 144–5.

[87] *The Life and Miracles of Saint William of Norwich*, ed. A. Jessopp and M. R. James (Cambridge 1896) p. 43.

[88] *Ibid* p. 26.

[89] Brett pp. 162–4.

[90] *Diplomatarium* pp. 608–10; Barlow pp. 196–8.

likely to have wanted to come to it. The piety of the day may have expressed itself in devotion to, and in, great churches as well as small. Indeed, the more home churches became very local and so very small, the more people may have felt the need at least occasionally to attend grander establishments. Small churches may well, as Brooke suggests, have led to an intimate relationship between priest and people, but one defect of a church sixteen feet by thirteen is that you cannot put on much of an ecclesiastical show in it.[91] So, perhaps the gigantic nave of Norwich cathedral and the swarms of new small parish churches in East Anglia were complementary.

The relationship between the English church and English towns was affected for many centuries afterwards by what had happened in the Anglo-Saxon period. Many early arrangements and rights were long perpetuated, largely thanks to twelfth-century developments in canon law and to the Reformation, which long preserved the *ecclesia anglicana* from Roman rationalisers. The effects of the distant past are to be seen in large towns and in small. For example the famous ministry of W. F. Hook in Leeds was possible because when he was presented in 1837 almost the whole of the city comprised one vast parish. The great size of the parish was probably due to Leeds having been a major ecclesiastical centre at a very early date; it has recently been convincingly argued that it was the *Campodunum* where Edwin built the *basilica*.[92] That it was not divided reflects the great difficulty found in creating new parishes in England between the twelfth century and the nineteenth. A curious instance of the effect of the Anglo-Saxon past on the history of a small town is that of Hadleigh in Suffolk. Hadleigh has a moderaely conspicuous role in Anglican history: Rowland Taylor, the martyr was its rector (1544–55); so too was David Wilkins of the *Concilia* (1719–45); and so too was Hugh Rose who in July 1833 held there the 'conference' which had some significance in the rise of the Oxford movement.[93] That there was something very remarkable about Hadleigh can be seen from its revenues. In the early nineteenth century its tithes were commuted for an annual charge of £1,325.[94] It was not only a very rich living, but a Canterbury peculiar which formed part of the exempt jurisdiction of the deanery of Bocking. The association with Canterbury antedates the Conquest and may go back to a grant from Byrhtnoth the hero of the battle of Maldon.[95] Its ecclesiastical history may be taken back further yet. One of the few valuable fragments in the

[91] Brooke (1970) pp. 80–1.
[92] See note 15 above. I owe this identification with *Campodunum* to a so far unpublished paper by Miss Margaret Faull.
[93] H. Pigot, 'Hadleigh', *Proceedings of the Suffolk Institute of Archaeology* (Ipswich 1863) pp. 30–81.
[94] *Ibid* p. 79.
[95] Hist. Mss. Commission *Eighth Report* p. 322.

twelfth-century *Annals of Saint Neot's* records that Guthrum, the Danish king of East Anglia, was buried in 890 at the *villa regia* of Hadleigh.[96] The importance of Hadleigh in the history of the church derives in the end almost certainly from its having been an important royal church under the East Anglian kings; with its revenues being preserved and coming into the gift of the archbishops of Canterbury. When one considers the threads which link the Saxon church with later centuries there is a certain symbolic weight in the fact that among the churches held by Regenbald, who served the Confessor so profitably and came so quickly and effectively to terms with the Conqueror, was Bray.

[96] *Asser's Life of King Alfred together with the Annals of Saint Neots*, ed W. H. Stevenson (new impr Oxford 1959) p. 140.

Additional Bibliographical Note

For the church of St Paul-in-the-Bail, Lincoln (p. 139 above) now see B. Silmour, 'The Church of St Paul-in-the-Bail, Lincoln'. *Medieval Archaeology*, xxiii (1979), pp. 214–8. In regard to Hadleigh (p.153 above) reference should have been made to A. Hoffman, *Bocking Deanery* (Chichester, 1976). C. N. L. Brooke, 'The Medieval Town as an Ecclesiastical Centre. General Survey', in *European Towns. Their Archaeology and Early History*, ed. M. W. Barley (1977), pp. 459–74 is an important survey.

10

Observations on English Government from the Tenth to the Twelfth Century

Prudent historians, when they consider the ordered power of the late Anglo-Saxon state, are apt to indulge a professional instinct, to hedge their bets. Such phrases as 'specious uniformity' and 'rudimentary precocity' have found favour.[1] It has long seemed likely, and it has by now become certain, that such caution is superfluous.

Some of the most solid, and the earliest, evidence for a powerful and elaborate system of government in England has been provided by recent investigation of the forts of the 'Burghal Hidage'.[2] Nearly all thirty-three have been identified. It has been shown that some are very big, enclosing over eighty acres. Their earthworks were massive and sometimes revetted with timber. The lengths of the fortifications often correspond, sometimes closely, to those which may be deduced from the 'Burghal Hidage' by using its formula of a hundred and sixty hides to the furlong. So Alfred, or he and his son, not only built a vast system of fortifications, but also devised elaborate means of serving them, of which the 'Hidage' is the record. By the beginning of the tenth century West Saxon kings were capable of a feat of government on the largest scale.

The coinage from the end of Edgar's reign demonstrates how successfully the English could manage a system of great sophistication. Its main characteristics have been generally known since 1961.[3] An abundant silver coinage was kept under complete royal control. Every six or seven years (later every two or three) a new type was issued and previous types were then normally demonetized. The evidence of hoards is that such demonetizations, involving the frequent replacement of a coinage of millions of silver pennies, were very thorough, though less so in the Confessor's reign. Not the least remarkable feature of the system was that a new type might be lighter, or heavier, than its predecessor, sometimes markedly so. Historians have been inclined to boggle at what numismatists show them to have existed here. Their difficulty is that of making sense of the evidence without attributing more sophistication

---

[1] F. Barlow, *The Feudal Kingdom of England* (London, 1955), pp. 42, 46; V. H. Galbraith, *The Making of Domesday Book* (Oxford, 1961),pp. 46, 47.

[2] C. A. Ralegh Radford, 'The Later Pre-Conquest Boroughs and their Defences', *Medieval Archaeology*, xiv (1970), pp. 83–103, and the articles cited there.

[3] R. H. M. Dolley and D. M. Metcalf, 'The Reform of the English Coinage under Eadgar', *Anglo-Saxon Coins*, ed. R. H. M. Dolley (London, 1961), pp. 136–68.

than seems plausible. The evidence is nevertheless such as to render the implausible irresistible. The English kings were running the earliest known, and the best, example of the system of *renovatio monetae* which by 1200 had come into use in many states from Poland to Portugal.[4] A ruler could use a currency controlled in this way to bring in profits exceeding those of simpler systems. The currency became a means of taxation and subjects would sometimes, as in Aragon in 1236, grant heavy property taxes to be rid of *renovatio monetae*.[5]

For the best results it was desirable that there should be a close connection between the monetary and fiscal systems. A passage (possibly interpolated) in *Dialogus de Scaccario* supports the supposition that in England the Crown insisted that all payments to itself should be in coin of the current issue.[6] Such a requirement would not only help to enforce the demonetization of old types; it could also provide the Crown with the means to play 'heads I win, tails you lose' by, for example, at some times requiring payment by weight and at others by tale. The variety of methods of payment, by tale, by weight and blanch, recorded in Domesday suggests the possibility of such a system. Its presence would accord with Miss Sally Harvey's suggestion that the payments in an *ora* of 20d., rather than of 16d., recorded from royal demesne in Domesday represented the means whereby the king averted loss when the weight of the penny was reduced from about 21.5 gr. to 17 gr. in *c.* 1062.[7] A converse explanation may account for the great increase in the weight of the penny, from 18 gr. to about 26 gr., in *c.* 1051. Various explanations have been offered for such increases. For example, the wish to 'avoid the creation of a bullion reserve of embarrassing magnitude'.[8] Or, in the case of the increase under discussion (granted a likely connection with the suspension of the geld and the standing down of the fleet) that Edward 'calculated that fewer coins would be needed and decided that the opportunity should be taken to produce a heavier coin which would give enhanced prestige'.[9] It seems more likely that the heavier coin was a substitute for the tax,

---

[4] H. Bertil A. Peterson, *Anglo-Saxon Currency. King Edgar's Reform to the Norman Conquest* (Lund, 1969). *Cf.* A. Suchódolski, '*Renovatio Monetae* in Poland in the Twelfth Century', *Wiadomści Numizmatyczne*, v (1961), pp. 57–75 of the supplement and C. S. S. Lyon, 'Variations in Currency in Late Anglo-Saxon England', *Mints, Dies and Currency*, ed. R. A. G. Carson (London, 1971), pp. 101–20.

[5] S. Bolin, 'Tax Money and Plough Money', *Scandinavian Economic History Review*, ii (1954), pp. 5–21, esp. p. 17.

[6] Ed. C. Johnson (London, 1950), p. 9; on the assumptions that *instantis monete* (last line) means 'of the current issue' and that the chronology is, as elsewhere in the *Dialogus* (*cf.* p. xx), unreliable.

[7] S. Harvey, 'Royal Revenue and Domesday Terminology', *Economic History Review*, 2nd ser., xx (1967), pp. 221–28.

[8] M. Dolley, *The Norman Conquest and the English Coinage* (London, 1966), p. 10.

[9] F. Barlow, *Edward the Confessor* (London, 1970), pp. 183–84.

and intended to increase the value to the Crown of payments by tale. The late Old English coinage system was probably highly remunerative. If it is true that Ethelred II did not introduce a hidage tax until *c.* 1012, it may have been his new system of exploiting the currency which did most to enable him to buy off the Danes.[10]

'The Anglo-Saxon financial system, which collected the Dane-geld, was not run from a box under the bed.'[11] Indeed, it demonstrates the power of the state. A powerful instance of the fiscal system at work has been provided by Dr Hart in an analysis of a reassessment of Northamptonshire carried out between a date probably not long after the Conquest and 1086.[12] The assessment was not only reduced, but also reallocated between hundreds. This reallocation was such as to restore a balance among the hundreds which had existed at the time of the 'County Hidage', but had since been upset by a reduction of the burden on some hundreds, but not on others. The restoration of the earlier balance required the reduction of the hidages of different hundreds in different proportions: in some in the ratio 2 : 1; in others 5 : 2; in others 9 : 3½; otherwise in yet others. What must have been a central decision and plan was executed in an elaborate and orderly way at the local level.

Few financial documents survive which are older than Domesday Book. Of these the Northamptonshire Geld Roll is the most important. In addition Miss Harvey has shown that Domesday was preceded by, and partly dependent on, hidage lists, some of them arranged as it is, and some older than the Conquest. Such records are known to have been kept in the Treasury with Domesday.[13] Otherwise there is very little.[14] But it is likely, as Galbraith suggests, that late Old English administrative documents were numerous, and that nearly all have been lost, partly because they were commonly in English, as the Northamptonshire Geld Roll is.[15] Miss Robertson's collection of charters in Anglo-Saxon contains some twenty documents which are not charters, agreements, or records of law-suits, but public and private administrative records of other kinds. Though few, they are very varied: a list of services for the repair of a bridge;[16] a memorandum on

[10] *Two of the Anglo-Saxon Chronicles Parallel*, ed. C. Plummer and J. Earle, (Oxford, 1892), p. 173.

[11] V. H. Galbraith, *Studies in the Public Records* (London, 1948), p. 45.

[12] C. Hart, *The Hidation of Northamptonshire* (Leicester, 1970), esp. pp. 39–43. It seems reasonable to take such a post-Conquest instance as indicative of English practice, especially as the key document, the Northants Geld Roll, is in English.

[13] S. Harvey, 'Domesday Book and its Predecessors', *English Historical Review*, lxxxvi (1971), pp. 753–73.

[14] But *cf.* pp. 177–8 below.

[15] *Studies in the Public Records*, pp. 37–40.

[16] *Anglo-Saxon Charters*, ed. A. J. Robertson (Cambridge, 1956), no. LII (possibly post-Conquest).

the recruitment of a ship's crew in Ethelred II's time;[17] estate lists and surveys;[18] lists of treasures;[19] stock inventories;[20] the Northamptonshire Geld Roll; the 'Burghal' and 'County' hidages. The chances for the preservation of such documents were poor. The best lay in their being copied into a cartulary, as the Northamptonshire Geld Roll was. But cartulary-making became widespread only in the twelfth century. Only one pre-Conquest cartulary survives and only two others of before 1100.[21] Many of the documents are of types which are not found in Latin in the Old English period. It is reasonable to deduce that those collected by Miss Robertson are indeed the survivors from a much larger number and that English was the ordinary language for much written business.[22]

The use of written English went with a considerable degree of lay literacy; no doubt as both cause and effect. Æthelweard's translation of the Chronicle was the first book written by an English nobleman and, for nearly four centuries, the last.[23] Two of Ælfric's theological treatises were written for thegns.[24] The relative abundance of inscriptions, not only on churches but also on, for example, brooches and rings, is suggestive.[25] A layman who learned to read in the Confessor's reign would be able to make out his father's will, the king's writs, the boundary clause of a charter, or a monastery's inventories. In Henry II's day mere literacy would have won him none of these advantages. If he wanted them he had to learn Latin. There is no doubt that some did so;[26] but it would be unwise to be confident that they were more numerous than those who were literate in English a century or more earlier. If the late Anglo-Saxon state was run with sophistication and thoughtfulness this may very well be connected with the ability of many laymen to read.[27]

It would be tediously easy to multiply instances of the power of the late Old English kings. Nothing is more remarkable about them than the long series of innovations which they introduced and the power of

[17] *Ibid.*, no. LXXII.

[18] *Ibid.*, nos. LIV, LXXXIV, CIX, CX and App. I and IV and V, for which see pp. 50–51 below.

[19] *Ibid.*, nos. XXXIX, CIV and App. II nos. II–IX. *Cf.* p. 49 below.

[20] *Ibid.*, nos. XXXIX, CIV, App. II nos. III, IX and *cf.* J. Earle, *Hand-Book of Land Charters and other Saxonic Documents* (Oxford, 1888), pp. 275–77.

[21] G. R. C. Davis, *Medieval Cartularies of Great Britain* (London, 1958), pp. xi–xii.

[22] *Cf.* Professor Dorothy Whitelock's suggestion on the survival of letters in English, *English Historical Documents c. 500–1042* (London, 1955), p. 577.

[23] But see H. G. Richardson and G. O. Sayles, *The Governance of Mediaeval England* (Edinburgh, 1963), p. 273.

[24] Whitelock, *English Historical Documents*, p. 849.

[25] E. Okasha, *Hand-list of Anglo-Saxon Non-Runic Inscriptions* (Cambridge, 1971).

[26] Richardson and Sayles, *op. cit.*, pp. 265–84.

[27] *Cf.* Galbraith, *Studies in the Public Records*, p. 57.

experiment and of creation so displayed. The shires of the Midlands, the hundredal system, the burghal system, planned towns, Danegeld and the currency reveal a capacity for change and for order hardly matched until the nineteenth century. Those who find themselves unable to believe that this was so draw attention to, for example, inequalities in the taxation system and provincial differences in law and administration. But such inefficiencies and variations appear in fact to have been less marked than they were in most of the states of Europe in the eighteenth century.

Prima facie the Dark Age state most readily comparable with the English is that of the Carolingians. The best account of the relations between them remains that of Stubbs.[28] He pointed out the numerous and obvious similarities which suggest direct connection. Carolingian counties and *centenae* with their courts bear a resemblance to those of England which extends to matters of detail. The earl like the count took a third of the profits of justice. Danegeld in England is preceded by similar taxes in Francia. Prescriptions which appear in ninth century Carolingian capitularies reappear in tenth century English laws.[29] He also drew attention to the dynastic and other relationships which would have enabled one area to influence the other. Nevertheless he warned that 'the parallels between Frank and English law must not be pressed without allowing for the similarity of circumstances which prompted them and the fundamental stock of common custom and principle which underlay them'. His conclusion was masterly: 'it is wiser and safer to allow the coincidences to speak for themselves, and to avoid a positive theory which the first independent investigator may find means of demolishing'.

For a generation after Stubbs the question was regarded as open. For example, Maitland took it for granted that Danegeld might have a Carolingian origin.[30] But in 1912 Helen Cam published her M.A. thesis, addressed to the question Stubbs had raised. She concluded that in reply to the question: ' "Did the West Saxon kings borrow from the Carolingian emperors?", we can only reply that it is possible, but hardly probable.'[31] Her evidence hardly justified her conclusion, not least because she gave virtually no consideration to Stubb's suggestions on, for example, Danegeld, general oaths and the relationship between English laws and Frankish capitularies. At the same time Liebermann's *Gesetze* were appearing and his inclination was to find early or common

[28] W. Stubbs, *The Constitutional History of England*, i (Oxford, 1891), pp. 223–27.
[29] To the instances cited *ibid.*, p. 226, add those mentioned on pp. 45–47 below and by J. Yver, 'Les premières institutions du duché de Normandie', *Settimane di studio del centro italiano sull'alto medioevo*, xvi (Spoleto, 1969), p. 319. Some capitularies and some Anglo-Saxon 'codes' resemble one another fairly closely in general form.
[30] F. W. Maitland, *Domesday Book and Beyond* (Cambridge, 1897), p. 518.
[31] H. M. Cam, *Local Government in Francia and England* (London, 1912), p. 156.

Germanic origins for institutions where he could, while he was only marginally concerned with some of the relevant evidence. The strange consequence has been that for sixty years the question of the relationship between English and Carolingian institutions has been only rarely and barely considered. In seeking the origins of English institutions scholars have preferred to look north and to later texts, rather than south and to earlier. For example, Dr Richardson and Professor Sayles suggest a Scandinavian origin for the earl's third penny, referring to the *Heimskringla*, even though the count's third share is a well-known Carolingian institution.[32]

Stenton wrote of the Danegeld that it was 'the first system of national taxation to appear in western Europe' and that 'as a piece of large scale financial organisation it has no parallel in the Dark Ages'.[33] In fact on several of the twelve or thirteen occasions when large payments were made to the Danes in Francia the money was raised by national taxation which, if it was more complex than Danegeld, nevertheless in some respects resembled it.[34] For example in 866 Charles the Bald levied 6d. on every *mansus ingenuilis*, 3d. on every *mansus servilis*, 1d. on every *accola* and on every two *hospitia*. He required all free Franks to pay the *heribannus* and merchants a tenth of their possessions.[35] (The levies on the *mansus* may have applied only to lands held as benefices or even only to monastic lands so held.[36]) It seems that the *mansus indomicatus* was generally exempt from such taxes, suggesting comparison with the exemption of manorial demesne in England.[37] The existence of such Carolingian taxation does not prove that English Danegeld has Frankish origins. But it is at the very least in sufficiently strong contrast to Stenton's statements to suggest that even one of the most eminent of English historians could lose sight of what happened beyond the Channel.

Undoubtedly evidence for direct connection is to be found in the coinage. It is generally agreed that the introduction of a penny coinage into England in the eighth century and the extension of royal authority over the coinage in the ninth and early tenth centuries reflect and partly depend on Carolingian policy.[38] For example when Athelstan introduced a penalty for false coining it was the unusual one of striking

---

[32] *The Governance of Mediaeval England*, p. 26, n. 1; F. L. Ganshof, *Frankish Institutions under Charlemagne* (Providence, R.I., 1968), p. 29.

[33] F. M. Stenton, *Anglo-Saxon England*, 3rd edn. (Oxford, 1971), pp.645, 648.

[34] E. Joranson, *The Danegeld in France* (Rock Island, 1923).

[35] *Ibid.*, pp. 72–73; *cf.* pp. 45–58, 62–92.

[36] F. Lot, 'Les tributs aux Normands et l'église de France au ixe siècle', *Bibliothèque de l'École des Chartes*, lxxxv (1924), pp. 58–78.

[37] Joranson, *op. cit.*, p. 191; R. Welldon Finn, *An Introduction to Domesday Book* (London, 1963), p. 254.

[38] M. Dolley, *Anglo-Saxon Pennies* (London, 1964), pp. 14–15.

off the hand, which is required for the same offence in the capitularies.[39] The most remarkable feature of the later development of the English coinage, the successive demonetizations, also had Carolingian precedent. On several occasions between the time of Charlemagne and that of Charles the Bald an emperor gave orders for the demonetization of previous types in favour of a new one.[40] The edict of Pîtres, 864, gives detailed instructions on how such a demonetization was to be accomplished.[41] There is evidence that it was attended with some measure of success.[42]

There are other points of resemblance between the English and Carolingian systems where the evidence suggests something more than common origins and common needs. The earliest is an instance of English inflence on the empire. When Charles the Bald introduced compulsory work on fortifications, which was well-known in England, but not in Gaul, he did so, he said, *iuxta antiquam et aliarum gentium consuetudinem.*[43] In the next century the case for English kings having Frankish precedent in mind when they established the hundredal system is strengthened by the word 'hundred' itself. Many of the features of the system appear new in England, but some of them had appeared earlier across the Channel.[44] No instance is known before the tenth century of the word 'hundred' (or of any word, in English or Latin, meaning a numerical hundred) being used in England to denote a unit of government or of jurisdiction.[45] The argument from silence carries weight here because we have so many early laws. It was on the Continent that such words were used to denote governmental divisions not dissimilar from later English hundreds.[46] Before the tenth century the English do not appear to have had either the institution or the name.

---

[39] Yver, 'Les premières institutions du duché de Normandie', *op. cit.*, p. 343, nn. 109, 110. Frankish moneyers were at work in the Danelaw in the late ninth and early tenth centuries, M. Dolley, *Viking Coins of the Danelaw and of Dublin* (London, 1965), pp. 17–20.

[40] K. Morrison and H. Grunthal, *Carolingian Coinage* (American Numismatic Society Notes and Monographs, no. 158, 1967), pp. 1–8.

[41] *Capitularia Regum Francorum*, ii, ed. A. Boretius and V. Krause (*Monumenta Germaniae Historica, Legum, Sectio II* (Hanover, 1890)), pp. 314–18.

[42] Morrison and Grunthal, *op. cit.*, p. 6.

[43] N. Brooks, 'The Development of Military Obligations in Ninth and Tenth Century England', *England before the Conquest*, ed. P. Clemoes and K. Hughes (Cambridge, 1971), p. 81.

[44] H. R. Loyn, 'The Hundred in the Tenth and Early Eleventh Centuries', *British Government and Administration*, ed. H. R. Loyn and H. Hearder (Cardiff, 1974), pp. 1–15, esp. 2–3; H. Dannebauer, 'Hundertschaft, Centena und Huntari', *Historisches Jahrbuch*, lxii–lxix (1942–49), pp. 155–219, esp. pp. 163–65.

[45] F. Liebermann, *Die Gesetze der Angelsachsen*, ii, pt. ii (Halle, 1912), p. 516.

[46] In important aspects and areas the *centena* may have been an innovation of Charlemagne's time: Loyn, *op. cit.*, pp. 2–3; Ganshof, *Frankish Institutions under Charlemagne* p. 32; B. Guérard *Le Polypytque de l'abbé Irminon* (Paris, 1844), i, pp. 43–44.

The case for the institution, when it appears in the tenth century, having been developed under Continental influence is supported by the adoption of a corresponding name.

There is similarly a good *prima facie* for direct connection in regard to general oaths. The first possible reference to such an oath in England appears in Edward the Elder's Exeter code which refers to 'the oath and pledge which the whole nation has given' in a context which has to do with the prevention of theft.[47] Athelstan's fourth and fifth codes refer to an oath or oaths in a similar context 'given to the king and his councillors' and 'given at Grateley'.[48] In *c.* 943 Edmund's Colyton code gives the text of an oath by which 'Omnes', were to swear fidelity to the king, 'sicut homo debet esse fidelis domino suo'.[49] From Cnut comes the famous requirement that every man above twelve years 'take an oath that he will not be a thief nor a thief's accomplice'.[50] It is not clear how these references to oaths should be related together. But it is clear that they can be so related by considering them in comparison to what is known of Carolingian oaths. Charlemagne introduced or reintroduced the general oath in 789, taking elaborate precautions in 792 or 793 to ensure that every adult male above the age of twelve took it. In 802 a new text for the oath was introduced. All were to swear '. . . fidelis sum, sicut homo per drictum debet esse domino suo'. There was another general oath taking and the instructions to the *missi* make it clear that the oath was regarded as one not to engage in any unlawful activity.[51] There is no certain reference to a general oath in England before Edmund, while it had a much older history in Gaul. There is an important textual resemblance between the core of Charlemagne's oath and the core of Edmund's. The age limit mentioned by Charlemagne and Cnut is the same. Granted then that all the English references make sense if taken as referring to an oath of the Carolingian type, it would seem that in the absence of definite proof the onus should lie on those who maintain that we do not see here a Carolingian institution imported into England.

Such an importation would not be surprising. The dynastic and cultural relationships between England and the Carolingian world were close from at the latest the later ninth century. In the age of Alfred and Charles the Bald, Asser, Grimbald and Hincmar the nexus of

---

[47] F. L. Attenborough, *The Laws of the Earliest English Kings* (reprint, New York, 1963), p. 121.

[48] *Ibid.*, pp. 149, 153.

[49] A. J. Robertson, *The Laws of the Kings of England from Edmund to Henry I* (Cambridge, 1925), p. 12. The text is preserved only in a later Latin version.

[50] *Ibid.*, p. 185.

[51] F. L. Ganshof, *The Carolingians and the Frankish Monarchy* (London, 1971), pp. 112–17.

relationships between the successful West Saxon and the struggling Carolingian realms was sufficient to ensure that many of the achievements of Alfred and his circle must be placed in a Carolingian context. Alfred's biography is exactly in the tradition of Carolingian royal biography.[52] The Chronicle recalls the Carolingian royal annals.[53] Professor Wallace-Hadrill has suggested that Alfred's producing a law code was a consequence of his resuming 'a practice that had been lost in England because he knew that, up to the time of Charles the Bald, the Carolingians had found a use for it'.[54] The suggestion is a very important one in the present context. At the time when the West Saxon dynasty was acquiring new scope for the exercise of power it came into a relationship with Frankish circles which were devoted to the memory and to the collection of the records of Carolingian glory.

In the tenth century dynastic relations with the sub-Carolingian world continued to be important; but Carolingian influence is most readily demonstrable in the thought and institutions of the English church, especially in the time of the monastic reformers and in the next generation. The writings of Wulfstan and Ælfric were deeply influenced by Carolingian thought.[55] A bishop writing a letter in the reign of Ethelred II could copy the larger part of it from one of Alcuin.[56] The monastic reformers looked to contemporary models of observance; but in establishing a series of monasteries which was integral to the state and in drawing up such a document as the *Regularis Concordia* they looked much further back, to Louis the Pious and Benedict of Aniane.[57] Stubbs fairly commented: 'It would be very rash to observe that while the bishops who composed so large a part of the Witanagemot sought foreign models for their canons they did not also seek foreign models for their secular laws.'[58]

The seriousness of the difficulties, but also the importance of the possibilities, which are intrinsic to the attempt to consider Old English government in a Carolingian and sub-Carolingian context are most apparent in the case of Domesday Book. The Carolingians had written surveys made for a wide variety of purposes, often using the sworn

---

[52] D. A. Bullough, The Educational Tradition in England from Alfred to Ælfric', *Settimane . . .*, xix (Spoleto, 1971), p. 455, n. 2.

[53] J. M. Wallace Hadrill, 'The Franks and the English in the Ninth Century', *History*, new ser., xxxv (1950), pp. 212–14.

[54] *Idem, Early Germanic Kingship in England and on the Continent* (Oxford, 1971), p. 148.

[55] *E.g.* D. Bethurum, *The Homilies of Wulfstan* (Oxford, 1957), esp. p. 61; P. Clemoes, 'Ælfric', *Continuations and Beginnings*, ed. E. G. Stanley (London, 1966), pp. 182–83.

[56] F. E. Harmer, *Anglo-Saxon Writs* (Manchester, 1952), p. 22.

[57] D. Knowles, *The Monastic Order in England* (2nd edn, Cambridge, 1966), p. 42.

[58] *Constitutional History*, i, p. 224.

inquest.[59] They had *mansus* lists. In 843 the empire was divided *per descriptas mansas*. A hundred and twenty commissioners toured to make the necessary *descriptio*, part of which probably survives.[60] The emperors had surveys made, in great detail, of particular estates. They pursued careful inquiries of other kinds. For example, in 864 Charles the Bald ordered a detailed inquiry into markets, past and present, the results of which were to be returned in writing, on *breves*, a term not unfamiliar to students of Domesday.[61] Carolingian taxation involved the listing and valuation of property.[62] There is very little about Domesday, considered as a piece of administration, which would have seemed unfamiliar to a Carolingian official of the period between Charlemagne and Charles the Bald. When the wide variety, the sometimes wide extent, and the techniques of Carolingian surveys are considered it is very difficult to avoid the conclusion that theirs is the tradition in which Domesday, somehow or other, must lie. The possibilities of connection are numerous; the gap in the evidence is wide. No one knows when (no one indeed really knows if) surveys ceased to be used by the Continental rulers; no one knows when English rulers began to use them.

If such techniques fell into desuetude in sub-Carolingian states some of them were preserved in the church. The tradition of the estate survey, the polyptych (or *descriptio*, another term familiar to students of Domesday Book) was continuous there from the ninth century to the twelfth.[63] Guérard, the founder of the study of such surveys, saw Domesday Book as one of them: 'De tous les documents qui peuvent être rangés dans la classe des polyptyques, le plus étendu et le plus remarquable'.[64] Something of what he meant can be seen in considering, for example, the compilation of the polyptych of the

---

[59] W. Metz, *Das Karolingische Reichsgut* (Berlin, 1960), pp. 11–90; Ganshof, *The Carolingians and the Frankish Monarchy*, pp. 130–32.

[60] Ganshof, *op. cit.*, pp. 292–95.

[61] *Capitularia*, ii, *op. cit.*, pp. 317–18. For *breve* in its common Domesday meaning of schedule or return see Ganshof, *The Carolingians and the Frankish Monarchy*, p. 293 and E. Lesne, *Histoire de la propriété écclésiasique en France*, iii (Lille, 1936), pp. 1–30, esp. 1–6. It was the term almost invariably used by Carolingian government in such contexts as: 'per omne regnum suum litteras misit, ut episcopi, abbates et abbatissae breves de honoribus suis quanta mansa quisque haberet . . . deferre curarent' ('Annals of St. Bertin', *s.a.* 869, ed. F. Grat, J. Vielliard and S. Clémencet (Paris, 1964), pp. 152–53.

[62] Joranson, *The Danegeld in France*, p. 49.

[63] Lesne, iii, *op. cit.*, pp. 1–30. The early meanings of *descriptio* commonly have to do with a record or survey made for purposes of taxation (Ducange, *Glossarium, s.v.*). In the Carolingian period it denotes a survey, e.g. of the kind which was made for the division of the empire in 843 (p. 48 above) or inventory *e.g.* such that 'by consulting it the king could discover not only what he possessed, but also what his possessions were worth' (Ganshof, *The Carolingians and the Frankish Monarchy*, pp. 293–94). For its use to denote an estate survey, see Lesne, *op. cit.*, iii, 11–20.

[64] *Polyptyque de l'abbé Irminon, op. cit.*, i, p. 25.

abbey of Prüm, in Lorraine, in 893, or somewhat before. Commissioners were sent to all the abbey's demesnes (which were scattered over some hundreds of square miles) to inquire into the number of manses of every description, into mills, and into other sources of income.[65] Perrin has shown, from variations in the text as it applies to different areas, that a number of different sets of commissioners were despatched and he discusses the way in which their original returns were put together and edited.[66] He goes on to emphasise the almost universal practice of writing out a polyptych in a book, rather than on the rolls normal for other kinds of record, and the status of such a survey as public record.[67] There is an echo of Domesday here, not too faint, and not inconceivably answering.

It may be then that the Carolingian techiques which are seen at their apogee in Domesday Book were tansmitted to England by the church. True, there is no sign of a complete *descriptio* having been made for the lands of any pre-Conquest monastery. Such surveys were far from universal on the Continent. But Continental houses which did not have complete surveys could still make use of the techniques of written record which came from the world of the *Capitulare de Villis* and the *Brevium Exempla*. They could make inventories of stock and lists of treasure and survey their estates piecemeal, as occasion arose.[68] The handful of administrative documents from English monasteries, which have been argued to be the survivors from many more, are of just such kinds. Doubtless it is unremarkable that one list of men, oxen and flitches of bacon resembles another, even if one comes from Æthelwold's Ely and the other from the *Brevium Exempla*.[69] But there are somewhat more specific resemblances between English and Continental documents. In particular there are Continental precedents for two English documents in which a list of treasures is followed by a list of sources of income.[70] In general the English documents do look as if they came from milieux whose techniques in the use of writing in estate management were in a Carolingian tradition.

Most of the documents in question come from monasteries, especially from Ely; and none is earlier than the end of the tenth century. English monastic reform is well-known to have owed much to Continental houses, especially Fleury, St Peter's, Ghent, and the reformed houses of Lorraine, notably Gorze and Verdun. From such houses could be learned, not only how monks should rightly live, but

[65] C.-E. Perrin, *Recherches sur la seigneurie rurale en Lorraine* (n.p., 1935), pp. 3–93.
[66] *Ibid.*, pp. 47–64; *cf.* pp. 600–3.
[67] *Ibid.*, pp. 614, 607.
[68] Lesne, *op. cit.*, iii, pp. 19–20, 76–77.
[69] Robertson, *Anglo-Saxon Charters*, no. XXXIX; *Capitularia*, i, pp. 250–52.
[70] Robertson, *op. cit.*, nos. XXXIX and CIV (pp. 19497); *Capitularia*, i, *loc. cit.*; Lesne, *op. cit.*, iii, p. 156.

also, and no less important, how the property whereby monks lived should be looked after. Abbo of Fleury had much to do with the English reform. He well knew the value of a polyptych. In a letter to a fellow abbot he described the good use to which he had put *libri politici a temporibus Magni Caroli*, even though, *pene vetustate consumpti*.[71] The surviving documents from the Lorraine houses, especially Gorze and Verdun, show the careful use of writing in estate management. Better record keeping could indeed be directly associated with reform.[72] It is reasonable to suppose that English reformed houses were influenced by their foreign exemplars in this respect as in others. What such a potentate as Æthelwold learned in the church he could have applied in the state.

The use of the inquest is almost intrinsic to the Carolingian tradition of inquiry and survey. The possibility of the inquest's use in late Anglo-Saxon England is widely admitted, though there are differences of opinion on how formal it was and on whether it was used by the Crown.[73] There is a little evidence which has not been used by the main authorities. It has been acutely observed that the early part of what is called Ethelred's fourth code looks like a reply to an inquest on the customs of London.[74] In addition there are two surveys, one dating from between the Conquest and Domesday, the other of about the time of Domesday, recording dues owed to, respectively, the bishop of Winchester at Taunton and the church at Lambourne.[75] Both are in English, and witnessed. A witnessed survey of dues comes close to a record of a sworn inquest, especially when, as in the Taunton document, they are dues owed in the past. It relates to the state of affairs on the day of the Confessor's death, so recalling Domesday. The other claims royal participation in some way. These documents strengthen, though they do not clinch, the case for the pre-Conquest inquest and for its use by the Crown. It is curious, but characteristic, that while it has long been admitted that the English inquest may have had a Carolingian ancestor, it has nearly always been assumed that the descent could only be via the Normans.

It is sobering to consider what account historians would have given of the history of English administration had Domesday and the early records of the Exchequer been lost. Left to squeeze what they could from charters and annals they would gravely have underrated the English state. One may wonder how far other European states have been

---

[71] *Patrologia Latina*, ed. Migne, cxxxix, col. 442.

[72] Perrin, *Recherches sur la seigneurie rurale en Lorraine*, pp. 101–239, 599.

[73] R. V. Turner, 'The origin of the medieval English jury', *Journal of British Studies*, vii (1967–68), no. 2, pp. 1–10.

[74] H. G. Richardson and G. O. Sayles, *Law and Legislation from Æthelberht to Magna Carta* (Edinburgh, 1966), p. 28.

[75] Robertson, *Anglo-Saxon Charters*, App. I, nos. IV, V.

underrated by their historians, lacking financial records older than the thirteenth century. That administration on the Continent in the tenth and eleventh centuries may have been more sophisticated than is commonly assumed multiplies possible explanations for the resemblances between Carolingian and English government. While it is very likely that some important developments in England reflect the influence of the ninth-century empire, its memory, or its records, others may derive from France, Germany or Normandy. Nevertheless, if it is granted that when the Domesday survey was made and the *breves* incorporated in the great *descriptio*, this was much more likely to have been the fruit of a strong administrative tradition which had been continuously maintained from Carolingian times than of the adoption of *ad hoc* procedures, and if it is asked where that tradition had found a home in the century preceding 1086, the answer must be: just possibly Normandy,[76] but much more probably England.

The framework of the Old English state lasted long. Some of it still endures. Nevertheless it came under heavy strain in the twelfth century, which was not a period of universal progress in English administration. It is possible that the Anglo-Saxon fiscal system was never afterwards so efficient, or oppressive, as it had been under Ethelred and Cnut;[77] it is likely that Stephen's reign did much to ruin it; but it was Henry II who actually dismantled it. Henry I had continued the Danegeld. It is not known whether Stephen levied it. Henry II did so for the last time in 1162. Although the old assessment continued to be used occasionally for shire *dona* and hidage or carucage taxes were revived between 1194 and 1220, the balance of the fiscal system shifted towards scutage, the exploitation of feudal incidents and the sale of royal rights.[78] Regular changes of coin type continued until 1158, '1158 and not 1066 is the year for the numismatist to have always in mind'.[79] In that year Henry completely abandoned the system of *renovatio monetae*. The coinage of ugly and ill-struck pennies of the 'Tealby' type which was then introduced was maintained until 1180. By the end of the century the English coinage had gone over to the sub-Carolingian simplicity of the *type immobilisé*.

It is possible to regard both these changes as reforms. Yet though Danegeld was, as we are often assured, riddled with anomalies (which Henry increased), it was the largest item in the king's not very large revenue; and the Angevin fiscal system, as we follow it along the road to

[76] Yver, 'Les premières institutions du duché normand', p. 339 for recent work on the early Norman fiscal system.
[77] Maitland, *Domesday Book and Beyond* (1960 reprint), pp. 25–26, 514; Dolley and Metcalf, 'The Reform of the English Coinage under Eadgar', p. 157.
[78] Painter, *Studies in the History of the Medieval English Feudal Barony* (Baltimore, 1943), pp. 74–79; J. C. Holt, *Magna Carta* (Cambridge, 1965), pp. 19–42.
[79] Dolley, *The Norman Conquest and the English Coinage*, pp. 35–36.

Runnymede, is not without anomalies of its own. It is highly probable that Henry lost money by the currency revolution of 1158.[80] It may be that both abandonments were concessions. Certainly, in both instances, something which was, or once had been, very elaborate and orderly was replaced by something simpler to administer.

A marked change, certainly in the frame of mind in which England was governed, arguably in the power and coherence with which it was governed, may be seen in the treatment of administrative areas and boundaries. Tenth-century government created new units and suppressed old. The shires it made lay orderly on the map until 1 April 1974. On that map were elements of disorder: the foolish little shire of Rutland and the oddly disposed counties of the north west. These were not Saxon, but Angevin muddles. Although Rutland had a distinct status in the Anglo-Saxon period, its rise to the status of shire and the dignity of a sheriff was the product of a confused process in the twelfth century.[81] Similarly in the north west. Until John's reign Westmorland was treated in an anomalous way, having a sheriff only when one of the two lordships which made it up was in the king's hand.[82] The odd northern boundary of Lancashire is that between the fiefs of Roger of Poitou and Ivo Taillebois in 1094; among other eccentricities it bisects a parish. The early history of Lancashire is anomalous in other ways. For a time it was a kind of private shire, Roger of Poitou having his own sheriff. The Angevin Exchequer treated it as a unit of lordship rather than of administrative geography, in that the other lands of Roger were always included with it for Exchequer purposes.[83] These were shires which Old English government had not reached. What appears in them is not its system, organised in a way which seems rational to the modern eye, but a different one, whose instinct was to organise *ad hoc*, and largely by reference to who owned what.

The same contrasts can be seen, on a wider scale, between the way in which the English kings ordered their acquisitions in the tenth century and that in which the Capetians ordered theirs from the twelfth. In the one there is a reduction to uniformity; in the other the superimposition of royal government on whatever already existed, with as a consequence the France of the *ancien régime*, in some ways formidably united, in others with anomalies numberless and, for example, far more provincial distinctions in law than anyone has found in eleventh-century England. That the essential difference between the two states

[80] D. F. Allen, *A Catalogue of Coins in the British Museum. The Cross-and-Crosslets ('Tealby') Type of Henry II* (London, 1951), p. lxxxviii.
[81] F. M. Stenton in *Victoria County History of Rutland*, i (London, 1908), pp. 134–36; J. M. Ramsay, *ibid.*, pp. 165–71.
[82] J. C. Holt, *The Northerners* (Oxford, 1961), p. 199.
[83] J. Tait, in *Victoria County History of Lancashire*, ii (London, 1908), pp. 181–82, 187–88.

lies in the time of their unification can be seen in considering that astonishing survival of *ancien régime* attitudes, the independent status allowed the Channel Islands and the Isle of Man, or the centuries for which Berwick-on-Tweed was left with a totally anomalous status, or the long delay in shiring most of Wales. Lands which were added to England after 1200 were treated in the spirit with which the Capetians treated their acquisitions.

The church presents a similar contrast between what happened before and after the twelfth century. Edward the Elder and Athelstan could create new dioceses on what appears a rational plan. If what they did was sometimes undone by amalgamations in the following century one can in either case see that innovation was possible and that administrative units were not regarded as immutable.[84] In the late Anglo-Saxon and Norman periods new parishes were created, at least in the east, almost at will, and as necessity or greed required.[85] In the twelfth century new bishoprics ceased to be created; Ely (1108) and Carlisle (1133) were the last. It became very much harder to make new parishes.[86] In consequence the disproportions between English sees remained unquestioned through the middle ages; while the distribution of parishes in the nineteenth century remained what it had been in the twelfth (a phenomenon which had an effect on the geography of the Liberal vote).[87]

A serious effort to explain why medieval states were in important ways less powerful, less capable of thorough organisation and reorganisation, than those of a Carolingian type would extend this paper too far. It may be that much in the regularity of the earlier period was very old indeed. Orderliness in the disposition of men and land is not necessarily the fruit of progress. Something of the answer may perhaps be glimpsed in the reasons for the cessation of the creation of new parishes. This was the result of the development of canon law and of papal jurisdiction, which secured innumerable vested interests and so half froze the church. The number of vested interests, and of individuals, which kings had to respect may similarly have increased. It is worth noticing that the Anglo-Normans seem to have been the last rulers in England to have used forced and unpaid labour to build great earthworks and the last to employ harrying as an instrument of government.

For whatever reasons the attitudes and powers of government and its approach to institutions and to boundaries changed. The changes which

---

[84] Stenton, *Anglo-Saxon England* 3rd edn, pp. 438–40; F. Barlow, *The English Church 1000–1066* (London, 1963), pp. 162–65.

[85] *Ibid.*, pp. 183–208.

[86] E.g. J. H. Round, *Family Origins and Other Studies* (London, 1930), pp. 272–74.

[87] H. Pelling, *The Social Geography of British Elections 1885–1900* (London, 1967), pp. 108, 206, 289.

can be traced in twelfth-century England are not simply to be explained as a transformation of the archaic, if sometimes oddly regular, into the more developed or modern. For the late Anglo-Saxon system of government had not been specious in its uniformity or rudimentary in its precocity. It was uniform and sophisticated and reflected not only power, but intelligence. It was in important ways the continuation and the heir of the Carolingian state and our knowledge of it may provide our nearest approach to apprehending what the Carolingian state was like. If, ultimately, England avoided the fate of the rest of *ancien régime* Europe it was largely thanks to a framework established by a regime yet more ancient.[88]

[88] I am indebted to Miss P. A. Adams for her help with this paper and to Dr D. M. Metcalf, who advised me on the Anglo-Saxon coinage but is not responsible for any errors.

A note on additional bibliography will be found on p. 189 below.

11

The Significance of the Anglo-Norman State in the Administrative History of Western Europe

The history of administration on much of the Continent between the eighth century and the thirteenth may be roughly divided into three phases. First, the Carolingian, with records indicating that the central authority aspired to organisation and control on a large scale. Second, an age of obscurity, when written sources for governmental administration hardly exist, and the temptation to equate lack of documents with absence of elaborate government is strong, maybe justifiable. Third, from the twelfth century the darkness begins to lift, and records appear indicating the development of administrations of some sophistication, for example, the first surviving central financial accounts from Normandy (1180), Flanders (1187) and France (1202–3). England is different. There are no records from the eighth and ninth centuries corresponding to the Carolingian capitularies and formularies. But from the eleventh century there is the incomparable Domesday survey (1086), proving England to have been a formidably organised state; and the first of our records for a twelfth century 'comptabilité centrale', the Pipe Roll of 1129–30, is two generations older than the earliest Continental counterpart. Such records make it possible to trace the partial transformation of a state of a Carolingian type into one of a twelfth century type without an intervening age of obscurity. They raise questions which are important, not only for England and for the age in which they were written, but also for other countries and periods.

Nearly the whole of the England which William conquered was divided in an orderly way into shires, and the shires into hundreds.[1] Almost all land was assessed in hides and the like for purposes of taxation and service.[2] Regular sub-division into units of local government and a

[1] The shires (counties) of Northumberland, Cumberland, Westmorland, Durham, Lancashire and Rutland were created after 1066. Otherwise a map showing the English shires as they were until 1974 represents to an astonishing degree the administrative geography of the early eleventh century, though there was considerable tidying of boundaries in the intervening period. Hundreds are more complicated. In some shires they remained largely unchanged from the Anglo-Saxon period on, in others they were reordered between the Conquest and the thirteenth century. For a general account of hundredal topography see O. F. Anderson, *The English Hundred Names*, Lund 1934, pp. XL–XLVII. In much of the Danelaw what was elsewhere called a hundred was called a wapentake.

[2] The best general account of the assessment system is still F. W. Maitland, *Domesday Book and Beyond*, Cambridge 1897; reprinted London 1960, Essay III. For more recent work see n. 9 below. In much of the Danelaw the carucate was the unit, not the hide.

near-universal system of assessment were of fundamental importance. That the country was divided into shires, each under a royal official, the sheriff, gave a degree of general control and made uniformity in administrative action possible. The system of assessment enabled kings to levy taxes on the country as a whole, sometimes at very high rates.[3] It was also used by the Anglo-Saxons to provide military and naval service; and its use to raise troops continued in the early Anglo-Norman period.[4] England was so organised as to give its eleventh century rulers powers which others lacked.

The assessment systems which were so important in the eleventh century had a very long history. They appear in the late seventh century, as soon as there are charters to provide descriptions of land. Of some thirty-five charters with any claim to authenticity granting land before 700, all but two describe it in terms of some Latin equivalent of the hide (in Kent, *sulung*). That the hidages of early grants are commonly in round numbers makes it implausible that they are other than fiscal assessments. That some are of scattered pieces of land, each with an assessment, like the Sussex charter giving 38 *cassati*, made up of estates of 12, 10, 11, 2 and 3, suggests a detailed assessment comparable to that of Domesday.[5] In a few instances it is possible to show that an estate had the same hidage in the eighth century and in Domesday.[6] This strengthens the case, if it needs strengthening, for the later systems of assessment having been in a continuous line of development from the earlier. To consider the long history of such systems in early England is to be reminded of how much of Dark Age government may have had its origins in very old systems of social organisation, and that some of the history of medieval administration may stretch back into the prehistoric past.[7]

Assessment systems in Anglo-Saxon England were old, but not unchanging. On the contrary, their recurrent reordering and flexible use were very important to the state. For example, the organisation of

[3] The first clear reference to such a tax is in the D version of the Anglo-Saxon Chronicle's annal relating to 1051, stating that in that year the *heregeld* was abolished in the thirty-ninth year after its institution, *Two of the Anglo-Saxon Chronicles Parallel*, ed. C. Plummer and J. Earle, Oxford 1892, I, p. 173; but it is generally and very plausibly supposed to go back at least to Ethelred II's payments to the Danes, F. M. Stenton, *Anglo-Saxon England*, 3rd ed. Oxford 1971, p. 644. It was levied on at least four occasions by William I, in 1083 at the high rate of 6/- on the hide (Stenton, loc. cit.) and it is suggested, on the basis on a Domesday reference, that it had become annual by the Conqueror's last years, as it certainly was by Henry I's time, V. H. Galbraith, *The Making of Domesday Book*, Oxford 1961, p. 42, cf. no. 42 below.

[4] C. Warren Hollister, *Anglo-Saxon Military Institutions*, Oxford 1962, Chapters III–VI, and his *The Military Organisation of Norman England*, Oxford 1965, Chapter VIII.

[5] W. de Gray Birch, *Cartularium Saxonicum*, 3 vols. and index, London 1885–99, no. 78; P. H. Sawyer, *Anglo-Saxon Charters. An Annotated List and Bibliography*, London 1968, no. 45.

[6] F. M. Stenton, *Latin Charters of the Anglo-Saxon Period*, Oxford 1955, p. 74, n. 1.

[7] J. Campbell, review of J. Morris, *The Age of Arthur*, see pp. 121–30 above.

the fortress system in late ninth and early tenth century Wessex must have required extensive redeployment of hidage assessments to produce the scheme set out in the Burghal Hidage, which we have evidence to show not to have been merely a parchment plan.[8] The creation of the shires and hundreds of the Midlands, with their assessments in neat multiples of 100 and 120 hides was a tenth century feat. In some areas we have evidence for orderly and complete reassessments between the tenth century and 1086, while the Domesday survey itself was probably intended towards a general reassessment.[9] The local variations in the patterns of hidages etc. which Domesday reveals, and the way in which one pattern can sometimes be traced overlying another are indications of the long history of systems of assessment and of successive changes in them.

What kind of central administration, with what records, went with all this? The Domesday survey must have stood in a tradition familiar with surveys on a significant scale and in some way connected with that of Carolingian government.[10] Recent work has shown that before Domesday the central authority had hidage lists, some of them arranged, like Domesday, on a tenurial basis, records of the farms of

[8] The Burghal Hidage probably dates from 914–18 and lists 30 of the *burhs* (fortified places) of Wessex and 3 of those of Mercia together with the hidages attributed to each for its maintenance and defence. A feature of special importance is the formula given at the end of the text indicating the basis of the hidage allocation. There were to be four men for each pole (5½ yds.) of rampart and each hide was to provide one man. Thus it is possible to calculate from the hidages what the perimeter of each fortification was deemed to be. Investigation of the sites concerned has shown that in a considerable number of cases there was a fairly, sometimes a very, close correspondence between what is implied by the Hidage and what is found on the ground. The most striking case is that of Winchester, where the perimeter implied by the Hidage is 9,900 ft., the real perimeter of the fortifications 9,954 ft. See especially David Hill 'The Burghal Hidage: the Establishment of a Text', *Medieval Archaeology*, 13 (1969), pp. 84–92 and his 'The Origins of the Saxon Towns' in *The South Saxons*, ed. P. Brandon, London and Chichester 1978, pp. 174–89, esp. 182–87; C. A. Ralegh Radford, 'Late Pre-Conquest Boroughs and their Defences', *ibid.*, 14 (1970), pp. 83–103; and M. Biddle, 'Towns', in *The Archaeology of Anglo-Saxon England*, ed. D. M. Wilson, London 1976, esp. pp. 126–34.

[9] Cyril Hart, *The Hidation of Northamptonshire*, Leicester 1970, is the most important recent study of late Anglo-Saxon assessment. Even if not all his conclusions are accepted the evidence for the regularities of the system and in the ways it was modified are inescapable, see e.g. Tables VII and VIII (pp. 38 and 41). The suggestions of W. J. Corbett, 'The Tribal Hidage', *Trans. Royal Hist. Soc.* new ser., 14 (1900), pp. 208–30, on tenth and early eleventh century assessment and its relation to hundreds remain important. For Domesday, S. P. J. Harvey, 'Domesday Book and Anglo-Norman Governance', *Trans. Royal Hist. Soc.* 5th ser. 25 (1975), pp. 175–93.

[10] J. Campbell, 'Observations on English Government from the Tenth to the Twelfth Century', esp. pp. 163–7 above. I should have observed on p. 164 that a letter of Bishop Denewulf of Winchester of 900/909 looks as if it may draw on a written list of the stock etc. on an estate, Birch, *Cartularium*, as at n. 5, nos. 618, 619, Sawyer, *Anglo-Saxon Charters*, as at n. 5, no. 1444.

royal demesne, and of what was due from boroughs.[11] Some of these records went back to the Confessor's reign; for example a surviving survey of the royal property in Winchester of c. 1110 is almost certainly based on a similar written survey of *c*. 1057.[12] Of particular importance are the 'Geld Rolls' preserved in the Exon Domesday. These are the record of an inquest into the payment of a geld (whether in 1084 or 1086 is disputed) in the five south western counties.[13] They are related to, but distinct from, the Domesday survey, and show that it was not unique as a large-scale fiscal inquiry. Among much else of interest they indicate that the writing of accounts probably accompanied the collection of geld, for the collectors for Somerset were allowed a deduction for the cost of a scribe.[14] That the Wiltshire record exists in three slightly differing versions is an indication of how much 'paper-work' could be associated with such an inquiry.[15] One other comparable record survives. The Northamptonshire Geld Roll, of some date between the Conquest and 1083, is probably a summary of the result of a somewhat similar inquest. That it is in English is suggestive that the making of such records went back before 1066.[16]

The question arises of how far back it went. We have three hidage lists from before the reign of Edward the Confessor: the Tribal Hidage (seventh or eighth century),[17] the Burghal Hidage (early tenth century)[18] and the County Hidage (tenth or early eleventh century).[19] There is no means of telling whether they are the chance survivals from many such or rather abnormal, even eccentric, productions.[20] It is not bizarre,

[11] S. P. J. Harvey, as at no. 9; and her 'Domesday Book and its Predecessors', *Eng. Hist. Rev.* 86 (1971), pp. 753–73.

[12] F. Barlow in F. Barlow, M. Biddle, O. von Feilitzen and D. J. Keene, *Winchester in the Early Middle Ages: an Edition and Discussion of the Winton Domesday (Winchester Studies*, I), Oxford 1976, pp. 9–10, cf. S. P. J. Harvey in *Medieval Settlement*, ed. P. Sawyer, London 1976, pp. 196–7.

[13] For these see especially R. Welldon Finn, *The Liber Exoniensis*, London 1964, Chapter VI and Galbraith, *The Making of Domesday Book*, as at n. 3, pp. 87–101, 223–30.

[14] *Domesday Book*, IV (Additamenta), ed. H. Ellis, London 1816, f. 526.

[15] R. R. Darlington in *Victoria County History of Wiltshire*, ed. R. B. Pugh and E. Crittall, II, London 1955, p. 171.

[16] A. J. Robertson, *Anglo-Saxon Charters*, Cambridge 1956, pp. 230–36, 481–84, cf. Hart, as at n. 9, pp. 16–21.

[17] W. Davies and H. Vierck, 'The Contexts of the Tribal Hidage: Social Aggregates and Settlement Patterns', *Frühmittelalterliche Studien* 8 (1974), pp. 223–93, refer to most of the previous literature.

[18] See n. 16 above.

[19] Hart, as at n. 9, though his precise dating (pp. 45–46) is disputable.

[20] The private administrative documents of the late Anglo-Saxon period are diverse, though not numerous, and suggest the fairly extensive use of writing for administrative purposes at least by the church, Campbell, 'Observations on English Government', see above pp. 157–8.

though one can well see why it is unusual, to entertain the supposition that the extensive use of written record for administrative purposes went back at least as far as the eighth century. Perhaps Anglo–Saxon government in the eighth and ninth centuries differed from Carolingian not so much in the extent to which it used writings as in the kind of record which has survived. (It is worth remembering that we only know that Offa issued a law code because Alfred mentions having used it.)[21] On the other hand, the older assessment systems are seen to be, the more it is necessary to admit that quite elaborate administration is possible without written records; as indeed it was in some African states as Europeans found them.[22]

The problem of origins is equally difficult for the central accounting system. The Pipe Roll of 1129–30 shows an elaborate system already established. One important part of this, the system of reckoning, using a squared cloth as a kind of abacus, which gave the Exchequer its name, was probably of fairly recent origin.[23] Yet Round showed in 1899 that some important elements in the financial system of Henry I's reign went back to the time of Edward the Confessor and that there were grounds for suspecting that others did so as well. It is certain that the elaborate procedure of 'blanching' is older than the Conquest, that there is 'a distinct allusion to the the "terrae datae" system' in Domesday, and that the commutation of *firma unius diei* and the like were already far advanced under the Confessor. 'There are hints, if not actual evidence' that the sheriff's farm was 'more or less in existence'.[24] Other suggestive details have been gleaned from Domesday by other scholars, in particular by Tait and Morris.[25] It is clear that Edward's income was to a large extent in cash. A wide range of royal revenues, both from

[21] F. Liebermann, *Die Gesetze der Angelsachsen*, 3 vols, Halle 1903–16, I, p. 47

[22] E.g. L. Mair, *Primitive Government*, Harmondsworth 1962, esp. Chapter VII. For observations on the possibilities of oral accounting, P. D. A. Harvey, *Manorial Records of Cuxham*, c. 1200–1359, London 1976, p. 15. It is noteworthy, however, that not only does the Tribal Hidage (cf. n. 17 above) quite likely go back to the seventh century but it has also recently been shown that a written assessment of ship-service from elsewhere in Britain, Dalriada, may well be equally old, J. Bannerman, *Studies in the History of Dalriada*, Edinburgh 1974, pp. 132–56.

[23] R. L. Poole, *The Exchequer in the Twelfth Century*, Oxford 1912, Chapter III; C. H. Haskins, 'The Abacus and the King's Curia', *Eng. Hist. Rev.* 27 (1912), pp. 101–6, where he shows that the technique might have been available in the reign of the Conqueror. The interest shown in the abacus from the tenth century (for which see G. R. Evans 'Difficillima et ardua. Theory and Practice in Treatises on the Abacus', *Journ. Medieval Hist.* 3 (1977) pp. 21–38) almost certainly had importance for administration; the early twelfth century tract on the subject by Turchill is of special interest since it was written with English royal financial administration in mind, Poole, pp. 48–50..

[24] J. H. Round, 'The Origins of the Exchequer' in *The Commune of London and Other Studies*, Westminster 1899, pp. 62–96, esp. pp. 65–74.

[25] W. A. Morris, *The Medieval English Sheriff*, Manchester 1927, pp. 28–34, 62–70; J. Tait, *The Medieval English Borough*, Manchester 1936, pp. 140–54.

estates and other sources, were framed for fixed sums and arrangements were made to reduce farms to take account of the alienation of lands or the incurring of expenditure on the king's behalf.[26] It is not clear that farms were consolidated in the farm of the shire rendered by the sheriff to the extent that they were under Henry I but even if the sheriffs 'did not as yet manage the farming system within their respective shires, they were very important in that system';[27] and to the extent to which farms were not concentrated in the hands of the sheriffs Edward would have had more financial agents to deal with than did Henry. The complexity of the royal finances as revealed by Domesday is such that if Edward the Confessor did not have some fairly good system of accounting using written record, he must have had chamberlains with singularly good memories. The balance of the evidence is that he did have some such system, though too much is unknown to permit a more precise statement. Here too the question arises of how far back the origins of such a system go. The problem is even more acute than that of when the use of written surveys and lists of what was due to the king begins. There is no English evidence for the keeping of accounts before the eleventh century, though there is some from the Carolingian period (even, perhaps, earlier) on the Continent.[28] One very important element in the accounting system revealed in the first Pipe Roll could have been of great antiquity, the use of tallies. A tally is a piece of wood, cut with notches to indicate sums of money or quantities of commodities and then so split as to leave both parties to a transaction with a verifiable record. It thus provides a means whereby transactions involving numbers can be recorded and authenticated in a manner decipherable by the illiterate. When their use begins is not, apparently, known; if it extends back into the Dark Ages this could have important implications for early fiscal administration. Richard fitz Nigel interestly says that the original name for the Exchequer was the Tallies.[29]

---

[26] Round, as at n. 24, p. 73, Morris, as at n. 25, p. 30.

[27] Morris, as at n. 25, p. 29. The interesting suggestions on the sheriff's farm made by R. W. Southern, 'The Place of Henry I in English History', *Proc. Brit. Acad.* 48 (1962), pp. 157–69, he has now withdrawn, see his *Medieval Humanism and Other Studies*, Oxford 1970, p. V. It is expected that the publication of Miss J. Aveyard (now Mrs Green)'s Oxford D. Phil. thesis on the administration of Henry I will add much to knowledge of these matters.

[28] A. Tautscher, 'Betriebsfhrung und Buchhaltung in den karolingischem Königsgütern nach dem Capitulare de Villis', *Vierteljahresschrift für Sozial- und Wirtschaftsgeschichte* 61 (1974) pp. 1–28; P. Gasnault, 'Documents financiers de Saint Martin de Tours de l'Epoque Mérovingienne', *Journal des Savants* (1970), pp. 82–93.

[29] H. Jenkinson 'Medieval Tallies, Public and Private', *Archaeologia* 74 (1923–4), pp. 280–351; D. Oschinsky, *Walter of Henley and Other Treatises on Estate Management and Accounting*, Oxford 1971, pp. 212–34. Cf. *Regesta Anglo-Normannorum*, II (1100–1135), ed. C. Johnson and H. A. Cronne, Oxford 1956, n. 1490, a charter of Henry I freeing a monastery from a rent *quatuor solidi . . . ponantur in tallia mea et ipsi inde sint quieti. Dialogus de Scaccario*, ed C. Johnson, London 1950 p. 7.

If it is hard to be sure how much of the financial administration revealed in the first Pipe Roll had been introduced in the Anglo-Norman period it is easier to observe development in the central writing-office. Dr. Chaplais has shown that throughout the Anglo-Saxon period royal charters (and even some, not impossibly all, of the sealed writs) were written by beneficiaries or by monastic scriptoria working for the king.[30] There is little doubt that substantial development had taken place by the reign of Henry I. Henry had a chancellor. (It is certain that the office existed early in his father's reign but if, as is just possible, it is older, it is not much older.) He had a number of clerks writing for him. The hands of some of these have been identified and it seems that four or more were sometimes employed at the same time.[31] This development can fairly be associated with the great increase from his reign in the number of surviving documents written for the king, though before too much is made of this a closer analysis of the determinants of survival than is so far available is required.[32]

The vast majority of documents issued for the king to survive from before the thirteenth century relate to the ownership of lands and rights. Those of other kinds, communicating information and instructions, can be more important in administration, and may have been much more numerous. It is demonstrable that a large number of these were issued in the twelfth century and have been lost. The Pipe Roll of 1129–30 contains references to over three hundred *brevia*, of which none survive. There is a great increase in the number of surviving royal letters, not relating to land or rights, after 1199, when first letters close are enrolled. It is difficult to avoid Dr Bishop's conclusion, that the number of such documents written in the twelfth century and since lost must have been 'immense'.[33] It could well be that more such letters were written at the same time as that from which we have more documents of types which

[30] Pierre Chaplais, 'The Origin and Authenticity of the Royal Anglo-Saxon Diploma', *Journ. Soc. of Archivists* III. 2 (Oct. 1965), pp. 48–61 and 'The Anglo-Saxon Chancery; from the Diploma to the Writ', *ibid.* III. 4 (Oct. 1966), pp. 160–76. For an interesting argument that from the tenth century the Anglo-Saxon kings kept copies of charters issued for them, C. Hart, 'The Codex Wintoniensis and the King's Haligdom', in *Land, Church and People. Essays Presented to H. P. R. Finberg*, ed. J. Thirsk, Reading 1970, pp. 7–38.
[31] T. A. M. Bishop, *Scriptores Regis*, Oxford 1961, pp. 30–31. H. A. Cronne, *The Reign of Stephen, 1135–54. Anarchy in England*, London 1970, adds valuable information and warnings and apparently holds (p. 217) that at least six clerks were writing for the king at the end of Henry's reign and the beginning of Stephen's.
[32] A rough count indicates that the annual average of acts issued of which texts survive for the kings of England is as follows: Ethelred II 3; Cnut 3; Edward the Confessor 5; William I 9; William II 13; Henry I 48; Stephen 37. These figures are rounded to the nearest unit exclude documents issued for Continental beneficiaries for Continental lands and do not include Matilda's charters.
[33] Bishop, *Scriptores Regis*, as at n. 31, pp. 32–33.

do survive. The nature of the handwriting of some of Henry I's clerks has suggested to experts that it was that of men who were kept busily employed. It is possible that Henry could have kept clerks busy simply in writing charters which recorded his giving things away, but it seems unlikely.[34]

The likelihood that documents, other than those which were in some sense title deeds, had a poor chance of survival does not raise problems for the twelfth century alone. It is known that the Anglo-Saxons used letters, not necesarily sealed, for administrative purposes from the ninth century at the latest. The relatively small number of writs surviving from the eleventh century Anglo-Saxon kings largely relate to ownership. This may be why they were preserved; they may be the atypical survivors of a much larger number, most of which dealt with more ephemeral matters of business.[35] The twelfth century evidence is sufficient to show the extent to which such letters can be lost. There is thus a possibility that government in the eleventh century, or even earlier, involved the fairly extensive use of administrative letters.

There are broadly analogous problems even in regard to judicial administration. It is certain that extensive developments in this took place in the twelfth century. Their extent is matched, though not disproved, by that of our ignorance of how the legal system actually worked before Henry II's time. Consider two points at which legal and financial administration meet. the Pipe Roll of 1129–30 shows that Henry I got much of his income from selling justice, or selling judicial procedures. There are no means of telling how far William I, or Edward the Confessor did the same thing, or, if so, how the relevant payments were made and accounted for. Similarly, there is evidence in Domesday Book indicating that, while fines for lesser offences were farmed, those for major offences were *extra firmas*.[36] Again, we do not know what procedures and records were involved.

The nearest approach which a certain philosopher ever made to a

---

[34] *Ibid.* p. 13; though note that the surviving Pipe Roll of Henry I is in the hand of a scribe who also wrote royal charters, ibid. p. 28. A specially important kind of document which may have had a poor chance of survival is that of writs embodying what is in effect legislation, widely circulated. Four such, apart from Henry I's coronation charter, survive from the Anglo-Norman period. There is evidence to suggest that there were others. It could be that there were many such. It could even be that the absence of law 'codes' after Cnut is attributable to legislation having been promulgated thereafter in writ form, as in the well-known writs of Henry I on the coinage and on courts, whose manuscript tradition suggests how easily other such could have been lost. See A. J. Robertson, *The Laws of the Kings of England from Edmund to Henry I*, Cambridge 1925, pp. 232–4, 235–7, 284–5, 285–6, and 227–8; H. G. Richardson and G. O. Sayles, *Law and Legislation from Æthelbert to Magna Carta*, Edinburgh 1966, pp. 30–33.

[35] *Journ. Soc. of Archivists*, III. 4 (as at n. 30), p. 170.

[36] Morris, *The Medieval English Sheriff*, as at n. 25, p. 30.

positive statement was to say: 'Not but what it may not have been, perhaps it was.' To consider, as by implication in this paper, such questions as 'How detailed a record, if any, did Offa have of hidage assessments?', or 'What system of written accounting, if any, did Cnut have when he collected his heregeld?' is to sympathise with this agony. Such questions verge on the perverse, in so far as they are largely unanswerable; but they are real questions, and if they are unanswerable, that is an important fact, showing how little we know, or can know, of early administration. The Anglo-Norman administrative records compel such questions, because they demonstrate how much in administration can escape notice altogether if sources of the right kind do not happen to survive. If the Domesday survey had not been made, or had not survived, we should have no idea that William's government was capable of such a feat, not to speak of much else about English government for which Domesday is the only, but incontrovertible, evidence – for example that elements in the accounting system revealed in the first Pipe Roll go back to the time of the Conquest. Similarly, were it not for the survival of the twelfth century Exchequer records it would be impossible to know the scale and complexity of Henry I's system of account and audit. No contemporary chronicle mentions the Exchequer or anything about the accounting system. A handful of charters would enable one to piece together that there was something called the Exchequer, whose barons appear once with judicial powers, that rolls and tallies were used in relation to royal accounts, and that devices existed for making allowance to an accountant for money which he would owe had not the king given it away; that is all.[37] In short, negative arguments about early medieval administration must be held suspect to the extent that they depend on the silence of sources of the type which commonly survive.[38]

It would be absurd to be so Pyrrhonian as to question that there were important changes between the tenth century and the twelfth. It is prudent to retain a very open mind on what may have existed and yet be entirely hidden; it is imprudent to be dogmatic about the generation or scale of any particular change; even the broadest generalisations may be hazardous. I hazard the generalisations which follow. In the earlier

---

[37] Poole, *The Exchequer . . .*, as at n. 23, pp. 37–41, *Regesta . . .*, as at n. 28, nos. 963, 1053, 1490, 1514, 1538, 1741. This handful of references is from some 1500 documents, far more than survive for any other king at the time.

[38] A powerful example of the extent to which a source of a kind which does not normally survive can provide information and insights not available in those which normally do is that of the Hebrew *responsa*, for which see I. A. Agus, *Urban Civilization in Pre-Crusade Europe*, 2 vols., Leiden 1966. Consider, for example, the light cast upon feudal warfare by the revelation that urban merchants dealt, apparently in an organised way, in booty, and provided the supplies necessary for sieges, I, pp. 99–100 (a document of *c.* 1007), cf. I, p. 325 for loans for the paying of ransoms.

part of the period the English state depended heavily on regularity in divisions of local government and in assessment systems. It displayed great power in ordering, reordering and exploiting these, more power than its medieval successor had. The central authority dealt with areas as much as with individuals. Tax and service were levied by shires and by hundreds. When assessments were altered it could be for a whole area; the assessment for a shire or hundred being moved up or down, changes in what was levied on individuals being consequential on the changes made in round numbers for large units. Most royal income was probably paid according to systems whereby it was known in advance what it ought to be, whether as geld or as farms. It looks like an administrative world in which regularity, even rigidity, in, for example, assessment systems, are the counterpart to, and in a sense necessary because of, the central authority's not having the staff or organisation to deal on any very regular basis with matters of detail, local problems, or individuals of no great consquence. Consonant with such an organisation are indications of the use of rota systems. It was on a rota basis that Alfred organised the service of his *fyrd* and of his *ministri*.[39] The fair (no more than fair) degree of regularity with which some eleventh century kings adhered to the routine of being at Winchester for Easter, Westminster for Whitsun and Gloucester for Christmas is another instance, in a general way, of the same kind of thing.[40] The twelfth century story that three abbeys provided the king's writing-office in rotation is false as it stands but still may well bear some correspondence to what actually happened in the tenth century.[41]

During the twelfth century the importance of regular assessment systems in terms of hides began to decline. Their use for taxation and other purposes continued in the earlier twelfth century; and although Danegeld was last levied in 1162 hidage assessments were used for certain kinds of levy thereafter and general taxes on a hidage or a similar basis were raised between 1194 and 1220. But by Henry II's reign the Crown had come increasingly to depend on revenue raised on different bases; and the fiscal significance of hidages, fundamental in the eleventh century had faded completely by the middle of the thirteenth.[42]

[39] *Two of the Anglo-Saxon Chronicles Parallel*, as at n. 3, p. 84; *Asser's Life of King Alfred*, ed. W. H. Stevenson (new impr. with introduction by D. Whitelock) Oxford 1950, pp. 86–87.

[40] Most recently discussed by M. Biddle in an unpublished, but, I believe, forthcoming paper, 'Seasonal Festivals and Residence', read to the Council for British Archaeology's conference on Archaeology and History of the European Town, Oxford, April 1975. He showed that a fairly regular itinerary was maintained by the Norman kings, when in England, until 1109. (It was to a degree anticipated under Edward the Confessor, but not before.)

[41] Chaplais, *Journ. Soc. of Archivists* III. 4, as at n. 30, pp. 175–6.

[42] For Danegeld in the twelfth century see e.g. S. Painter, *Studies in the History of the Medieval English Feudal Barony*, Baltimore 1953, pp. 74–79. According to John of

From the twelfth century the offices and offices of central authority were dealing directly with far more individuals than before. The developments in the legal system whereby more and more business was attracted to the central courts or to itinerant justices sent from the centre was characteristic of much else that was happening. To take one well-known example, as a result of the activity of an eyre early in John's reign the sheriff of Yorkshire was responsible to the Exchequer for recovering about a thousand debts.[43] Notwithstanding our ignorance of the scale on which the late Anglo-Saxon kings used written instruments the evidence for an increase in the amount of writing done for the Crown under Henry I is enough strongly to suggest that far more individuals received documents of one kind or another from the king in the twelfth century than had been the case earlier. If this was so it must have been in considerable measure a consequence of social changes. To take the simplest of these to quantify, in 1066 there were not more than sixty-one religious houses in England, but by 1216 there were between 640 and 748, every one capable of creating business for the central offices.[44] In this and other ways it can be seen that not only was the central government organised in such a way that it could deal directly with more men and institutions, there were also more men and institutions whose status and knowledge were such that they were capable of dealing directly with the central government.[45]

There are parallels between developments in royal government and in the organisation of great estates. In the eleventh century great estates were sometimes, perhaps usually, organised in such a way that particular parts of the estate provided in rotation what was required throughout the year; e.g. the estates were divided into thirteen monthly groups or fifty-two weekly groups. It was also common in the eleventh and twelfth centuries for great landlords to farm out their estates, so that they had predictable incomes and only a limited number of individuals to deal with.[46] From the late twelfth century such estates

Worcester, ed. J. R. H. Weaver, Oxford 1908, p. 34, Henry I abandoned it from 1130 but it was restored by Stephen. For taxation later in the twelfth century e.g. Maitland, *Domesday Book and Beyond* (reprint 1960), pp. 545–6, J. C. Holt, *Magna Carta*, Cambridge 1965, pp. 19–42; S. K. Mitchell, *Taxation in Medieval England*, New Haven 1951, esp. Chapter III.

[43] *The Great Roll of the Pipe for the Second Year of King John*, ed. D. M. Stenton (Pipe Roll Society, vol. L, 1934), p. 111; cf. Jenkinson, Medieval Tallies, as at n. 29, p. 300 n. 7.

[44] D. Knowles and R. N. Hadcock, *Medieval Religious Houses. England and Wales*, 2nd ed., Cambridge 1971, p. 494.

[45] The introduction of tenure by knight service of the kind revealed in the twelfth century records may have increased the number of relatively unimportant men who had direct dealings with the Crown, since there were a considerable number of such among the tenants in chief.

[46] R. W. Lennard, *Rural England 1086–1135*, Oxford 1959, Chapter V, esp. pp. 132–4.

began to be run directly by the landlord and his staff, who maintained detailed control by the extensive use of written record.[47]

The English evidence for the nature of the state in the Anglo-Norman period illuminates, and raises important question about, what happened on the Continent. First, in regard to Carolingian administration. The resemblances between English government in the tenth and eleventh centuries and that of the Carolingians earlier are manifold. The organisation of counties and hundreds, the system for raising troops and money, that of exacting general oaths and the methods of inquiry and survey all bear strong resemblances.[48] There are, naturally, significant differences, perhaps the most important being that from the tenth century England did not have, occasional instances apart, an equivalent of the Carolingian *comes*, in the sense of a man of high status at the head of an individual county.[49] Nevertheless the resemblances are so numerous and significant that late Anglo-Saxon government may fairly be described as of Carolingian type.

Because late Anglo-Saxon government is known to have worked effectively its resemblances to that of the Carolingians strengthen the case for supposing theirs to have worked effectively in an earlier period. It is understandable, granted that much of the evidence is more for aspiration than execution, that eminent historians have been inclined to doubt the effectiveness of Carolingian government. Professor Perroy went so far as to say 'The truth is that local administration was as non-existent as central administration'.[50] Even Professor Ganshof was disinclined to believe that most of the reports, lists and returns (of which he demonstrated many were made) were actually used; rather, he thought they were 'piled up in a confused heap, or vanished completely'.[51] Neither of these great historians had evidence categorically to prove all their mistrust of Carolingian efficiency. There is indeed evidence for inefficiency, impracticability and corruption, but so there is for many other governmental systems, which nevertheless worked quite well. It is not, I believe, unfair to suppose that an important factor in forming certain attitudes to Carolingian government has been an instinctive disinclination to take the sources at face-value, to accept that adminstration could have been as they show it.

[47] Harvey *Manorial Records of Cuxham*, as at n. 22, pp. 12–34. The introduction to this work now provides by far the best introduction to the history and records of estate accounting in the period with which it deals. See also Oschinsky, *Walter of Henley*, as at n. 28, pp. 212–34.

[48] 'Observations on English Government', pp. 159–65 above; Hollister, *Anglo-Saxon Military Institutions*, as at n. 4, pp. 42–43.

[49] H. M. Chadwick, *Studies on Anglo-Saxon Institutions*, Cambridge 1905, Chapter 5.

[50] E. Perroy, 'Carolingian Administration' in *Early Medieval Society* ed. S. L. Thrupp, New York 1967, p. 146.

[51] F. L. Ganshof, *The Carolingians and the Frankish Monarchy*, London 1971, p. 134.

The possibility that Carolingian administration was effective seems greater when the evidence is set beside that from a later period in England. Consider two examples from the reign of Charles the Bald. In the Edict of Pîtres Charles required, *inter alia*, replies to a detailed questionnaire on markets.[52] Counts were to list all markets and to provide by *proximum placitum nostrum* answers to a series of detailed questions: which markets had been founded in his grandfather's time, which in his father's, which in his own, which by authority, which without, which had been moved, and if so by what authority. One takes such a questionnaire more seriously when one considers Domesday Book, in which the answers to another such, far more extensive, but comparable, are preserved.[53] Or again, *s.a.* 869 the annals of St Bertin record that instructions were given that returns should be made of the number of manses held by ecclesiastics, by counts, and by the vassals of counts, and that every hundred manses were to provide a *haistaldum*, every thousand an ox-cart etc.[54] The return of *breves* recalls Domesday. The levy of service looks more realistic if one compares, for example, that of ship-service by Ethelred II in 1008 'a warship from 310 hides and a helmet and corselet from 8 hides', for the English evidence is just good enough to show that Ethelred's order was implemented.[55] It is the more instructive to compare Charles with Ethelred, for the English king was hardly less beset by Danes and by dissension than the Frank had been. Yet his threatened regime was capable of great administrative feats: the collection of Danegeld on a vast scale, the implementation of septennial changes in the coinage, important modifications in the fortress-system.[56] Elements in the late Carolingian administrative system

[52] *Capitularia Regum Francorum*, II, ed. A. Boretius and V. Krause. *(Mon. Germ. Hist., Legum Sect. II)*, Hannover 1890, pp. 317–8.

[53] The questionnaire preserved in the *Inquisitio Eliensis* is most conveniently available in W. Stubbs, *Select Charters*, 9th ed., Oxford 1901, p. 101.

[54] Ed. F. Grat, J. Vielliard and S. Clémencet, Paris 1964, pp. 152–3.

[55] *Two of the Anglo-Saxon Chronicles*, as at n. 3, p. 138, translated in D. Whitelock, D. C. Douglas and S. I. Tucker, *The Anglo-Saxon Chronicle*, 2nd impr. London 1965, pp. 88–89: '1008 In this year the king ordered that ships should be built unremittingly all over England'. '1009 In this year the ships we mentioned above were ready'. (For variations in the text and disputed points of translation, see Plummer's commentary and the works cited below). For evidence of the existence of ship-service related to hidage (and its probably antedating 1008 in some form) see Hollister, *Anglo-Saxon Military Institutions*, as at n. 4, pp. 103–15; F. E. Harmer, *Anglo-Saxon Writs*, Manchester 1952, pp. 266–7 and F. Liebermann, *Die Gesetze der Angelsachsen*, as at n. 21, II. 2, s. v. Schiff.

[56] For Danegeld see n. 3 above; for the coinage pp. 186–8 below. The most interest-evidence for modification of the fortress-system is that for the fortification of South Cadbury with a stone wall some twelve hundred yards in circumference, dated with some confidence by numismatic evidence to 1009-19, L. Alcock, *By South Cadbury is that Camelot... The Excavation of Cadbury Castle 1966–70*, London 1972, cf. M. Biddle in *The Archaelogy of Anglo-Saxon England*, ed. Wilson, as at n.8, pp. 140–41 and references.

which, though recognised, tend to be brushed somewhat on one side because they did not have a future, gather more weight when one looks at England, where they did. Most important are levies of taxation to pay Danegeld. These, recorded twelve or thirteen times between 845 and 926, are mentioned by Professor Ganshof 'for the sake of completeness', though he regards them as unimportant in relation to royal power because the money went to Danes.[57] This does not alter the fact that rulers who could raise such taxes were powerful in a way in which their successors, south of the Channel, are not known to have been.

The English evidence raises questions about their tenth and eleventh century Capetian successors also. Had not the Domesday survey been made and had many of the twelfth century records of the Exchequer survived the English evidence would have resembled more closely that from other states, and English administration would have looked more as theirs looks. It is therefore a question how far the apparent differences between English administration and that elsewhere reflect no more than differences in the survival of sources. In Flanders there is evidence for the central fiscal administration's having developed from the late eleventh century along the lines not dissimilar to those of the English;[58] while in Normandy the Exchequer can, at least in the twelfth century, reasonably be understood as developing *pari passu* with its English counterpart.[5] But what of the Capetian lands? No records of a 'comptabilité central' survive from before the reign of Philip Augustus. It is thus unsurprising that there is virtually no discussion of financial administration in recent works on Capetian government.[60] Professor Lemarignier is hesitant, and apprehensive of anachronism, in even using the word 'administration' in relation to later eleventh century Capetian government.[61] Professors Lot and Fawtier adopted a rather different approach. 'Dès 1190, au moins, il existe un compte des recettes des bailliages et des prévôtés royales. Il n'y a

[57] E. Joranson, *The Danegeld in France*, Rock Island 1923; Ganshof, *The Carolingians and the Frankish Monarchy*, as at n. 51, p. 100.

[58] Bryce (Lyon) and Adrian Verhulst, *Medieval Finance. A Comparison of Financial Institutions in Northwestern Europe*, Bruges 1967, esp. Chapter II. Although the sources for Flemish financial administration before the *Grote Brief* of 1187 are sparse indeed (the charter to the Provost of St. Donatian, 1089, a fragment of an account of 1140 and the information provided by Galbert of Bruges provide almost all there is) these survivals, with the providential preservation of the *Grote Brief* (otherwise no comparable account survives before 1255) suffice to show that there was quite a sophisticated 'comptabilité centrale' early in the twelfth century. Our knowledge hangs on a narrow thread and owes much to chance.

[59] Lyon and Verhulst, *Medieval Finance*, as at n. 58, pp. 41–52 for the literature on the Norman Exchequer.

[60] J. F. Lemarignier, *Le gouvernement royal aux premiers temps capétiens (987–1108)*, Paris 1965, E. Bournazel, *Le gouvernement capétien au XIIᵉ siècle (1108–1180)*, Paris 1975.

[61] Lemarignier, *Le gouvernement royal*, as at n. 60, p. 157.

pas de raison pour que Louis VII ait innové en ces matières. Il est vraisemblable que la monarchie a eu une comptabilité, plus ou moins développée, pour les revenus de son domaine aṗ artir de l'avènment de Hugues Capet; et comme celui-ci n'a voulu faire et fait que ce que faisaient ses prédécesseurs . . . les origines de la compatbilité royale française se perdent dans la nuit des temps.'[62] In the light of the English evidence their approach seems the more attractive. That Anglo-Norman and French government were very different hardly needs demonstration; but it is above all in relation to the 'comptabilité centrale' that the possibility that there were at least broad similarities becomes pressing. It seems that Louis VII's income at least was comparable to Henry II's.[63] Even if his immediate predecessors had less (and it is not clear that their income was of a different order of magnitude) both he and they drew their revenues from sources which were both numerous and diverse. It is easier to believe that there was a fairly developed 'comptabilité centrale' than that fiscal administration was a matter entirely of memory and rules of thumb.[64] That is to say that administration may have had an early role in the development of Capetian power whose possible importance cannot be dismissed on the ground that it appears largely unknowable. It could be, for example, that the appearance of 'prévoîs' and 'mandements' (not improbably related, as Professor Lemarignier has suggested[65]) in the later eleventh century indicates administrative development on a substantial scale.

Comparison can never prove; but it can strengthen possibilities. A case of particular relevance in the present context is that of Normandy. Here a key problem is that of how far any of the framework of Carolingian government could have survived the dark and disrupted generations after 911.[66] One may compare East Anglia, under Danish rule from 870 to *c.*918. During that period no charters were produced which have survived, and no narrative source. The episcopal succession was broken and the monasteries destroyed. Nevertheless, and largely thanks to Domesday Book, it is possible to be nearly certain that important elements in its system of local government and assessment

[62] F. Lot and R. Fawtier, *Histoire des institutions francqises au moyen âge,* II Paris 1958, pp. 185–6.

[63] M. Pacaut, *Louis VII et son royaume,* Paris 1964, pp. 119–60. J. F. Benton, 'The Revenue of Louis VII', Speculum 42 (1967), pp. 84–91.

[64] Lyon and Verhulst, *Medieval Finance,* as at n. 58, p. 50 are adamant that the Capetain central financial administration developed later than that of Flanders or England but the only evidence they have which is not *ex silentio* is an inference from the greater simplicity of the French system of farms as it appears in 1202–3.

[65] *Le gouvernement royal,* as at n. 60, pp. 157–62.

[66] The most recent survey is J. Le Patourel, *The Norman Empire,* Oxford 1976, pp. 3–5.

survived through the period of Danish rule.[67] Indeed one of the most striking features of recent work on early institutions in England is the extent to which it suggest the extreme resilience of certain structures of local government through manifold political vicissitudes. For example, it seems much more likely than not that much in the organisation of northern England in the early medieval period was of pre-Saxon origin, successive Anglo-Saxon and Scandinavian conquests and reconquests notwithstanding.[68] A complication if one is considering the relevance of English evidence to Norman possibilities is that in parts at least of the Danelaw the Danes probably introduced elaborate assessment systems of their own.[69] This does not alter the assistance which English evidence gives to those disinclined to understand the early administrative history of Normandy in terms of *tabula rasa* or of chaos.

To consider the transmission and diffusion of administrative techniques is to realise how little we know of what may have been. Even in the oft quoted case of the sealed writ, where there is something of a consensus that an English development was directly or indirectly influential in many parts of Europe in the eleventh and twelfth centuries, involved in its antecedents is the 'letter close', with a history going back at least to the eighth century, and a possible significance in Carolingian government much more considerable than the tiny number of surviving examples *prima facie* suggests.[70] At another level consider the problems raised by the Danish assessment system in terms of *herred* and *bol*. It bears obvious similarities to the English system of hundreds and hides. The question of how far these are systems with common and distant Germanic origins and how far the Danish system reflects a major administrative reorganisation, say by Cnut, under English influence, is probably insoluble.[71]

Perhaps the most interesting case is that of *renovatio monetae*. It is well known that in Germany, and in other areas in both eastern and western

[67] R. Welldon Finn, *Domesday Studies, The Eastern Counties*, London 1967, pp. 105–21; G. C. Homans, 'The Frisians in East Anglia' *Econ. Hist. Rev.* 2nd ser. 10 (1957), pp. 189–206; R. H. C. Davis, 'The Kalendar of Abbot Samson', Camden Soc. 3rd ser., 84 (1954), pp. XI–XLVII.

[68] G. W. S. Barrow, *The Kingdom of the Scots*, London 1973, pp. 7–68.

[69] C. Hart, 'The Hidation of Huntingdonshire', *Proc. Cambridge Antiquarian Soc.* 61 (1968), pp. 55–66 and his *The Hidation of Northamptonshire*, as at n. 9, pp. 43–45; C. F. Slade, *The Leicestershire Survey*, Leicester 1956, p. 77.

[70] R. A. Fletcher, 'Diplomatic and the Cid revisited: the Seals and Mandates of Alfonso VII', *Journ. of Medieval Hist.* 2 (1976), p. 330 and refs.; P. Chaplais, 'The Letter from Bishop Wealdhere of London to Archbishop Brihtwold of Canterbury: the earliest original Letter Close extant in the West', in *Medieval Scribes, Manuscripts and Libraries: Essays presented to N. R. Ker*, ed. M. B. Parkes and A. G. Watson, London 1978, pp. 3–23 and *Journ. Soc. of Archivists* III. 4,1 as at n. 30 above, p. 169.

[71] L. Musset, *Les peuples scandinaves au moyen âge*, Paris 1951, pp. 88–90; for the possibility of yet further complications, G. F. Ward, 'The English *Danegeld* and the Russian *Dan*', in *American Slavic and East European Review* 13 (1954), pp. 299–318.

Europe, from about the twelfth century, many rulers exploited the currency by requiring that all the coins in circulation should be withdrawn at intervals, sometimes frequent intervals, and a new coin-type substituted.[72] It is also known that on several occasions (the last in 864) Carolingian rulers sought to withdraw all the coin in circulation and to replace it by a new type.[73] It used to be usual to see no connection between the Carolingian recoinages and the later *renovationes*. It has become harder to do so since it has been discovered that the late Anglo-Saxon kings carried out the system of *renovatio* on a very large scale.[74] After the recoinage of 975 (perhaps 973) the whole coinage was withdrawn at regular intervals, first of seven years, later of less, and replaced by a new type, sometimes lighter, sometimes heavier than its predecessor. The evidence of hoards is that, particularly in the first generations, the withdrawals were to a large extent effective. The system was continued after the Conquest, though simplified by general adherence to a standard weight for the penny, and finally abandoned in 1158. *Renovatio* on the scale on which the Saxons carried it out was a major piece of administration, involving a coinage of many millions of silver pennies and the control of about sixty mints. It is striking, and a further illustration of the danger of resting negative conclusions on early administration on deductions from silence that it would be impossible to learn from written sources that this elaborate and sophisticated system of managing the currency existed. It is the coins themselves which prove it. It is hard to believe that so complicated a system was simply invented by the English. There surely must be some connection with the Carolingian currency changes. Consider how the Edict of Pîtres lays down the precise techniques for changing the currency and numerous other resemblances between English and Carolingian government.[75] The question of the ultimate origins of the system is of obvious interest and import-

---

[72] A. Suchodolski, 'Renovatio Monetae in Poland in the Twelfth Century', *Wiadomści Numizmatcyczne* 5 (1961), pp. 57–75 of the supplement, maintains that the system was introduced in Bohemia and Hungary in the late 11th century, and in Germany and Poland in the twelfth. S. Bolin, 'Tax Money and Plough Money', *Scandinavian Econ. Hist. Rev.* 2 (1954), pp. 3–21 argues for its introduction into Denmark c. 1075 (pp. 15–16). F. von Schrötter *Wörterbuch der Münzkunde*, reprint Berlin 1970, s. v. 'Münzverrufung' provides a general, if somewhat outdated survey.

[73] E. g.: R. Doehaerd, 'Les réformes monétaires carolingiennes', *Annales, E. S. C.* 7 (1952), pp. 13–20.

[74] The most recent general account of the late Anglo-Saxon coinage is [R. H.] M. Dolley, 'The Coins', in *The Archaeology of Anglo-Saxon England*, ed. Wilson, as at n. 8, esp. pp. 358–60, giving full references to earlier work, among which R. H. M. Dolley and D. M. Metcalf, 'The Reform of the English Coinage under Edgar' in *Anglo-Saxon Coins*, ed. R. H. M. Dolley, London 1961, pp. 133–68 and H. Bertil and A. Peterson, *Anglo-Saxon Currency. From King Edgar's Reform to the Norman Conquest*, Lund 1969, are of special importance. For the post-Conquest coinage see [R. H.] M. Dolley, *The Norman Conquest and the English Coinage*, London 1966.

[75] *Capitularia II*, ed. Boretius and Krause, as at n. 52, pp. 314–7.

ance but apparently remains mysterious. Looking forward, it seems
highly probable that there is a connection between English *renovationes*
and the system as it appears later elsewhere in Europe.

It is likely that *renovatio monetae* is characteristic of much else in the
history of administration in western Europe. Elaborate techniques were
used of which written sources of the ordinary kinds do not necessarily
tell us; and what we know of the origin and diffusion of techniques is
little more than enough to indicate the depth of the problems and the
width of the possibilities.[76] No doubt much in Anglo-Norman England
was unique. The juxtaposition there of structures and systems which go
back to the Carolingian age, or beyond, with others which were
characteristic of the medieval state marks a crucial stage in that
singularly continuous development which, as Stubbs showed, links
modern institutions to those of the Dark Ages in a way unparalleled
elsewhere. But the chief interest of Anglo-Norman England in relation
to the administrative history of western Europe does not lie in the
recognition that England differed from other states, but in the question
of how far it differed. The extent to which knowledge of what England
was like depends on sources of kinds which do not survive elsewhere
suggests that of primary value in the study of administration in early
Europe is *difficillima ars nesciendi*.

[76] A curious instance of alleged transmission of law from one country to another is
the observation in '*Leges Edwardi Confessoris*' (a compilation of the earlier twelfth
century) à propos of the legislation on usury, there attributed to Edward: *Hoc autem
dicebat sepe se audisse in curia regis Francorum, dum ibi moratus esset* . . ., Liebermann,
Gesetze, as at n. 21, I, p. 668.

Additional Bibliographical Note

H. R. Loyn, *The Governance of Anglo-Saxon England 500–1087* (1984) is a balanced survey. Simon Keynes, *The Diplomas of King Æthelred 'the Unready' 978–1016* (Cambridge, 1980) is important on the production of royal documents. To the bibliography on the late Saxon burhs now add C. A. Ralegh Radford, 'The Pre-Conquest Boroughs of England, Ninth to Eleventh Century', *Proc. British Academy*, lxiv (1978), pp. 131–54. M. K. Lawson, 'The Collection of Danegeld and Heregeld in the Reigns of Ethelred II and Cnut', *English Hist. Rev.*, xcix (1984), pp. 721–38 is very important. The latest work of D. M. Metcalf, 'Continuity and Change in English Monetary History *c.*973–1076', *British Numismatic Journ.*, l (1980), pp. 20–49, li (1981), pp. 52–90 marks new advances. On *renovatio monetae* in general see T. N. Bisson, *Conservation of Coinage. Monetary Exploitation and its Restraint in France, Catalonia and Aragon c.A.D. 1000–c.1225* (Oxford, 1979). A series of articles by P. Nightingale has illuminated in important ways the connections between government, coinage and economic management: 'Some London Moneyers and Reflections on the Organisation of English Mints in the Eleventh and Twelfth Centuries', *Numismatic Chron.*, cxlii (1982), pp. 34–50; 'The Ora, the Mark and the Mancus; Weight Standards and the Coinage in Eleventh Century England', *Ibid.*, cxliii (1983), pp. 248–57, cxliv (1984), pp. 234–48; Dr. Nightingale here provides a convincing explanation of the 20d. *ora* which differs from that accepted above, p. 156; 'The Evolution of New Weight Standards and the Creation of New Monetary and Commercial Links in Northern Europe from the Tenth Century to the Twelfth Century', *Econ. Hist. Rev.*, 2nd ser., xxxviii (1985), pp. 192–209. Dr. J. A. Green's thesis (above, n.27) is complete: 'Some Aspects of Royal Administration in England during the Reign of Henry I' (Oxford D. Phil., 1975). Some of its conclusions are published in: J. A. Green, 'The Last Century of Danegeld', *English Hist. Rev.*, xcvi (1981), pp. 241–58; 'The Earliest Surviving Pipe Roll', *Bull. Inst. Hist. Res.* lv (1982), pp. 1–17; 'The Sheriffs of William the Conqueror', *Proc. Battle Abbey Conference*, v (1982), pp. 129–45. W. L. Warren, 'The Myth of Norman Administrative Efficiency', *Trans. Royal Hist. Soc.*, 5th ser. xxxiv (1984), pp. 113–32 is very stimulating. For Professor M. Biddle's observations on royal itineraries (cf. n.40 above) see F. Barlow, *et. al.*, *Winchester in the Early Middle Ages*, as at n.12 above, pp. 295–6. M. T. Clanchy *From Memory to Written Record, England 1066–1307* (1979) is full of interest on many of themes discussed above.

NEEXAVDI
ORATIONEM MEAM.
ETCLAMOR MEVS
ADTE VENIAT

4. David and Goliath at the beginning of Psalm 101 in a Psalter produced in Christ Church, Canterbury between 1012 and 1023. *(British Library, MS. Arundel 155, f. 93'; 292 x 170 mm.)*

12

England, France, Flanders and Germany in the Reign of Ethelred II: Some Comparisons and Connections

In seeking to do something to put Ethelred's reign in its European context it is natural to begin by asking how far the king was like other kings of his day and how far the style of his regime and life resembled theirs. To consider in this connection Robert the Pious, king of France from 996 to 1031 as he appears in the *Vita* written not long after his death by Helgaud, a monk of Fleury, is to discover an apparent contrast.[1] Helgaud presents Robert not only as literate, reading his psalter every day, but as learned, *sapientissimus litterarum*, educated in the liberal arts by Gerbert.[2] He shows him as very generous to the church, of course; keeping up a *sanctorum collegium clericorum* (apparently of household clerks) and giving lavishly to monasteries, not only to his favourite St Aignan but to many others, and the gifts which are chiefly emphasised are not of land, but of treasures.[3] His holiness was such that although Helgaud does not quite call him a saint he ascribes the power of healing to him, and it is with this that the continuous tradition of *les rois thaumaturges* begins.[4]

So far, not much like our Ethelred , or so it seems. But we should not be too sure. It is perfectly possible that Ethelred was literate. Nor is it impossible that a talented clerk could have done as good a job for his memory as the Encomiast of Emma did for Cnut's or the author of the *Vita Edwardi* for Edward the Confessor's. It may be that Ethelred had not been generous enough to earn such treatment, but the extent of his gifts to the church remains to be determined; if there was such a *Vita* it could easily have been lost; Helgaud's survives only in the author's manuscript.[5] It would be foolish to exclude the obvious probability that Ethelred as an unsuccessful king was one whom no one sought to honour. But we should at least bear in mind that kings in this period can look very different in different types of source and that for Ethelred we have some types, but not others.

---

[1] *Helgaud de Fleury, Vie de Robert le Pieux*, ed. R. H. Bautier and G. Labory (Paris, 1965).

[2] *Ibid.*, p. 60.

[3] *Ibid., passim*, esp. pp. 68, 72, 86, 88, 108.

[4] M. Bloch, *Les rois thaumaturges* (repr., Paris, 1961), pp. 36–41.

[5] For Æthelred's gifts now (1985) see Simon Keynes, *The Diplomas of King Æthelred the Unready 978–1016* (Cambridge, 1980).

There are aspects of Robert's life as described by Helgaud which come closer to Ethelred's. The shadow of murder falls. We learn of twelve men who came to assassinate the king one Easter;[6] though it is Glaber who tells us how a party sent by Fulk Nerra ambushed and killed Robert's friend Hugh of Beauvais before his eyes.[7] It is a reminder that there is nothing special to England or to Ethelred's reign about such incidents as the murder of Æthelm or of the sons of Arngrim.[8] Even the killing of Edward the Martyr was not altogether extraordinary. Richard I of Normandy upon succeeding as a minor to his father William Longsword (murdered at the instigation of Arnoul I of Flanders) was said to have had a narrow escape, if not from being killed, at least from being deliberately crippled.[9] Helgaud is less than open about the king's marital affairs. He counts it for virtue that Robert put away an unnamed woman related to him in the prohibited degrees and describes his married life with Constance with a mixture of unction and *schadenfreude*. That is to say that he does not reveal that the unnamed lady was Robert's second wife, Bertha, and that he says nothing of his first wife, Rozala/Susanna, the widow of Arnoul II of Flanders, to whom, probably old enough to be his mother, Robert was married off within months of her husband's death.[10] Helgaud's suppression of Robert's first marriage recalls the Encomiast's failure to mention that Emma was Ethelred's wife before she was Cnut's and indicates that such unions were not universally regarded as proper. That they took place is an indication of what can readily be seen in Constance's attempts to determine the succession after Robert's death, as in the aftermath of the reigns of Edgar, Ethelred and Cnut (or for that matter of Otto II), the importance in this period of great dowagers.

If two of the striking elements in the prelude to Ethelred's reign, a murder and a dominant dowager, are easy to parallel elsewhere, so too is the third, a royal saint. Such saints seem to be particularly common in the period *c.* 950 to *c.* 1100. Of Ethelred's contemporaries Robert II was regarded as all but a saint, Henry II of Germany did come to be regarded as saint. Then we have St Olaf, Edward the Confessor, St Cnut and his son St Charles the Good. The Encomiast regards Alfred the Atheling as a saint.[11] By Ethelred's reign there was an attempt to get up a cult of Edgar;

[6] Helgaud, *op. cit.*, p. 62.

[7] *Raoul Glaber, Les cinq livres de ses histoires*, ed. M. Prou (Paris, 1886), p. 58.

[8] The circumstances of Æthelm's murder as described by 'Florence of Worcester' resembled those of Ralph's, *Chronicon ex Chronicis*, ed. B. Thorpe (2 vols. 1848–9), i, p. 158.

[9] William of Jumièges, *Gesta Normannorum Ducum*, ed. J. Marx (Rouen and Paris, 1914), pp. 47–8.

[10] Helgaud, *op. cit.*, pp. 92–6, C. Pfister, *Etudes sur le règne de Robert le Pieux* (Bibliothèque de l'École des Hautes Etudes, lxiv (1885)), pp. 41–84.

[11] *Encomium Emmae Reginae*, ed. A. Campbell (Camden Soc., 3rd Ser., lxxii (1949)), p. 44.

similarly in Normandy for William Longsword.[12] Sanctity was a kind of counterpart to violence: Cnut, Charles, Alfred and William, like the young Edward, were all recruited to the noble army of martyrs at the point of the assassin's sword. At the same time royal women who soon came to be regarded as saints were numerous. For example three of Edward the Martyr's fairly close female relations came into this category.[13] There was nothing new about royal saints, men or women. But they seem to be particularly numerous in this period as compared to the Carolingian. For example, though it is easy to find English royal women of the seventh century who were regarded as saints, it is much harder in the ninth. The first such in the tenth century seems to be Edmund's widow Aelfgifu.[14] Ethelred belonged to a generation in which royal persons seem to have been creeping nearer to God, if not in their lives, then in their *Vitae*.

The period seems to have seen a striking number of inventions and translations of saints and relics. Glaber describes a remarkable wave of such in France in 1008, the archbishop of Sens making a good start by finding part of Moses's wand, long lost.[15] In England also there seem to have been a number of inventions and translations and the tract on the resting place of the English saints which Liebermann published reflects just that pride and interest in the range and multiplicity of saints which Helgaud and Glaber show so strongly.[16] Nothing could be more absurd than to claim novelty for such emotions and it is hard to quantify inventions and translations because our knowledge is largely determined by the availability of sources (which, however, in itself tell us something). But Dr Christine Fell in a paper on the English hagiographical tradition has produced an excellent case for there having been a strong revival of hagiographical writing in this period and it looks as if what she describes and what Glaber describes may be part of one

[12] For Edgar see William of Malmesbury, *De Antiquitate Glastoniensis Ecclesiae* in Adam of Domerham, *Historia de Rebus Gestis Glastoniensibus*, ed. T. Hearne (Oxford, 1727), i, pp. 90–91. (I owe this reference and some others to F. Barlow, *The English Church 1000–1066* (1966)). For William Longsword see Dudo of St Quentin, *De Moribus et Actis primorum Normanniae Ducum*, ed. J. Lair (Caen, 1865), p. 208.

[13] *Vita Ædwardi Regis*, ed. F. Barlow (1962), p. xii.

[14] *Two of the Anglo-Saxon Chronicles Parallel*, ed. C. Plummer and J. Earle (2 vols., Oxford, 1892), i, p. 113, *The Chronicle of Æthelweard*, ed. A. Campbell (1962), p. 54.

[15] Glaber, *op. cit.*, pp. 68–71.

[16] F. Liebermann, *Die Heiligen Englands* (Hanover, 1889). I understand Mr D. Rollason is shortly to publish his conclusions on the date of this work. The earliest mss are of the earlier eleventh century, N. F. Ker, *Catalogue of Manuscripts containing Anglo-Saxon*, (Oxford, 1957), nos. 49B, 274, cf. 138. Cf. *Chronicon Abbatiae Ramseiensis*, ed. W. D. Macray (Rolls Ser. 1886), pp. 114–5, *Chronicon Monasterii de Abingdon*, ed. J. Stevenson (2 vols. Rolls Ser., 1858), ii, pp. 280–81, M. Biddle in *Tenth Century Studies*, ed. D. Parsons (1975), pp. 136–7.

movement.[17] As in this so in other ways England seems to fit into a wider pattern, how neatly one cannot tell because of the difficulty of distinguishing between differences in circumstances and differences in sources. For example in considering the 'anti-monastic reaction' it would seem unwise altogether to lose sight of the anti-monastic reaction in France most strikingly expressed by Adalberon of Laon in his poem attacking the Cluniacs, luxurious, grasping, led to battle by their king Odilo.[18] Other questions easily suggest themselves. Is not the legislation of the later years of Ethelred similar in some respects to that produced abroad in connection with the Peace of God? Would it not be more helpful in attempting to understand Dunstan to conisder how far he was like a great continental prelate such as Adalberon of Rheims rather than to repeat how far he seems unlike Ethelwold?

It is easy to ask questions. One way of getting on to a more solid footing is to consider the Chronicle of Æthelweard. This was, as is well-known, written early in the reign of Ethelred for Matilda, granddaughter of Otto I and to whom Æthelweard was distantly related.[19] It is important both as evidence for fairly close connection between England and north Germany at this period and in showing how Æthelweard's interests correspond to those of others elswhere. Comparison with the work of Widukind is particularly suggestive. Widukind was a monk of Corvey, some seventy five miles from Essen. He wrote his *Historia Saxonum* for Matilda, abbess of Quedlinburg a decade or so before Æthelweard wrote his history for Matilda's half-niece. In both works the presence of the noble lady is marked. Each of Widukind's three books had a dedication and a poem of praise for Matilda; each of Æthelweard's four books begins with a separate, though less grand, dedication to *his* Matilda.[20] Each is trying to describe

---

[17] C. E. Fell, 'Edward King and Martyr and the Anglo-Saxon Hagiographic Tradition', *Ethelred the Unready, Papers from the Millenary Conference*, edited by David Hill, (British Archaeological Reports, British Series 59, 1978), pp. 1–13.

[18] G. A. Hückel, 'Les poèmes satiriques d'Adalberon', *Bibliothèque de la Faculté des Lettres de l'Université de Paris*, xiii (1901), pp. 49 sqq.

[19] Ed. A. Campbell, *op. cit.* It is clear (p. 1) that Æthelweard had sent at least one letter to Matilda and had received at least one from her before he started to write. L. Whitbread has conjectured that the account of Otto II's campaign of 982 in the C version of the Anglo-Saxon Chronicle may have derived from a communication from Matilda to Æthelweard, including as it does a note of the death of their relative Otto of Swabia, 'Æthelweard and the Anglo-Saxon Chronicle', *Engl. Hist. Rev.* lxxiv (1959), pp. 577–89. The evidence is no more than circumstantial, but it is in any case of interest that the C version should contain an account of this campaign, which, if grossly misleading in reporting Otto as victorious, is fairly detailed and appears, as Whitbread (pp. 577–9) points out, to have been incorporated in the Chronicle before news of Otto's death in December 983 had arrived.

[20] W. Wattenback and R. Holtzmann, *Deutschlands Geschichtsquellen im Mittelalter*, i (Cologne and Graz, 1967), pp. 26–34.

the history of his people from its origins, with particular emphasis on the glories of the dynasty now ruling. Æthelweard seems occasionally to modify the vernacular chronicle which was his principal source in ways which suggest a somewhat different view of kings and of kingship from that of its authors. He gives an account of Alfred's services to learning, as the Chronicle does not, and while, in describing the accession of Edward the Elder the Chronicle simply says *feng Eadweard his sunu to rice*, he says *coronatur ipse stemate regalia primatis electis*, a statement which recent research on the coronation *ordo* suggests may not have been anachronistic.[21] There is other evidence for an interest in history in England at this time. The one copy of Asser's life of Alfred which is known to have survived till modern times seems to have been written in Ethelred's reign, possibly for the royal nunnery at Shaftesbury.[22] Nor were such interests confined to England and Germany. For example Dudo of St Quentin's history of the dukes of Normandy was written not long after 1015 and reflects interests and aims broadly similar to those of Widukind and Æthelweard. (It was written for Ethelred's wife's uncle and dedicated to Adalberon of Laon.)

Æthelweard's connection with Essen is part of a larger cultural relationship between England and parts of Germany. It is not possible to be sure how extensive this was, for the fragmentary evidence is capable of very varied interpretation. Perhaps the most striking fragment is the fact that one of the oldest manuscripts of the Old Saxon Biblical epic, the *Heliand*, was possibly written in England in the late tenth century and has certainly been here since about that time.[23] A

[21] *Op. cit.*, p. 51, Plummer and Earle, *op. cit.*, i, pp. 92–3, cf. C. E. Hohler, 'Some Service Books of the Later Saxon Church', *Tenth Century Studies, op. cit.*, pp. 67–9. (It is also of interest that Æthelweard calls Offa *vir mirabilis* (p. 24) – not the Chronicle's line by any means.)

[22] Shaftesbury had been founded by Alfred and regarded itself, quite likely rightly, as having been given a hundred hides by him Asser, *Life of King Alfred* ed. W. H. Stevenson (new impr. Oxford, 1959), p 98, A. J. Robertson, *Anglo-Saxon Charters* (Cambridge, 1956), no. XIII (cf. Sawyer, *op. cit.*, no. 357), C. Fell, *Edward, King and Martyr* (Leeds Texts and Monographs, New Ser. 1971), pp. xviii–xix). Humphry Wanley, as reported by Francis Wise, said that the first hand of the, since burned, Cotton Ms. was of *circiter annum domini 1000 vel 1001* (ed. W. H. Stevenson, *op. cit.*, p. xliv, n. 4). What is known of Wanley's methods suggests that he based his observation on comparison with a hand which he knew to be of that date and his '1000 vel 1001' suggests reference to a document dated 1001. Only two Anglo-Saxon charters definitely dated to that year are known and it has been suggested that he based his remark on comparison with Cotton Charter Augustus ii, 22 (*ibid.*, pp. xiv, n. 1, xxxiii, n. 1), the only one of the two to survive as an original. But it is curious that the other charter of this date is the well-known one granting Bradford-on-Avon to Shaftesbury and it is reasonable to entertain the supposition that the original of this survived long enough for Wanley to base his dating on it.

[23] Ker, *op. cit.*, no. 137. At about the same time there was another Old Saxon Biblical poem known in England, for the second version of the Old English *Genesis* is in part a translation of the Old Saxon poem of the same subject.

curious thing is that James, listing the manuscript in the seventeenth century, called it *Liber Regis Canuti*. Nothing about the manuscript as it is now indicates why he should have done so. R. Drögereit argued that the *Heliand* probably originated at Werden.[24] If so this would relate suggestively to Æthelweard's relationship with Essen, for Essen had close links with Werden, just on the opposite bank of the Ruhr. Drögereit's case has been powerfully opposed, though it remains possible that Werden was the home of the poem.[25] In any case Drögereit's account of the other connections or possible connections between Werden, Essen and England is of interest, particularly in relation to the maintenance of Anglo-Saxon cults in Germany (Werden was an Anglo-Saxon foundation of c. 800) and the apparent appearance of specifically Werden cults in south west England in the early eleventh century.[26] There were Continental Saxons in England in this period including, probably, the author of the first life of Dunstan ('B'), and, even if Mr Lapidge is right in reversing Stubbs' careful assessment of the balance of probabilities as in favour of this man's having been a Continental Saxon, 'B' had in any case probably been connected with the Saxon Ebrachar, bishop of Liege 959–71.[27] (This is a reminder that

[24] Drögereit, *Werden und der Heliand* (Essen, 1951), esp. pp. 83–111 and 'Sachsen und Anglesachsen', *Niedersächsisches Jahrb. f. Landesgeschichte*, 21 (1949), esp. pp. 24–62.

[25] B. Bischoff, 'Paläographische Fragen deutscher Denkmaler der Karolingerzeit', *Frühmittelalterliche Studien*, v (1971), pp. 127–9 (I owe this reference to the kindness of Mr [C.] P. Wormald). But see also J. Knight Bostock, *A Handbook on Old High German Literature*, 2nd ed. rev. K. C. King and D. R. McLintock (Oxford, 1976), p. 180).

[26] *Werden und der Heliand*, esp. pp. 108–10, 'Sachsen und Angelsachsen', esp. pp. 27–31. The west-work at Werden has been suggested as a parallel to that of the Old Minster at Winchester – though there were, of course, other comparable west-works overseas (M. Biddle, as at n.16 above, p. 138).

[27] *Memorials of St Dunstan*, ed. W. Stubbs (Rolls Ser. 1874), pp. xi–xxii, M. Lapidge, 'The Hermeneutic Style in the Tenth Century Latin Literature', *Anglo-Saxon England*, iv (1975), p. 81 n. 2. Mr Lapidge's rebuttal of Stubbs depends positively on the Old English rather than Old Saxon spelling 'hearpam' in the phrase 'cytharam suam quam lingua paterna hearpam vocamus' but this hardly serves conclusively to refute Stubb's suggestion (p. xii) that 'The terms "lingua paterna" and "lingua Saxonica" are used more generically for the common tongue of the continental and insular Saxon', granted that no great weight can be attached to such a choice of spelling in a manuscript tradition transmitted in all probability via Anglo-Saxon scribes. Negatively his case depends on two instances to refute Stubb's opinion that if the author is insular it is surprising that he should call himself 'vilis Saxonum indigens', 'a form which is scarcely ever used by an English writer without some qualifying limitation as in Angul-Saxones, West Saxones or Orientales Saxones' (p. xiii). Two instances hardly suffice, especially when one is from a much earlier source and the other is an exceptional instance from Æthelweard who in general *does* use *Saxones* to indicate either Continental Saxons, or Saxons in the invasion period. It is noteworthy that he even calls the West Saxons *Occidentales Angli*, though this involves departing from usages of the the vernacular chronicle which he was following, e.g. pp. 18, 28, 32, 35, 40. For the connection with Ebrachar see *Memorials*, pp. 385–8. Cf. Barlow, *The English Church, 1000–1066*, pp. 16–17.

the question of relations with Saxony at this time is complicated by there having been Saxon bishops in Lotheringia, e.g. Volkmar, abbot of Werden 971–74, bishop of Utrecht 977–90.[28])

Manuscripts, cults and poems are one thing, the realities of power another. To ask such very simple questions as 'In what sense could or did Ethelred have a foreign policy?' or 'How continuously was he in contact with foreign powers and manoevring to gain what he could from them?' is to realise how wide are the gaps in our knowledge. The Anglo-Saxon Chronicle says virtually nothing of the involvements of English kings with their Continental neighbours. Sparse though its record is for much of the tenth century it is still surprising how it is silent on events which one would have expected to seem of great importance to contemporaries. Thus it provides no contemporary account of the series of marriages of Edward the Elder's daughters to the greatest potentates in Europe, nor for that matter of the marriage of Alfred's daughter Ælfthryth to Baldwin II of Flanders.[29] It is not as if some of these marriages did not have political consequences. Athelstan sheltered his nephew the later Louis IV, played an important part in his accession to the French throne in 936, and sent a fleet to help him in 939.[30] His brother Edmund threatened to intervene against Hugh the Great on behalf of Louis in 946.[31] Otto I was heavily involved in the affairs of France at this time and it was probably in connection with this crisis that the two embassies to Edmund from the *regnum oriens*, presumably Germany, came, which are mentioned in the first life of Dunstan.[32] One of them came to put what Stubbs calls a 'matrimonial proposition'. That these embassies are known only through incidental references in a saint's life is a reminder of how much diplomatic activity there may have been of which we know nothing. It is likely, for example, that such activity lies behind the commercial privileges which 'the men of the Emperor' are found enjoying in Ethelred's fourth law-code.[33]

---

[28] *Werden und der Heliand*, p. 108. (Arnoul II of Flanders, for whose important English contacts see below, was partly Saxon, for his mother Matilda was the daughter of Hermann Billung.)

[29] The reference to Edith's marriage to Otto I in the 'Mercian Register' is almost certainly simply the product of a guess by a later copyist, *The Anglo-Saxon Chronicle*, ed. D. Whitelock, D. C. Douglas and S. I. Tucker (2nd impr. 1965), p. 68, no. 9. The C version does refer to this marriage in its annal for 982; see n. 19 above.

[30] F. M. Stenton, *Anglo-Saxon England* (3rd edn, 1971), pp. 346–7.

[31] *Ibid.*, p. 360; R. Holtzmann, *Geschichte der Sachsischen Kaiserzeit* (2 vols. reprint, Munich, 1971), i pp. 128–30; Richer, *Historiarum Libri IIII*, ed. G. Waitz (Hanover, 1877), pp. 64–5.

[32] *Memorials* . . . pp. 23, 46, xvi.

[33] A. J. Robertson, *The Laws of the Kings of England from Edmund to Henry I* (Cambridge, 1925). (Similarly with the privileges of the men from Normandy, France and elsewhere.) For a suggestion about who 'the men of the Emperor' may have been, Drögereit, 'Sachsen und Angelsachsen', p. 54.

That such privileges could be treated for at a high level we know from Cnut's letter of 1027.[34] Another instance of an embassy to England known of only by a chance survival is that which Arnoul of Flanders (on balance probably Arnoul II (964–88)) mentions in a letter to Dunstan as about to be despatched.[35] So, in considering Ethelred's reign and mis-adventures, it is prudent to bear in mind that they may have a lost European and diplomatic dimension.

The actual evidence for Ethelred's relations with powers other than the Danes and the Normans amounts to one sentence of Ralph Glaber's. He says that Ethelred, Rudolph of Burgundy and Sancho of Navarre sent gifts to Robert the Pious and sought his help.[36] It would undoubtedly have made sense for Ethelred to have sought Robert's help, not least because of Robert's close relationship with Richard II of Normandy. England had at least one steady stream of relationship with Robert's dominions through the connection between Fleury and the monasteries founded by Oswald. Abbo of Fleury was both well-known in England and a prominent figure at Robert's court. A good example of the maintenance of the link with Fleury is that, during the crisis of Edward the Martyr's reign, Germanus, abbot of Winchcombe, once a monk of Fleury, returned for a period to his old monastery.[37] But of the details of Ethelred's relationship with France and with Robert we can recover nothing.

Where we can recover something is in relation to Normandy. The Anglo-Saxon Chronicle tells us that the Danish fleet was in Normandy in 1000, of Ethelred's marriage to Richard II's sister Emma in 1002 and then of Ethelred's flight to Normandy in 1014.[38] This account can be filled out somewhat from other sources. The agreement of 991 between

---

[34] Robertson, *Laws* . . . pp. 148–9.

[35] *Memorials*, p. 360; for the date see P. Grierson, 'Relations between England and Flanders before the Norman Conquest', *Trans. Royal Hist. Soc.* 4th Ser. xxiii (1941), p. 91, n. 5.

[36] Glaber, *op. cit.*, p. 59.

[37] *Chronicon Abbatiae Ramseiensis*, p. 73, D. Knowles, C. N. L. Brooke and V. C. M. London, *The Heads of Religious Houses in England and Wales 940–1216*, (Cambridge, 1972), p. 78. The important sacramentary, Orleans Ms. 127, produced at Winchcombe before the end of the tenth century and later at Fleury, which had crossed the Channel by 1009, is probably a relic of the link between the two houses, D. Gremont and Fr. Donnat, 'Fleury, Le Mont Saint-Michel et l'Angleterre à la fin du Xe siècle . . .', *Millénaire Monastique du Mont Saint-Michel*, i, ed. J. Laporte (1966), pp. 751–93, N. R. Ker, *Medieval Libraries of Great Britain* (2nd ed. 1964), p. 199. Manuscripts provide other evidence for Englishmen on the Continent at this period; thus it seems likely that *c.*1000 an itinerant Anglo-Saxon was responsible for illuminating manuscripts at Fleury, St Bertin and elsewhere, A. Boutemy, 'Un monument capital de l'enluminure anglo-saxonne, le manuscrit 11 de Boulougne-sur-Mer', *Cahiers de Civilisation Médievale*, i (1958), pp. 179–82, cf. F. Wormald, *English Drawings of the Tenth and Eleventh Centuries* (1952), pp. 73–4, no. 45.

[38] Plummer and Earle, *op. cit.*, i, pp. 133, 134, 145.

Ethelred and Richard II made, according to the letter of John XV's in which is preserved, at the instigation of the pope and with the aid of a papal legate (Leo, abbot of St Boniface) relates to circumstances of which otherwise nothing would be known. Ethelred and Richard agreed to be at peace and not to shelter one another's enemies.[39] Were it not for this document we should not even know that they had been at enmity. And why should John XV have intervened to make peace between England and Normandy? A possible guess is that it had something to do with the troubles over the see of Rheims which broke out after the death of Adalberon in 989. The dates would fit well enough. Hugh Capet's ambassadors left for Rome to seek help against Arnoul in July 990. It was clear by the autumn that they were not going to get it. If John had then sent Leo north of the Alps (as he used him on another mission in connection with the Rheims dispute in 992) there would have been time to have reached Ethelred by Christmas, when we know him to have done so. All the same one would have thought that John's interest at this time by no means lay in helping Hugh's ally Richard to make peace with England.[40]

The next piece of additional evidence is provided by William of Jumièges, writing in about 1075. He describes the defeat of an English invasion of the Cotentin aimed at capturing Richard II, putting the date not long after Emma's marriage to Ethelred in 1002.[41] As often with William's work it is hard to know quite what to make of what he says. It would be imprudent to go much further than did Sir Frank Stenton in his account of the passage: 'There was a tradition in Normandy that . . .'[42] But one can edge somewhat nearer to belief. That the Cotentin as the most Danish part of Normandy might have been the right part to invade and that the Nigel who is described as leading resistance was a real man in the appropriate place does not get us much further.[43] William's description of the Anglo-Saxon

---

[39] *Memorials*, pp. 397–8. For (slightly later) references to Norman exiles in England see L. Musset, 'Relations et échanges d'influences dans l'Europe du Nord-Ouest (X^e– XIe siècles)', *Cahiers d'Histoire Médiévale*, i (1958), p. 76. I regret that I have not seen R. L. Graeme Ritchie, *The Normans in England before Edward the Confessor* (Exeter, 1948).

[40] F. Lot, *Etudes sur le règne de Hugues Capet et la Fin de Xe siècle* (Bibliothèque de L'Ecole des Hautes Etudes, (Paris, 1903), pp. 14–30, 83–91, 249–65 (pp. 100–102, 103, 115 for later missions of Leo's).

[41] *Gesta Normannorum Ducum*, pp. 76–77. A. Campbell, *Encomium*, p. xlii suggests that the date indicated by William is wrong and that the incident probably belongs to the period of hostility implied by the treaty of 991; but we do not know enough of the course of relations between England and Normandy to judge what is plausible and what not. Sudden reversals of policy were in any case common enough in the politics of this period.

[42] F. M. Stenton, *Anglo-Saxon England* (1971), p. 397.

[43] L. Delisle, *Histoire du château . . . de Saint-Sauveur-le-Vicomte* (1867), p. 2. The landing seems to have been near Val-de-Saire.

expedition is a shade more helpful. He says that Ethelred ordered a very large number of ships to put to sea and a large number of *milites* from his whole kingdom to join the fleet, appropriately equipped with helmets and hauberks, on a day he ordained. The way in which the collection of the fleet and the summons to the army are described separately recalls the Chronicle annals for 999 ('the king . . . determined they should be opposed by a naval force and also by a land force') and for 1000 ('the king went into Cumberland and ravaged nearly the whole of it . . . and his ships went out round Chester').[44] The reference to helmets and hauberks recalls the annal for 1008: 'The king ordered . . . a helmet and a corselet from [every] eight hides'.[45] Granted these similarities and that the Cotentin expedition would represent the same kind of forward policy as that of 1000, it seems reasonable to regard the story as at least something more than an empty tradition.

William's next possibly hard piece of information comes in a longish, though demonstrably inaccurate, account of the Danish wars in England from the massacre of St Brice's Day (which could, incidentally, be regarded as an indication of English administrative efficiency – what other king of the time could have organised simultaneous massacres in several places on the same day?) up to 1014. He says that at one stage Swegn came from northern England, with a few men, to seek peace with Richard. He got it and it was agreed that whatever the Danes captured would be taken to Normandy for sale and that wounded Danes would be tended in Normandy.[46] There is no other evidence about this; though it is certainly true that the Danes needed somewhere to sell their booty. Compare the E version of the Chronicle for 1048: 'and then they went East to Baldwin's country and sold whatever they had got from their raid.'[47] The next possible shred of evidence comes from Henry of Huntingdon who says that in 1009 Ethelred sent to Richard asking for his advice and help.[48] It is plausible enough that he did and the story is made the more plausible by Huntingdon's just stating it as a bare fact without any attempt to weave it into a larger tale. There are one or two other suggestive remarks in Continental sources. Dudo, writing at about the end of Ethelred's reign puts into the mouth of one of Richard I's enemies the words 'The English also are obediently subject to Richard'.[49] Doubtless they never had been; but that Dudo should have put this statement in his book is a hint that there was more to Anglo-Norman relations than we know. Glaber, writing a

---

[44] Plummer and Earle, *op. cit.*, p. 133.
[45] *Ibid.*, p. 138. (Translation, Whitelock, Douglas and Tucker.)
[46] *Op. cit.*, p. 80. Cf. A. Campbell, *Encomium*, p. xlii, n. 4.
[47] Plummer and Earle, *op. cit.*, p. 171.
[48] *Historia*, ed. T. Arnold (Rolls Ser. 1879), p. 176.
[49] Ed. Lair, *op. cit.*, p. 265.

little later, gives an account of the accession and deeds of Cnut; he emphasises the close relations between Cnut and Richard II and says that during much of Cnut's reign if any crisis threatened the duke of Rouen a numerous army was brought to his aid from over the sea.[50] It is obvious that most of the sources which supplement the account of Anglo-Norman relations which appears in the Anglo-Saxon Chronicle are of mixed and doubtful value. The sum of what they suggest is more important and more credible than any particular scrap of alleged information they proffer. It is, that involved in Ethelred's troubles with the Danes may be a complex relationship with Normandy most of the details of which are lost, but whose course could have been significant in the determination of events.

The history of the connection between England and Normandy can be taken a little further on the ecclesiastical side. The first reform of the Norman monasteries came at the same time as and under some of the same influence as that in England.[51] Gerard of Brogne's disciple Mainard became abbot of St Wandrille's in 960 and in 966, having expelled a community of canons from Mont Saint-Michel, became abbot there. St Ouen seems to have been reformed at about the same time and this is probably reflected in a begging letter to Edgar from the community there.[52] They pray for him, they say, just as they do for their own illustrious count, night and day. They have heard of his generosity to all widows, orphans, churches and those in need. They are themselves a church in need of restoration and invite a subscription. (There is a similar letter to Edgar from the church of St Geneviève at Paris, thanking him for a gift and asking for more.[53]) A quite different connection with St Ouen appears in a post-Conquest story that Edgar had actually bought the body of that saint from four clerks who had brought it to England; he had at first found it hard to believe that it was genuine, but upon two test cures being performed, concluded the transaction.[54]

[50] Ed. Prou, *op. cit.*, p. 29.

[51] J. Laporte, 'Les origines du monachisme dans la province de Rouen', *Révue Mabillon*, xxxi (1941), pp. 49–52.

[52] *Memorials*, pp. 363–4; it is not clear from the letter whether it is from the reformed or the unreformed community. The former seems more probable and if so this letter helps to give some indication of the date of the reform of St Ouen about which there is some doubt, Laporte, p. 52, J. F. Lemarignier, *Les privilèges d'exemption des abbayes normandes* (Paris, 1937), pp. 28–29, 38–39.

[53] *Memorials*, pp. 366–8.

[54] *Edmeri Cantuariensis Cantoris Nova Opuscula de Sanctorum Veneratione*, ed. A. Wilmart, *Rev. des Sciences Réligieuses*, xv (1935), pp. 362–4. For the cult of St Ouen at Canterbury see W. Levison, *England and the Continent in the Eighth Century* (Oxford, 1946), p. 213. It is worth noticing that the charter by which Edward the Confessor grants land to St Ouen (Sawyer, *Anglo-Saxon Charters . . .* , no. 1015) although described by Dr D. Mathew as unimpeachable, *The Norman Monasteries and their English Possessions* (Oxford, 1962), pp. 143, 24, had in fact been impeached by Levison, *England*

continued

Another aspect of the ecclesiastical relationship between England and Normandy has recently been drawn attention to in studies by Mr Lapidge and Professor Musset. In publishing three Latin poems, which he showed to be from Aethelwold's school at Winchester, Mr Lapidge has drawn attention to the strong similarities between one of them in particular, the *Altercatio*, and satiric poems written by Garnier of Rouen, who was in the circle of Ethelred's brother-in-law, Robert, Archbishop of Rouen.[55] He concluded that although the resemblances are too close to be coincidental it is impossible to conjecture what the relationship was. Musset has recently shown that the resemblances are even greater than Lapidge had observed and is the more strongly inclined to believe in a direct relationship.[56] He has drawn attention to further evidence for relations between England and certainly Gaul, probably Normandy, in this period in the account of the miracles of St Swithin by Lantfrith (who was certainly in the circle in which the Anglo-Latin poems in question were written and may have written one of them himself). Lantfrith says that the fame of St Swithin extends beyond the sea and gives three examples: one is of a robber, in prison and in chains in Gaul, awaiting execution who heard from some merchants that there was a saint called Swithin *noviter inventus in transmarinis partibus*, invoked him, and got out. The second is of a woman who was ill and who took what proved to be the reliable advice of an English priest who was passing through, to invoke St Swithin. The third is of a woman beset by demons, who went from Gaul to Swithin's shrine in England and was cured there.[57] A particularly interesting reference to the English relationship to a Norman church comes in an account of the life of William of Volpiano in the chronicle of St Bénigne at Dijon. In describing William's reform at Fécamp it says that among his community there was an Englishman, of noble, indeed royal, stock, called Clement who was so frequently visited by men from his country that he removed himself to Dijon in order to serve God in peace.[58] This cannot be dated more closely than to 1001–1030 and it could be that the Englishmen who pestered him were exiles

continued
and the Continent . . . , p. 212 n. 2, who detected elements in it more characteristic of the tenth century and in particular of the reign of Edgar.

[55] M. Lapidge, 'Three Latin Poems from Æthelwold's School at Winchester', *Anglo-Saxon England*, i (1972), pp. 85–137, esp. pp. 101–2.

[56] L. Musset, 'Rouen et l'Angleterre vers l'an mille', *Annales de Normandie*, xxiv (1974), pp. 287–90.

[57] *Sancti Swithuni . . . Translatio et Miracula*, ed. E. P. Sauvage, *Analecta Bollandiana*, iv (1885), pp. 399–402. (One of the ways in which wandering Englishmen would have turned up as exiles overseas was as penitential exiles; the existence of *pro forma* letters for such suggests that they could have been numerous, Barlow, *The English Church 1000–1066*, pp. 271–2.)

[58] *Patrologia Latina*, ed. J. P. Migne, cxli, col. 864. (Another reference which I owe to Professor Barlow.)

rather than passing visitors. Fécamp was, of course, the great ducal monastery at this period. It was there, for example, that Robert the Pious spent Ascensiontide with Richard II in 1006; and it was to Fécamp that Cnut gave land in England, explicitly fulfilling a promise made by Ethelred.[59]

The ecclesiastical connections of which we know most are those with Flanders. The role of the great Flemish monasteries is too well-known to dwell on here.[60] Similarly the importance of Flemish and Picard cults in England has been rightly emphasised by Professor Barlow.[61] Further important aspects of the relationships are brought out in correspondence printed by Stubbs which in particular brings out the importance to Flemish monasteries of English patronage.[62] Consider the letters from Flemish abbots to archbishops of Canterbury. The first is from Wido, abbot of Blandinium, to Dunstan and was written between 981 and 986.[63] Wido says he would not have written so soon after sending a messenger to England but he is forced to do so because the crops have failed and he relies on Dunstan's benevolence. The next is from Fulrad, abbot of St Vaast, to Dunstan's successor Æthelgar. He congratulates him upon being made archbishop and says he hopes to find another Dunstan in him.[64] What this means is soon spelled out; he wants a present. Then comes a letter from Odbert, abbot of St Bertin, also to Æthelgar.[65] He thanks him for his promises and points out that the benefactions he has already given will soon be exhausted. More are required. (Notice how quick off the mark these prelates are: Æthelgar was archbishop for only eighteen months, but St Bertin had already got through one benefaction and was after more.) On Sigerics's following Æthelgar as archbishop Odbert wrote straight away.[66] Dunstan, says he, had been a great friend, Æthelgar a greater yet; the implication of what it was up to Sigeric to be is unmistakable. He expresses the hope that Sigeric will stay at St Bertin's on his way to Rome for the pallium. We do not know whether he did or not; but he certainly did not stay there on his way home. It may be that, as Stubbs suggests, he thought Flemish hospitality might prove too expensive a luxury.[67] The most striking thing about these letters is that they suggest not just gift-

---

[59] C. Pfister, *Etudes sur le règne de Robert le Pieux*, p. 212; Sawyer, *Anglo-Saxon Charters*, nos. 940, 982, cf. Mathew, *Norman Monasteries and their English Possessions*, p. 19.

[60] For English relations with Flanders in general, Grierson, 'The Relations between England and Flanders before the Norman Conquest', as at n.35 above, is of great importance.

[61] F. Barlow, *The English Church, 1000–1066*, pp. 19–20.

[62] These are from the collections in British Library Mss Vespasian A XIV (written for Wulfstan II of York) and Tiberius A XV.

[63] *Memorials*, pp. 380–81.

[64] *Ibid.*, pp. 383–4.   [65] *Ibid.*, pp. 384–5.   [66] *Ibid.*, pp. 388–9.

[67] *Ibid.*, pp. 391–5, 389, n. 2.

giving, but continued dependence on the gifts, which the abbots expect
to keep coming. It could be an important thing about Dunstan and his
immediate successors, even perhaps an important thing about English
policy, that major Flemish abbeys seems to much in their patronage.

A notable feature of these letters and other associated correspondence
is the literary art displayed. They are in fancy Latin and four or five of
those to Dunstan are in whole or in part versified. These seem to be
circles in which the hopeful cleric sings for his supper with as much
elaboration and polish as he can muster. The Anglo-Latin documents of
the period and in particular some of the verse show a rather different
side of the late tenth century English church than do its vernacular
productions: they bring out more of the courtly and less of the pastoral.
Considerable store was set by literary accomplishment. The Ramsey
history says that Oswald's nephew, also called Oswald, who was later
abbot, received his early education at Ramsey but was then sent to
Fleury to study letters. It then, for once becomes a contemporary
source, and says that they still had 'in archivis nostris liber eius
versificus, multiformis peritiae ipsius et perspicacis ingenii testis'.[68] The
importance of the Continent as a source for Latin learning in this period
is apparent when one considers how many Latin works at this time and
in the generations immediately following were produced for English
use by foreigners: for example, the B life of Dunstan, written probably
by a Continental Saxon and then sent to Abbo of Fleury to be
improved; the *Vita Sancti Edmundi* also by Abbo, who was a very
talented performer indeed, witness the astonishing triple acrostic verse
to Dunstan. (Characteristically he produced another like it for Otto
III).[69] The miracles of St Swithin were written up by a foreign clerk, the
Encomium Emmae Reginae by yet another. Then in the next generation
there were Goscelin, Folcard and the author of the *Vita Edwardi*.

Our sources are so sparse that they give no more than glimpses even
of ecclesiastical relationships with foreign lands. What they do tell us is
often chiefly valuable as an indication of how little we know. A good
example is a letter in one of the collections printed by Stubbs from an
unknown English ecclesiastic to Arnoul Count of Flanders.[70] This
prelate had had an evangeliary stolen from his monastery by two clerks,
who had sold it to the count for three mancuses. They had by a miracle
owned up and so the letter is sent asking for the return of the book. The
circumstances of their trip to Flanders are explained. They had been
sent to search for a certain girl *captam a Danis vestris*. An interesting
thing here is the reference to Arnulf's Danes. *Vestris* makes it sound as if
they were in his service, not just Danes who happened to be about the

[68] *Chronicon . . . Ramseiensis*, ed. Macray, pp. 159–60.
[69] *Memorials*, pp. 410–12.
[70] *Ibid.*, pp. 361–2.

place. They are not otherwise, I believe, heard of, and their presence could have been an important element in Anglo-Flemish relations. A kind of counterpart in the reference in Ottar the Black's poem on Cnut to Frisians fighting for Edmund Ironside against Cnut at Sherston in 1016.[71]

The letter to Arnoul to which reference has just been made draws attention to two important articles of commerce: holy objects and slaves. The scope of this paper does not afford an opportunity even to sketch the evidence, fairly copious as to range, very sparse as to scale, for English commerce in this period. Still, it is important to emphasise the likelihood that commercial activities formed in various ways, not all obvious, an integral part of the web of relationships which linked the various parts of northern Europe. Many episodes and incidents seem to have a commercial dimension of some kind. For example Ælfeah was martyred at Greenwich in 1012. The Danish fleet was there again in 1013, 1014 and 1016.[72] The name, Greenwich, is suggestive, the *wic* element being in the palatalized form which Ekwall regards as the most likely one to be associated with the meaning 'trading-place'.[73] The nature of the places where the Danish fleet is mentioned as lying suggests that it moored in harbours rather than lay on beaches and this would be specially understandable if the ships were as ornate as the Encomiast of Emma says.[74] In the Chronicle's account of Ælfeah's martyrdom it is said that the Danes got drunk because 'wine from the south had been brought there'.[75] All this suggests that Greenwich may well have been an important trading place. It is therefore of some interest that it was among the places given to St Peter's Ghent by Edgar in 964. When Cnut made a grant of English property to Fécamp and the Confessor one to Mont Saint-Michel each included a *portus* (in the sense of *portus maris*).[77] One may then reasonably wonder whether these monasteries may not have been particularly concerned to own maritime trading-places and reflect what a coup it must have been for Christ Church Canterbury when Cnut gave it Sandwich itself.

Consideration of the murder of the archbishop leads to another chain of Continental connection some of the links in which are probably commercial. One of the best accounts of the atrocity is provided by Thietmar, bishop of Merseburg, in his chronicle.[78] He had, he says,

[71] Trans. D. Whitelock, *English Historical Documents c. 500–1042* (1955), p. 308. I am obliged to Mr M. K. Lawson for this reference.

[72] Plummer and Earle, *op. cit.*, i, pp. 144, 145, 149.

[73] E. Ekwall, *The Old English Wic in Place Names* (Uppsala, 1964).

[74] *Encomium* . . . , I, 4 and II, 4, cf. pp. 94–96.

[75] Plummer and Earle, *op. cit.*, i, p. 142. It is not stated how the wine had got there.

[76] Sawyer, *Anglo-Saxon Charters* . . . , no. 728.

[77] See Sawyer and Mathew as at n. 59 above.

[78] *Thietmari Mersebergensis Episcopi Chronicon*, ed. J. M. Lappenbergh and F. Kurze (Hanover, 1889), pp. 214–5, 218–9.

gained his knowledge of this and of other near-contemporary events in England from an Englishman called Sewald. Thietmar was the grandson of Henry, count of Stade (on the left bank of the Elbe). Another Henry, Thietmar's uncle, succeeded as count. Some of his coins survive and are imitated from those of Ethelred.[79] Another scrap of information links Stade with England. The *Annales Stadenses* under the year 1112 relate the shipwreck there some two generations earlier of people who were *navigantes de Anglia*.[80] Even in the worlds of learning and monasticism commerce played its part. A satirical poem, mentioned earlier, by Garnier of Rouen raises curious possibilities in this regard.[81] He denounces an Irish scholar called Moriuht, and offers an account of his early life. Moriuht had, it is alleged, been captured by the Danes and sold as a slave, sold to a nunnery at a place which may be Corbridge; and there he seduced several nuns. He made off overseas, was taken by the Danes again and sold at an unknown Saxon market, being bought by a widow, who bought him with false money. He seduced her and others. He had finished in Normandy where he set up as a scholar. Clearly, this is satirical travesty; but it has the air of being travesty of the kind of thing which actually happened and the poem ranks as the earliest evidence for the slave-trade in Normandy. No one can tell what is fact and what is farce in such a work. Still, it is an engaging thought that the Scandinavian slave-trade could have worked in such a way as to bring an Irish scholar to the court of Richard II of Normandy. A more certain and more commonplace reminder of the connection between commerce and learning comes from Helgaud.[82] He has very kind words to say about Gauzelin who followed Abbo as abbot of Fleury in 1004. Gauzelin, he says, was very charitable, so much so that one very cold winter, he positively took off his furs and gave them to the poor. This edifying episode not only tells us of the luxury of a great Benedictine house but also, granted that the main sources of furs lay in the far north and east, indicates another possible commercial thread.

These are scraps; indeed a very large part of what evidence there is for the relation between England and North West Europe is scraps. Nearly always much can be made of them, or little. But when the diversity and in some degree the scale of the range of relationships

[79] *Ibid.*, pp. vii–viii, A. Suhle, *Deutsche Münz – und Geldgeschichte* . . . (Berlin, 1964, p. 61). (In the light of Professor Dolley's remarks (*Ethelred the Unready*, as at n.17 above, pp. 125–6) I should say that I do not know whether these imitations are direct or indirect.) Cf. Drögereit, 'Sachsen und Angelsachsen', p. 55, also for the possible implication of English connection in the dedication of a church at Stade to St Pancras.

[80] *Mon. Germ. Hist. Scriptores*, xvi, ed. G. Pertz (Hanover, 1868), pp. 320–21.

[81] See notes 55 and 56 above and L. Musset, 'Le satiriste Garnier de Rouen et son milieu', *Rev du Moyen Age Latin*, x (1954), pp. 237–58.

[82] Helgaud, *op. cit.*, p. 120.

which these limited sources indicate are considered it seems likely that England resembled and was linked with its neighbours to a larger extent and in more important ways than can categorically be proved.[83]

---

[83] *Addendum*. Professsssor Barlow (F. Barlow *et al.*, *Leofric of Exeter* (Exeter, 1972) p. 14 n. 2) draws attention to a litany of the eleventh century which includes an Ethelred among the martyrs, and hints that this might be Ethelred II. However, as Mr M. K. Lawson has pointed out to me, the conjunction of this name with Ethelbert makes it almost certain that a much earlier Kentish prince is intended, cf. e.g. *Symeonis Dunelmensis opera . . .*, i (Surtees Soc. 1868) ed. H. Hinde, pp. 2–8.

Additional Bibliographical Note

Knowledge of many aspects of Ethelred's reign has been increased by Simon Keynes, *The Diplomas of King Æthelred the Unready 978–1016* (Cambridge, 1980). For relations with Germany see K. [J.] Leyser, 'Die Ottonen und Wessex', *Frühmittelalterliche Studien*, xvii (1983), pp. 73–97. Dr Rollason's study of the tract mentioned in n.19 above has been published: D. W. Rollason, 'Lists of Saints' Resting-Places in Anglo-Saxon England', *Anglo-Saxon England*, vii (1978), pp. 61–94. For the role of dowagers see now P. Stafford, *Queens, Concubines and Dowagers in the Early Middle Ages* (1983), pp. 143–74. I should have referred, in relation to royal saints, to Janet Nelson, 'Royal Saints and Early Medieval Kingship', *Studies in Church History*, x (1973), pp. 39–44, for both its observations and its references. There is a new edition of Adalberon's work (p. 194 above): C. Carozzi, ed., *Adalberon de Laon. Poème au Roi Robert*, (Paris, 1979).

5. A fourteenth-century plan of the high altar and east end of the abbey church of St. Augustine, Canterbury. At the far east stood the altar-tomb of Augustine, flanked by those of his immediate successors as archbishop, Laurentius, Mellitus, Justus, Honorius, Deusdedit and Theodore. Other Anglo-Saxon archbishops were buried further west. On the high altar lay 'the books sent by Gregory to Augustine'. The bodies of the early archbishops were moved to these positions in the new Norman church on its completion in the early twelfth century. See p. 210 below. (*Cambridge, Trinity Hall, MS. I, f. 77a*)

13

Some Twelfth-Century Views of the Anglo-Saxon Past*

The greatest advances in the study and understanding of Anglo-Saxon history made before the nineteenth century were those of the twelfth. They were in large measure accomplished by historians working during the reigns of Henry I and Stephen: William of Malmesbury, Henry of Huntingdon and the author traditionally called Florence of Worcester, but whose name was probably John. William and 'Florence' were monks and their work forms part of that flowering of Benedictine historiography which matches the flowering of Benedictine architecture in the generations after the Conquest. The motives of such men in writing of the Anglo-Saxon past have been discussed, with perceptive eloquence, by Sir Richard Southern. He speaks of the 'outrage, resentment and nostalgia' of 'men who had known pre-Conquest England'. We are listening, he says, to 'the voice of a whole generation of literate men who had English ancestors', of monks who found claims and cults, hitherto taken for granted, now threatened and scorned and who thus were driven to the task of 'bringing fragmentary and dispersed material together and extracting from it a story which would impress hostile or indifferent contemporaries'. The historical movement, he maintains, 'drew its inspiration and gained its momentum from the necessities of corporate survival', for what had been brought into question was 'the survival of an ancient monastic culture, a religious and intellectual tradition, and a position in the world'.[1]

There is much that is powerfully suggestive in this view. The consequences of the Conquest were indeed such that threats were posed to the monastic legacy from the Anglo-Saxon past. When Wulfstan II of Worcester, the last survivor of Edward the Confessor's bishops, caused his monk Hemming to put together a cartulary in about 1095 explicitly among his motives was a wish to counter 'the violence of the Normans . . . who have unjustly deprived this holy church' (though it was not of the Normans alone that he thought ill).[2] The ways in which men whom William had put in power in the English church questioned its

---

* This chapter was originally delivered as a Denis Bethell Memorial Lecture.
[1] R. W. Southern, 'Aspects of the European tradition of historical writing: 4, the sense of the past', *Trans Roy His Soc ser 5* 23 (1973) 243–63: 246–9.
[2] ibid., 249–50.

209

traditions must have been alarming indeed: for example, Lanfranc conceived doubts about the sanctity of his predecessors Aelfeah and Dunstan; abbot Walter of Evesham submitted venerable relics of his house to verification by fire; abbot Warin expelled from the church at Malmesbury some of the relics of its saints.[3]

But too much can be made of such episodes. If Lanfranc had his doubts about Aelfeah, in time he came round. True, Professor Brooke has brilliantly suggested how, in his rebuilding of Christ Church Canterbury, the archbishop expressed in architectural form a new, more universal, and less provincially rooted view of the church. 'In the short space of seven years he built a new cathedral to present a new image of the church in which none of the local shrines was visible to obscure the vista of the altar of Christ and the throne of the archbishop'.[4] But then Christ Church by no means forgot its saints and did not have the best hand of saints to play. The trump cards were a few hundred yards away, at St Augustine's; and there the Norman rebuilding was such as to turn the abbey church into a vast shrine to Gregory, Augustine and the early kings and archbishops of Kent. Abbot Scotland and his Norman successors at St Augustine's did not make less of Saxon saints and the Saxon past than their native predecessors had done. They made more of them, almost theatrically so.[5] Abbot Walter of Evesham had indeed had qualms about the, to him unknown, saints of his monastery. But Walter was to find he needed such saints. He was, says the Evesham chronicler, given to new things; although the old abbey church was one of the most beautiful in England, little by little he knocked it down and built anew. Funds, however, ran out and the building work came to a standstill. What should the abbot do but send out a pair of monks to raise money on the stump, equipped with the shrine and relics of St Egwin, previously doubted.[6] In the last resort no abbot, be he never so Norman, could in prudence scorn the saints and holy history of his own monastery.

If defensive nostalgia for the Anglo-Saxon past played a part in the inspiration of the Anglo-Norman historians there are, nevertheless, other motives, by no means less important, to be reckoned with. For monastic historians the threats they had to meet came not only from Norman intruders, but also, and perhaps to a greater extent, from

---

[3] David Knowles, *The monastic order in England* (2nd ed., Cambridge 1966) 119; Margaret Gibson, *Lanfranc of Bec* (Oxford 1978) 171–2.

[4] C. N. L. Brooke, 'Historical writing in England between 850 and 1150', *Settimane di Studio del Centro Italiano di Studi sull'Alto Medioevo* 1711 (1970) 223–47: 238.

[5] For references to the literature see H. M. Taylor and J. Taylor, *Anglo-Saxon architecture* (3 vols., Cambridge 1965–78), i 142–3.

[6] W. D. Macray (ed), *Chronicon Abbatiae de Evesham*, Rolls Series 29 (1863) 55. For the source see Antonia Gransden, *Historical writing in England c. 550 to c. 1307* (London 1974) 111–13.

bishops and their agents, from canons, secular clergy and new orders.[7] The interest of monks in the Anglo-Saxon past was by no means exclusively defensive or negative. It had its positive side; to be seen almost immediately after the Conquest in the ways and the extent to which the re-establishment of monasteries in the North sought to recreate what had been there in the distant past.[8] Furthermore the interests of such a monk-historian as William of Malmesbury extended far beyond subjects which were in some way related to monasteries and to monasticism. Such writings on Anglo-Saxon history as his must be considered as part of a wider movement which included important works by men who were not monks. Pre-eminent among these secular authors was Henry of Huntingdon who devoted two thirds of his *Historia Anglorum* to the period before 1066. Henry's work (he was writing at the end of Henry I's reign and during Stephen's) is a powerful corrective to any view which puts too exclusive an emphasis on yearning for a lost part as a motive for writing about the Anglo-Saxons. Henry could have been partly English (though there is no direct evidence for this) but the patron for whom he wrote was Alexander bishop of Lincoln, and among the emotions which affected that prelate's hard head and not always soft heart, it is unlikely that nostalgia for the Anglo-Saxons worked strongly. Gaimar's *L'Estoire des Engleis* gives further cause for thought. Gaimar was a secular clerk. His work is the first history ever to have been written in French. For the most part it is an indefatigable rendering into French verse of the *Anglo-Saxon Chronicle*. It was written, shortly before 1140, for Constance Fitzgilbert, the wife of an Anglo-Norman land-owner in Lincolnshire.[9] Clearly, by early in Stephen's reign interest in Anglo-Saxon history extended beyond monasteries, beyond the church and beyond the wish to preserve the memory of a lost world.

Dr Thomson is surely right in emphasising that the flowering of historiography in early twelfth century England must be seen as part of wider intellectual movements, and as involving many strands of the intellectual history of the twelfth century. One of these is the classicizing tendency described by Sir Richard Southern in another admirable paper: the urge to write histories in a style resembling that of Sallust, works of art, sources of pleasure, stirring and entertaining in their use of fine language.[10] William of Malmesbury says he sought to savour his work

[7] Martin Brett, 'John of Worcester and his contemporaries', R. H. C. Davis and J. M. Wallace-Hadrill (ed), *The writing of history in the middle ages: essays presented to Richard William Southern* (Oxford 1981) 101–26: 125–26.

[8] Knowles, *Monastic order*, chapter 9.

[9] A. Bell (ed), Anglo-Norman Text Society 14–16 (1966); M. D. Legge, *Anglo-Norman literature and its background* (Oxford 1963) 27–36.

[10] R. W. Southern, 'Aspects of the European tradition of historical writing: 1, The classical tradition from Einhard to Geoffrey of Monmouth', *Trans Roy Hist Soc ser 5* 20 (1970) 173–96.

'with Roman salt'.[11] Henry of Huntingdon begins his with a quotation from Horace.[12] These were fit contemporaries for Henry of Blois, bishop of Winchester, with his collection of Roman statues, 'the Cicero of our day' as a contemporary was kind enough to call him.[13]

These historians did not, however, seek principally to entertain. They sought to inform, and not least by clarity in exposition. The creation of an ordered framework is of the essence of their work and among the weightiest of their contributions. Consider, for example, Henry of Huntingdon's intelligent and original re-arrangement of early Anglo-Saxon history. Most medieval writers were, and not a few modern writers have been, content to construct a narrative by interweaving Bede and the Anglo-Saxon Chronicle. Many problems of exposition arise in this; for the number of the early kingdoms and the complications of their conversions make the sequence and pattern of events hard to follow. Anyone who reads Bede from Book III onwards, anyone who tries to lecture on early Anglo-Saxon history, finds difficulties here.

Huntingdon faces them head on. What he does is this. In Book II of *Historia Anglorum* he describes the beginning of each of the Anglo-Saxon kingdoms. At the end of the book he sums up, telling the reader that he has taken the history of kings and kingdoms up to the time of the Conversion. In the next book he will, he says, explain which preachers, by the objurgation of whom, by what miracles and teaching, converted which kings, in what order, to the faith of our Lord. He is a very orderly writer and one who takes methodical pains to let the reader know exactly where he is. Thus, before he closes Book II he says that he does not think it will be *taediosus* to the reader, but rather, on the contrary, *apertior et gratior*, if he briefly recapitulates the names of all the kings of England, which up to this point in his book have been *confuse dispersa*.[14] He duly does it, providing a list of kings for each kingdom.

Then, on to Book III. Huntingdon begins, as usual, by making sure that the reader knows where he is going. I am about, he says, to deal with the conversion of England. He then lists seven crucial royal conversions; and thereafter sets off to deal with each in detail. He uses extensive extracts from Bede; but Bede has been rearranged. Huntingdon has taken all the pieces of the *Ecclesiastical History* which deal with conversions and has arranged them under kingdoms. Each new section begins with a clear indication that it *is* a new section, e.g. 'Secunda pars incipit qua aperitur quomodo rex et populus Estsexe . . .' and so on. Book III is entirely devoted to conversions; ecclesiastical

[11] William Stubbs (ed), *Gesta Regum*, Rolls Series 90 (2 vols, 1887–9) i 2.
[12] Thomas Arnold (ed), *Historia Anglorum*, Rolls Series 74 (1883) 1.
[13] Lena Voss, *Heinrich von Blois, Bischof von Winchester 1129–71* (Berlin 1932) 135.
[14] Arnold, 63–4.

history has been completely separated from secular. At the end of the book Huntingdon reminds his reader that this is what has been done but that in the next book he will return to the *contextum* of the kings of England. So indeed he does: end of Book II, death of Centwine; beginning of Book IV, reign of his successor Caedwalla.[15]

I have dwelt on an example of Henry of Huntingdon's methods of exposition because it is so significant that he faces historians' problems as well as historical problems. His book is in part a work of imagination, especially in its battle pieces; at what may be a deeper level it is one with a serious and an almost despairing moral purpose.[16] No less significant is the extent to which it reads as a text-book or a set of careful lectures. Its author is often anxious to sort out, reorder, clarify, to make sure that the reader knows where he has got to and where he is going. It is characteristic of Huntingdon that it was he who introduced the idea of the Heptarchy which so many generations have found so useful, if in part so misleading, in seeking a thread to follow through the early English centuries.[17]

If Henry of Huntingdon's *Historia* is in large measure a work of exposition, the historian working at Worcester (whom I shall call, for convenience, 'Florence') wrote something much more like a work of reference. He produced, as part of a world chronicle, an annalistic history of England, drawing not only on Bede and the Anglo-Saxon Chronicle but on much more beside. Modern scholars often chiefly value his work for its use of sources which no longer survive and for them the great desideratum is its dissection to reveal what these were. But the most significant thing about his book is not so much his use of sources now lost, as the width of the range of sources upon which he drew. It is important that he was capable of overtly contrasting his sources when they differed. Thus under 672 he points out that the English chronicle gives an account of what happened in Wessex after the death of Cenwalh which differs markedly from that of Bede.[18] Similar concern is to be found on occasion in William of Malmesbury's works.[19] For example, he notes that the Chronicle and Bede give different lengths for the reign of Ethelbert of Kent. In such matters

[15] Arnold, 77, 63, 103, 105. The division between Book III and Book IV appears misplaced in Arnold's edition, 103.

[16] N. F. Partner, *Serious entertainments: the writing of history in twelfth-century England* (Chicago 1977) 11–50 provides the best account of Henry of Huntingdon and draws attention to the orderliness mentioned above; I am much indebted to her.

[17] Arnold, 64–66. The Heptarchy according to the *Oxford English dictionary* s.v. first appears *eo nomine* in print in the work of Lambarde, 1576, twenty years before Savile first printed Huntingdon, whose work must, however, have been known in manuscript; cf. Arnold's introduction, xxxvi–xliii.

[18] Benjamin Thorpe (ed), *Chronicon ex chronicis* (2 vols, London 1848–9) 30.

[19] Rodney M. Thomson, 'William of Malmesbury as historian and man of letters', *J. Ecclesiast Hist* 29 (1978) 387–413: 393.

these historians are intellectually in advance of their predecessors. Bede, for example, never, in his historical works, contrasts two sources; but, when he had conflicting evidence, as not infrequently he must have had, worked either by silent conflation, or by silent discarding.

One of the most valuable and original features of 'Florence's' work is the extensive collection of reference materials which he provides.[20] First, he has lists of *nomina episcoporum* for all the English sees. These are not simply cobbled together; his accounts of, in particular, the East Anglian and the Mercian sees embody research. There follows his most striking effort: *Regalis prosapia Anglorum*. In this he sets out the genealogies of all the English royal families. A notable feature is the extent to which he had, partly by drawing on hagiographic materials, been able to include the *wives* of a number of kings. He sets out his materials in the diagrammatic form of family trees rather as we are familiar with them. He next provides outlines of the history of the five principal kingdoms, lists the shires and bishoprics which in his own day occupied the lands of each of those kingdoms, and provides a summary account of the shires in each diocese. His is indeed a work of reference. His table and trees are not just materials for the *Handbook of British Chronology*; they are its true ancestor.

William of Malmesbury was perhaps the greatest, and is certainly the most admired, of the Anglo-Norman historians. His account of early Anglo-Saxon history is not in all respects so thorough as those of Huntingdon and 'Florence' but presents some of the same features: a wrestling effort to order chaotic circumstances, care to establish what and where the early kingdoms were. William's *History of Glastonbury* is perhaps the most remarkable piece of historical research of its day.[21] Particularly interesting is chapter 71, *Nomina abbatum Glastonie*, for here he sought to tabulate the names, years of ordination and lengths of abbacy for all the abbots since the foundation of the abbey. Here as with 'Florence's' lists and tables we are provided with the means of looking things up. Here is the ancestor of Knowles, Brooke and London, *The Heads of Religious Houses*.

Not the least of William of Malmesbury's triumphs was his *Gesta pontificum*. This account of the histories of all the dioceses of England stands out as a methodical account of the ecclesiastical history of a whole country, of a kind previously attempted for no other. It is also, up to a point, a topographical survey. Most of our earliest descriptions of English cities come from William, and very interesting they are too.

---

[20] This material is printed in the edition of 'Florence's' work by Henry Petrie, *Monumenta historica Britannica* i (London 1848) 627–34, but in 'Florence's' autograph manuscript (Corpus Christi College, Oxford, MS 157) his tables and trees appear not at the end of his work, as Petrie prints them, but at the beginning (pp 37–54); and are very beautifully drawn up and decorated.

[21] John Scott (ed), *The early history of Glastonbury* (Woodbridge 1981).

To take but one example, his account of Carlisle, in particular of the Roman ruins there, including a hall still standing in defiance of the weather and the demolition gangs; this is the only description from this period of Roman buildings still standing in England and nearly the only one which gives an idea of the crucial date lacking for most of the cities of Roman Britain: the date of demolition.[22] Such topographical arrangement and topographical interests appear elsewhere in this period. The (largely unprinted) hagiographical section of Henry of Huntingdon's *Historia, De miraculis,* is in part topographically arranged.[23] It is thought that there may once have existed a work by Conrad, archdeacon of Salisbury, *Descriptio utriusque Britaniae,* which sounds as if it could have been a precursor, for other areas, of Gerald of Wales's works on Wales and on Ireland.[24]

Taken together the works of the Anglo-Norman historians are hard to parallel in other lands. Of course there is no difficulty in finding examples abroad of a classicizing style: one does not have to read much further into Thietmar of Merseburg than into Henry of Huntingdon to find a quotation from Horace.[25] Topographical interest; yes, one can find that, for example (earlier) in Flodoard's account of the Roman antiquities of Rheims.[26] Extensive annalistic compilations; yes indeed, take for example Marianus to whom 'Florence' owed so much. But no other land produced such a group of works thought out in such advanced ways – one could almost say such modern ways. Nowhere else is there, for example, such comprehensiveness in the topographical approach. It is one thing to give a history of the bishops of one see, as Adam of Bremen did, quite another to provide histories of all the sees in a kingdom, as William of Malmesbury did. Why was English historiography so outstanding? The answers must be sought in the needs of the day; the problems facing those who sought to meet them; and the intellectual equipment with which historians faced the problems.

The learned men of Anglo-Saxon England had left their country very ill-provided with histories. No work of history of any weight was written by an Englishman between the death of Bede and the Norman Conquest, unless, and indeed at what a pinch, the *Chronicle,* Aethelweard's work, or the *Vitae* of the tenth century saints are so regarded. One can be tempted by the idea that there may have once been substantial works which now are lost. It is spine-chilling to consider the manuscripts of which, but for a series of happy chances, the Cottonian fire of 1731 could have destroyed all knowledge: the only

---

[22] N. E. S. A. Hamilton (ed), *De gestis pontificum Anglorum,* Rolls Series 52 (1870) 208.
[23] Gransden, *Historical writing . . .,* 197–8.
[24] L. Fleuriot, *Les origines de la Bretagne* (Paris 1980) 233–4.
[25] I. M. Lappenberg and F. Kurze (ed), *Thietmari . . . chronicon* (Hanover 1889) 2.
[26] J. Heller and G. Waitz (ed), *Flodoardi historia Rememsis ecclesiae,* MGH SS 13 (1881) 412–3.

known manuscripts of *Beowulf*, of the *Battle of Maldon* and of Aethelweard, the only manuscript of Asser known to have survived the middle ages. How easily, one must reflect, could other works, equally important, have been lost without trace, then, or earlier. It is certain that some sources have been lost: for example, the East Anglian annals drawn upon in the F text of the *Chronicle* and certain accounts of tenth-century history used by William of Malmesbury and by 'Florence'. Nevertheless, it is demonstrable that, for all the pains they took to search for sources, the Anglo-Norman historians were to a very large extent dependent on no works other than those which still survive. It is virtually certain that for large areas of Anglo-Saxon history the inquirer of *c.* 1100 had no source apart from Bede or the wretched annals of one or more versions of the Chronicle.

The impression that English ecclesiastics were backward in writing works of history is reinforced by Dr Fell's account of the English hagiographical tradition.[27] As she describes it, it was extraordinarily meagre and extraordinarily conservative. There is no surviving Latin life of an English saint composed between the earlier eighth century and the late tenth, though later hagiographical works may contain limited traces of compositions from this long period of apparent silence. The martyrology in Old English which appears in the ninth century and which was still being copied in the eleventh includes no Anglo-Saxon saint other than those indicated as such by Bede or by some hagiographical source which still survives. As authors, English clerics were inert. Another indication of this is that so many of the Latin biographical works relating to England and produced in the immediate pre-Conquest generations were the work of foreigners: Abbo's life of St Edmund, *Encomium Emmae Reginae*, the 'B' life of Dunstan, *Vita Edwardi Confessoris*, the first lives by Goscelin.[28]

The lack of historical or hagiographical works is the more striking when one considers how important early saints and early kings were to the great monasteries. In late Anglo-Saxon England realignments of saints went with realignments of power. The consolidation of the power of Aethelflaed and of Ethelred in West Mercia in the early tenth century is marked by the translation of Oswald's body from Bardney to Gloucester and Werburg's from Hanbury to Chester.[29] In the later tenth and earlier eleventh century some great communities, especially Glastonbury and Durham, were very active in collecting and/or

[27] C. Fell, 'Edward king and martyr and the Anglo-Saxon hagiographical tradition', D. Hill (ed), *Ethelred the Unready: papers from the millenary conference*, Br Archaeol Rep Br Ser 59 (1978) 1–14.

[28] Gransden, *Historical writing . . .*, 42.

[29] A. Thacker, 'Chester and Gloucester: early ecclesiastical organisation in two Mercian burhs', *Northern History* 18 (1982) 199–211.

claiming saints, an activity which had much to do with the nature and extent of other claims made by them and by their patrons.

Consider Glastonbury. This great house does not always get its due from historians, who seem sometimes unable to rid themselves of a feeling that it was something of a backwater. It was, however, the richest monastery in late Anglo-Saxon England.[30] It was the place of burial for Edgar, the most imperial of the late Anglo-Saxon rulers. He was a maritime king for whom a main area of action was the Irish Sea. His subordinated kings rowed him on the Dee; according to 'Florence' he circumnavigated Britain every year; it was later believed that he had intervened in Ireland.[31] The grandeur and the nature of the saints assembled at his favoured monastery of Glastonbury, on its holy island looking north to the Bristol Channel, matched his activities and ambitions: Patrick, David, Gildas, Aidan.[32]

Glastonbury was also a place with some tradition of learning, including at least gestures towards classical learning. (It is curious that, in the most famous Glastonbury manuscript from the period of tenth century reform, the longest passage in the hand which has been suggested to be that of Dunstan is a page from the *Ars amatoria* of Ovid, outlining the general principles of seduction.)[33] Yet the power, aspirations and learning of this very rich monastery were not reflected in compositions of an historical or hagiographical kind, or indeed, of any other kind, so far as we can tell. When William of Malmesbury came to write the history of Glastonbury he found very little there to draw on which had been composed at the abbey, charters apart.

Here, and generally, one major impulse behind the great Anglo-Norman historiographical effort was that the Anglo-Saxons had left so many gaps to fill. The very scale of the challenge may have helped to determine the nature of the response. Anglo-Saxon history had elements which made it specially intractable. For example, serious difficulties arose from there having been so many kingdoms; to create an intelligible narrative from chronologically parallel series of events was an awkward matter. This partly accounts for the vigour and emphasis with which Huntingdon and, to a limited but still marked degree, Malmesbury keep advising the reader of the way in which problems of exposition are being handled, in a plain indication of the self-consciousness of their struggles to order confusion.

Yet greater difficulties were caused by the nature of the

---

[30] Knowles, *Monastic order*, 702.

[31] F. M. Stenton, *Anglo-Saxon England* (3rd ed., Oxford 1971) 369; *Chronicon* (ed. Petrie) 576–8; E. John in J. Campbell, E. John and P. Wormald, *The Anglo-Saxons* (Oxford 1982) 255.

[32] Scott, *The early history of Glastonbury*, 54–71.

[33] R. W. Hunt (ed), *St Dunstan's classbook from Glastonbury. Cod.Bibl. Bodl. Oxon. Auct. F 4.32*, Umbrae Codicum Occidentalium 4 (Amsterdam 1961) xx–xxiii and f 47.

hagiographical data. Straightforward *Vitae* of Anglo-Saxon saints were few and far between. But there was a very large number of saints: some of these had at least a little recorded about them in writing; more had nothing but oral traditions to sustain their reputations. A good example of the kind of problem posed is that of the traditions associated with the so-called 'Kentish legend', recently, and well, explored by Dr Rollason.[34] Its core is the story of how Ecgbert (king of Kent, 664–73) was involved in the murder of two of his young cousins; of how he made restitution by granting their sister land to found the monastery at Minster; and of how her daughter Mildrith became abbess of that monastery, affording miraculous evidence of sanctity. The earliest surviving version comes in a Ramsey source of c. 1000, which may perhaps have drawn on eighth-century materials. It is one of a large number of hagiographical legends, which might be called those of the holy cousinhood. Many of them do not appear until the eleventh century or later. They relate to a singular galaxy of saints, all placed in the later part of the seventh century, all descended at various removes from one or more of three kings (Ethelbert of Kent, Penda of Mercia and Anna of East Anglia) and most of them women. Dr Rollason, in a *simplified* tree, lists fourteen saints in this cousinhood: SS Mildrith, Mildburg and Mildgith were sisters; St Werburg was their cousin, as was St Osyth; St Eanswith was their great-aunt. Her sisters-in-law were SS Aethelthryth, Wihtburg and Seaxburg. Seaxburg was the mother of SS Eormenhild and Earcongota, of whom the first was the mother of St Werburg; and so it could go on.

Many, perhaps all, of these saints were real people. There is no later parallel to such a cluster of relations being regarded as saints. Their legends, when we have them, often contain folkloric elements which take us a long way from Bede. Nevertheless an Anglo-Saxon saint with a documentary record of any kind was doing well, relatively speaking. There were scores of them who were remembered, but not written about. A typical case is that of the cult of St Rumonus at Tavistock.[35] William of Malmesbury wrote of this that 'no written testimony strengthens belief'; and, he added, you will often find this in England. The violence of enemies has swept everything away, leaving nothing but *nuda tantum sanctorum nomina* and tales of modern miracles. Many of these shadowy saints belonged to the age before the Viking invasions. Their story is part of the more-than-half-lost history of English monasticism between the age of Bede and the tenth century reform. Their cults were not infrequently associated with the communities of secular clerks which were common in late Anglo-Saxon England. Such

---

[34] D. W. Rollason, *The Mildrith legend: a study in early medieval hagiography in England* (Leicester 1982) 45.

[35] Hamilton, *Gesta pontificum*, 202.

communities sometimes had a long past in which they seem to have begun as double monasteries founded and ruled by great royal ladies. Whatever their origins, or their original grandeur, these institutions have often left no more than the faintest footsteps in the sands of time. Sometimes they can be traced in Domesday; sometimes the remains of one of their churches can be identified; sometimes they show up at the point when, as not infrequently happened, an Anglo-Saxon holy place became the site of a new house of Augustinian canons. The members of such communities did not write books – at least, not that we know of, though some or much Anglo-Saxon poetry could be theirs. They very seldom received charters: Ethelred II's grant to St Frideswide's, Oxford, is a most exceptional instance.[36] It was such communities which had done much to ensure that, if England was poor in *Vitae*, it was rich in saints, and in stories of saints.

It was not easy in the post-Conquest generations for men who demanded more than *nuda sanctorum nomina* to cope with such cults. One obvious response was the composition, not to say fabrication, of *Vitae* of individual saints. An impressive number of such were produced by Goscelin and by others. More comprehensive historians were well aware of the problems. 'Florence' made an effort to get material from the 'Kentish legend' into his annals; and made use of hagiographical materials in compiling his genealogical trees. One of the most effective ways of dealing with such materials was topographical. A start along such lines had been made before the Conquest with the Old English tract 'The resting places of the English saints'.[37] Possibly compiled in two stages, one in the tenth century, the other in the eleventh, it lists the shrines of fifty-one saints, some well-known, others hardly known at all. In the twelfth century it continued to be used, in a developed Latin form. Henry of Huntingdon's *De miraculis* was a more extended account, partly on a topographical basis, of many English saints. A wish to cope with the saints and miracles of England was part (though not the main part) of the reason for William of Malmesbury's topographical approach in *Gesta pontificum*.

The topographical approach is one aspect of the peculiarly comprehensive treatment of England which the Anglo-Norman historians adopted: describing and listing and numbering. England was their *patria* and they were proud of it. William of Malmesbury says that he writes 'propter patriae caritatem'.[38] It was a *patria* which had characteristics which marked it out from other kingdoms. Its political unity and geographical distinctness were, if by no means complete,

---

[36] For editions and accounts of which see P. H. Sawyer, *Anglo-Saxon charters: an annotated list and bibliography* (London 1968) no. 909.

[37] D. W. Rollason, 'Lists of saints' resting places in Anglo-Saxon England', *Anglo-Saxon England* 7 (1978) 61–94.

[38] Stubbs, *Gesta regum*, i 2.

then elsewhere unmatched. No subjects of Louis VII or Lothar II, Henry I's contemporaries when William of Malmesbury was writing, could, had they determined on similar enterprises to the *Gesta pontificum*, have been by any means so certain what the limits of their descriptions should be. Not only was England well defined, its administrative arrangements were notably orderly, compared to those of continental states. Its thirty-five shires could be neatly listed; it was easy approximately to specify the boundaries of ancient kingdoms or of modern dioceses by reeling off the shires involved. Such specifications in Malmesbury or in Huntingdon are a kind of counterpart to the way in which the shires determine the framework of the Pipe Rolls. The historians' descriptions of England as a whole had something in common with Domesday Book; they partly reflect the unity, the regularity, the compassability of the England the Normans conquered.

The most striking quality of the Anglo-Norman historians is intellectual grasp. Everywhere there is order and method, intellect applied to the creation of books which are genuine works of reference and research. Whence do these qualities come? Partly from the works of the past. Much was owed to Bede, but Bede was in important ways not more, but less, sophisticated than those who revered him in the twelfth century. Something, above all in style, was owed to classical authors. Something, notably the interest in the compilation of lists, may have been owed even to Nennius, whom they believed to have been Gildas. More particularly, the works of these historians, and especially those of Malmesbury and of Huntingdon, deserve to be set beside others more frequently mentioned as characteristic of the intellectual endeavours of the twelfth century.[39]. Intrinsic to many of these endeavours was bringing things together and sorting them out: this is what Gratian, Abelard and Peter Lombard do, and in their way, it is what the historians do. In England the book which most recalls the intellectual qualities of Malmesbury and Huntingdon is, I would suggest, *De legibus Anglie*, attributed to Glanvill, above all in its orderly exposition, in the way in which it imposes patterns on an intricately related chaos. There is even something to be learned from a comparison between the *Dialogus de scaccario* and Huntingdon: the latter is sometimes nearly as didactic in style as the former; and 'Are you with me?' is the question which both repeatedly indicate.

An important set of questions, which I am not competent to answer, is raised about the role of history in education and in the intellectual attitudes of the day. A common view seems to be that it played little part in the one and was not highly regarded in the other. But William of

---

[39] Rodney Thomson, 'William of Malmesbury's Carolingian sources', *J. Mediev Hist* 7 (1981) 321–27 points out the desirability of seeing Malmesbury in a European context.

Malmesbury, describing his own education at the beginning of Book II of *Historia regum* says that he studied logic a little, medicine quite a lot, ethics well, *historiam praecipue*.[40] Henry of Huntingdon did not allocate history a low place in his intellectual and moral world. Knowledge of the past, he says, marks the distinction between brutes and rational creatures. Brutes, whether animals or men, neither know nor wish to know whence they came, they do not know their own origins nor 'patriae suae casus et gesta'.

Well might Huntingdon and Malmesbury speak well of History; they had served it well. Their work laid the foundations for all who have followed them. But not the least interesting thing about the story of the recovery of knowledge of the distant past of England is that it is by no means one of continuous progress. In important ways the gains made by the Anglo-Normans were permanent. Manuscripts of their works continued to be used and copied. There are, for example, twenty-five medieval manuscripts of Henry of Huntingdon's *Historia*. In some monasteries the serious study of Anglo-Saxon history continued. At St Augustine's Canterbury in the early fifteenth century the work of Thomas Elmham on the history of his house reached heights not to be exceeded for over two hundred years. His was the first history written in England to be illustrated by a local map and by a plan of a church, the first to provide facsimiles of charters, the first to include a serious discussion of diplomatic, and the first to solve the problem of the explication of concurrent chronological series by setting the dates out in parallel columns.[41] Indeed in general the great monasteries kept their heads, and a pretty sane view of their own past, while all around a flood of nonsense rose.

But a rising tide of nonsense there was. It had several elements. One was, of course, the work of Geoffrey of Monmouth; for several centuries from its publication *c.* 1136 *Historia regum Britanniae* poisoned most educated Englishmen's view of their own past. His fictions were exposed by Polydore Vergil, who, however, failed to kill them completely.[42] The latest example I have found of large parts of Geoffrey's farrago being presented as cold truth is in a work hopefully entitled, *A million of facts*, published by the Society for the Diffusion of Useful Knowledge in 1833.

[40] Stubbs, *Gesta regum*, i 103.

[41] A. Gransden, *Historical writing in England, c. 1307 to the early sixteenth century* (London 1982) 350–55; Michael Hunter, 'The facsimiles in Thomas Elmham's history of St Augustine's Canterbury', *The Library ser 5* 28 (1973) 215–20. The layout of 'Florence's' episcopal lists in the first pages of his manuscript of his *Chronicon* is extremely careful, rather like that of canon tables, and is plainly designed to permit chronological correlation but is nothing like so precisely detailed as Elmhan's *Chronologia Augustiniensis* (Charles Hardwick (ed), *Historia Monasterii S. Augustini Cantuarinensis*, Rolls Series 8 (1858) 1–73.

[42] T. D. Kendrick, *British Antiquity* (London 1950) especially chapters 1, 5 and 6.

It is possible to extend a large tolerance towards twelfth-century fictionalizing history, and perhaps we should extend it. Monmouth's work is undoubtedly of great brilliance. To the extent that it is presented as truth it is a fraud; but Dr Flint's view that Geoffrey was really writing a kind of satire – not least one on his historian contemporaries – which was taken as truth has much to commend it.[43] In any case Geoffrey's history *was* very soon accepted; one effect of its acceptance was, to a degree, to put much of Anglo-Saxon history in the shade. It was so much less interesting than Geoffrey's account of an earlier period. The popularity of other fictionalizing history which also appears in the twelfth century is no less comprehensible. Some of these tales provided a more or less Anglo-Saxon past for areas knowledge of whose real Anglo-Saxon past was lost. For example, the story of Havelock the Dane provided an interesting history, otherwise lacking, for Grimsby. It is hardly surprising, though rather striking, that three characters from the story, Havelock, Goldbury and, naturally, Grim, appear on the town's first seal (temp. Edward I) duly labelled.[44] The rise of this kind of history, or rather, its first appearance in written form, is of course connected with the development of epics and romances in French and, somewhat later, in English. These in turn are connected with developments in hagiography. Some hagiographers wrote for the same audiences and used the same techniques as those of romance. History, fictionalized history, romance and hagiography stood, by the late twelfth century, in a complicated relationship to one another;[45] and one which did little to help that good cause, the discovery of the truth about the past.

Of the Anglo-Norman historians he whose attitude towards the legends of the saints is most interesting is William of Malmesbury. He retails some most extraordinary stories and his 'credulity' has been emphasised. Its nature has been brilliantly discussed by Dr Thomson.[46] He points out that a high proportion of Malmesbury's more astounding miracle-stories are attributed to 'a decade or two previous to his writing'; and that he is at his most restrained and 'intellectual' when dealing with the remote past. For example, in his account of the remote, allegedly apostolic origins of Glastonbury he is 'restrained, rational and cautious, with elaborate citation of his sources'. He is unlike many medieval historians in that he 'introduces marvels when his source-material is most abundant, and gratuitously, to the extent that they contribute little or nothing to his main theme'. Dr Thomson suggests tentatively, but

[43] Valerie I. J. Flint, 'The Historia Regum of Geoffrey of Monmouth: parody and its purpose, a suggestion', *Speculum* 54 (1979) 447–68.

[44] W. de Gray Birch, *Catalogue of seals in the Department of Manuscripts in the British Museum* (6 vols, London 1887–1900) ii no. 4958.

[45] M. Dominica Legge, 'Anglo-Norman hagiography and the romances', P. M. Clogan (ed), *Medievalia et Humanistica* n. s. 6 (1975) 41–50.

[46] 'William of Malmesbury as historian and man of letters', 398–401.

illuminatingly, that there was a degree of inner conflict in William in these regards. On the one hand he had a truly and strongly critical sense. On the other: 'When he came to his own time he could hardly dismiss miracles, signs and wonders without provoking questions from others and distress in his own psyche.' He illustrates this suggestion, powerfully, by showing how, although Malmesbury's 'Miracles of the Virgin' by its very nature makes plain his commitment to belief in alleged episodes of a flabbergasting description, nevertheless he is both judicious, and explicitly troubled, about the failure of ancient authorities to say anything about the assumption or ascension of the Virgin. This analysis does much to explain how it could be that a man so critical as Malmesbury, so doubting on occasion of *opiniones volaticae* as opposed to good evidence,[47] could appear on other occasions as so flagrantly credulous. It has been suggested that Malmesbury 'attempted to harness hagiography to history' and even 'took the romancer's freedom to invent, including precise dates and proper names'.[48] some of his stories help to explain such judgements. But his work as a whole by no means suggests that he was a historian who wrote without regard for fact or critical assessment of sources. Rather does it seem that, as Dr Thomson suggests, there were certain contexts in which he chose not to judge, or dared not judge, as in most other circumstances he did.

The debate about the extent and nature of William of Malmesbury's 'credulity' is of narrow significance only if one believes that an understanding of history, in the sense of the attainment of a secure understanding of how what can be known about the past, *can* be known, came easily into the intellectual tradition in which we live. Another view can be taken: that the discovery of the means of finding the true nature of the past has been no less important, and no less difficult, than the discovery of the means of understanding the physical world. For those who think in this way Malmesbury, at his frequent best, stands for a real intellectual advance. The extent to which, later in the twelfth century, approaches other than his became prominent can seem disquieting. It is crude, but not meaningless, to see his approach, which could be at times almost that of a lawyer judging evidence, being rivalled or even dominated by another, much more akin to that of the historical novelist. Consider, for example, two twelfth-century hagiographical feats: the development of the accounts of St Edmund and of St Osyth.

Not much is known of St Edmund apart from his having been killed by the Danes in 870. His cult was early, but the clerks who guarded his shrine, characteristically of such communities, left no writings about him. In the 980s appears a *Vita*, by Abbo of Fleury. The story he had to

---

[47] Scott, *Early history of Glastonbury*, 21.

[48] Peter Carter, 'Miracles of the Virgin Mary', R. H. C. Davis and J. M. Wallace-Hadrill (ed), *The writing of history in the middle ages; essays presented to Richard William Southern*, 127–66: 163.

tell is in various respects astounding; but he fairly clearly told it as he got
it. His account of the historical background is reasonable and moderate
even if it occasions difficulties. He has to make a little information go a
long way, but he does not fill the gaps with fiction, using verbiage rather.
A century later comes Archdeacon Hermann's account. It is not very
different from Abbo's; he has a few more details and some recent
miracles, but no pseudo-history. Hermann's spirit is not unlike that of
Malmesbury, who drew on him. Sixty years later (c. 1150) appears the
work of Geoffrey of Wells. Now there is no shortage of information on
the political background; rich and fascinating indeed are the
circumstances and the details with which Geoffrey regales us.[49]

Singularly interesting is his account of Edmund's origins.[50] It begins
with Offa, king of the East Angles, and said to have reigned before
Edmund. He had no heir and went on pilgrimage to Jerusalem. On his
way he passed through the dominions of the king of the (continental)
Saxons, a relative of his. At his court he met a most worthy young
man, Edmund indeed, whom he adopted as his son and made his heir.
(I abbreviate.) With a good deal of pseudo-history we do not know to
what extent its authors actually believed what they wrote or were
making sense according to their lights of odd and often oral sources
which they had no means of verifying. This particular story however
must be conscious fiction, concocted by Geoffrey of Wells or someone
not long before. We can be sure of this, because we can see its starting
point: a misunderstanding of Abbo's statement that Edmund was 'ex
antiquorum Saxonum nobili prosapia oriundus'. What Abbo almost
certainly meant was that Edmund came from an ancient Anglo-Saxon
family. But because in English usage *Angli* was used for the Anglo-
Saxons, (*Antiqui*) *Saxones* for the continental Saxons, he was taken to be
indicating an immediate continental origin and the appropriate tale was
made up. Made up; the role of plain (or fancy) fiction in hagiography was
extensive. To an extent it always had been. But there was something
fairly new about the extent and superficial plausibility of such fictitious
or semi-fictitious history as Geoffrey of Wells provides; and what was
new about it was much the same as what was new about Geoffrey of
Monmouth.

My second instance comes from the feats of the canons of Chich in
Essex in writing up the *Vita* of their foundress St Osyth.[51] St Osyth
was one of the great late seventh-century cousinhood of saints. Her cult
appears to have survived at Chich, no one knows how. In 1121 an
Augustinian house was founded there; it was an important one; its first

[49] Dorothy Whitelock, 'Fact and fiction in the legend of St Edmund', *Proc Suffolk Inst Archaeol* 31 (1970) 217–33.
[50] M. Winterbottom, ed., *Three Lives of English Saints* (Toronto, 1972), pp. 67–87.
[51] Denis Bethell, 'The lives of St Osyth of Essex and St Osyth of Aylesbury', *Analecta Bollandiana* 88 (1970) 75–127.

prior was within three years to become archbishop of Canterbury. Little if anything was recorded in writing about Osyth, proper *Vitae* and *Legendae* were plainly needed and the canons set to work with a will. A number of *Vitae* were produced at Chich (and elsewhere). One of the authors was William de Vere, brother of the earl of Oxford, brother-in-law of Geoffrey de Mandeville and Roger Bigod. So great an Anglo-Norman grandee could not neglect an obscure Anglo-Saxon saint: not if she was St Osyth and he was a canon of Chich he couldn't. He and others made a bad job of the life of St Osyth. The story as they present it is this. Osyth was a grand-daughter of Penda, king of Mercia. She was married off to Sighere, king of East Anglia (or, more plausibly, of Essex). Having miraculously avoided his matrimonial embraces she became abbess of Chich. The monastery was then attacked by the Danes, who cut her head off. She showed considerable fortitude in not dying at once, but carried her head into the church first. The most striking feature of the story is the gross chronological dislocation. First William de Vere and others put Osyth into the seventh century, then they attribute her martyrdom to the Danes Inguar and Ubba who belonged to the ninth.

It is this which is shocking. Some may boggle at the story of the severed head; but that is the kind of hagiographical topos which was accepted. But no one consciously believed in miracles of chronology; it was not normal to accept the idea of two pasts: one human with real dates and events; the other divine with saints and wonders floating freely through the generations. The authors of these *Vitae* were writing chronological nonsense; and what is more, avoidable nonsense. A careful look at Bede would have enabled them to substitute a fairly reliable approximate date for Osyth for the wild guesses some of them actually provided.[52] The work of the Anglo-Norman historians was available by the time William de Vere wrote (after 1163) and would have enabled him and others to make more chronological sense than they did. They did not care: or anyway, they did not bother. The great Anglo-Norman historians did care and did bother about just such things. They had a sense of evidence.

Why trouble about such false stories and careless misadventures as those of Geoffrey of Wells or the canons of Chich? One can find one serious reason in considering a work written in another East Anglian monastery in the same generation. Thomas of Monmouth's *De vita et passione Sancti Willelmi Martyris Norwicensis*.[53] This most interesting work (rather surprisingly not in the bibliography of David Knowles's *The monastic order in England*) describes the mysterious death in 1144 of a

---

[52] For actual dates in the *Vitae* see, especially, Bethell, 'Lives of St Osyth', 87 n 2. C. Plummer (ed), *Venerabilis Baedae Opera historica* (2 vols, Oxford 1896) i 199, 218, 322 permit the approximate dating of Sighere of Essex.

[53] A. Jessopp and M. R. James (ed), *The life of St William of Norwich* (Cambridge 1896).

boy called William, and of how a majority of the monks of Norwich convinced themselves and others that he had been ritually murdered by the Jews. It is of sharp interest in the history of Europe because it marks the point in which the deadly lie of Jewish ritual murder comes to the surface: and does so in a big, well-endowed, not unsophisticated house of Black Monks. One need not be an enemy of the Black Monks in saying: 'They should have known better'. One would be less than a friend if one did not say: 'One wishes they had known better'. It is important that some of the monks of Norwich did indeed know better. It is clear from Monmouth's book that there was opposition within the monastery to the adoption of the cult. It seems that monks were among those 'who allow that he was cruelly killed but who are uncertain by whom, or why, he was made an end of, and do therefore not presume to affirm that he was either a saint or a martyr'.[54] I would maintain that there is a parallel between those decent doubters at Norwich and William of Newburgh who would not swallow Geoffrey of Monmouth; and a parallel between on the one hand the monk of Bury who made up the story of Edmund's German origins and the canons of Chich who so readily wrote avoidable nonsense and on the other those at Norwich accepting the story of ritual murder. It may be contended, and understandably contended, that it is anachronistically beside the point to criticise the imaginative flights of medieval hagiography. Understanding, rather than condemnation, may be called for. At least in such an extreme case as that of the monks of Norwich and St William the force of another approach can be felt, one well summed up in an observation by the Duc de Broglie which Lord Acton was fond of quoting: 'We must beware of too much understanding lest we end by too much forgiving'. More generally, one of the charges which the Reformers levied against the medieval church was that it was insufficiently concerned to distinguish truth from falsehood. Its open vulnerability to this charge derived in part from the extent to which its hagiography was fictitious. Too much had been composed in the spirit of Geoffrey of Monmouth. Lies about saints were not new to the twelfth century; but the literary development of the age enabled them to be supplied on a larger scale and in a better style. Such a man as William of Malmesbury often stood for the pursuit of truth, zealous supporter of the cults of saints though he was. In such works as those of Geoffrey of Wells that pursuit was set on one side in favour of warmly interesting and richly circumstantial fiction.

The problems and possibilities raised by early twelfth-century approaches to the Anglo-Saxon past are numerous, and many of them have been no more than touched upon, if that, in the present paper. For example, interest in Anglo-Saxon history extended beyond monastic or

---

[54] Jessopp and James, 88.

native circles poses questions about the assimilation of 'Norman' and 'Anglo-Saxon'. The cult of Edward the Confessor needs consideration here. A curious result of that cult, and of an Angevin king's regard for an Anglo-Saxon saint, was king John's being buried at Worcester. It was believed that after the Conquest Lanfranc had intended to depose bishop Wulfstan II on the ground that he was *illiteratus*. (The story first appears in Osbert of Clare). The threatened bishop had gone to the tomb of Edward the Confessor and laid his staff upon it. It sank into the tomb as though the tomb were made of wax and was held fast. The king and confessor who had made Wulfstan bishop had provided a miraculous demonstration which could be regarded as bearing on the right of kings to appoint bishops.[55]

It has been suggested above that one of the most interesting things about the work of early twelfth-century historians of England is its relationship to intellectual endeavours in other fields and what it indicates about the role of historiography in the history of learning and of culture. Such a suggestion is by no means original and I would emphasise how much what is written above owes to the work of others, in particular of Dr Thomson and Dr Partner. The 'extraordinarily complex historical activity' which characterizes the early twelfth century, the way in which 'earlier historians were carefully studied, contemporaries were copied out and annotated almost as soon as written',[56] what can fairly be called William of Malmesbury's professional sense,[57] tell part of an important story. At least for some, and at least for a time, history was not a subordinated study, at best the poor relation or the country cousin of theology or law. In their endeavours to recover and to explain to others the past, and not least the pre-Conquest past, these historians stood for something very serious.

In our attempts to understand them, and their subjects, one of the greatest difficulties which stands in the way is the complex intractability of the hagiographical materials. A paradigm case is that of those relating to St Osyth. It was Denis Bethell who, by acute intelligence, and much hard work made sense of these. His so doing was but one among his many services to historical learning, and not even among the greatest of them. For, of lasting weight though his published works are, yet more important is the help and inspiration which he gave to other historians.

[55] F. M. Powicke, *Stephen Langton* (Oxford 1928) 85–88.
[56] Martin Brett, 'John of Worcester and his contemporaries', 125, 103.
[57] R. R. Darlington, *Anglo-Norman historians* (London 1947) 9–10.

I should have indicated that the suggestion that such communities as those mentioned on p. 219 may have produced verse derives from P. Wormald, 'Bede, Beowulf and the Conversion of the Anglo-Saxon Aristocracy', in *Bede and Anglo-Saxon England*, ed.

continued

R. T. Farrell (Br Archaeol Rep Br Ser 46 (1978)), esp. pp. 53–54. Mr J. B. Gillingham, in a kind communication, pointed out to me that, in emphasising the importance of Dr Thomson's demonstration of the difference between William of Malmesbury's treatment of the distant past and his treatment of the recent past (pp. 222-3 above), I should have brought out how far this must complicate contention about the transferability in the twelfth century between attitudes to the past and attitudes to the present (cf. p. 226 above). So I should.

Index

abacus, 179
Abbo of Fleury, 166, 204, 206, 216, 223-4
Abbotsbury, 141
Abelard, Peter, 220
Absolution Sunday, 152
accounts, 176; *see also* Exchequer; Pipe Roll;
    tallies
Acton, 114
Acton, Lord, 226
Adalberon, archbishop of Rheims, 194, 199
Adalberon, bishop of Laon, 194, 195
Adam of Bremen, 146, 215
Adamnan of Coldingham, 10
administration, Anglo-Saxon, 155-70, 171-89;
    see also abacus; accounts; administrative areas
    and boundaries; African administration;
    Angevin government; assessment systems;
    Burghal Hidage; clerks, royal; coinage;
    Continental relationships; County Hidage;
    Danelaw; Edward the Confessor; France,
    comparisons with; *gafol*; geld; *gwestfa*;
    hundred; judge; laws; letters close; *scir*;
    shire; writs
Ad Murum, 108, 109n., 116
administrative areas and boundaries, 168
Adomnan, abbot of Iona, 35
Adon, 57
adoption, significance of, 75
Adventus Saxonum, 123, 124
Ad Villam Sambuce, see Sambuce
Aelfeah, archbishop of Canterbury, 205, 210
Aelfflaed, 108
Aelfgifu, queen of England, 193
Aelfric, 149, 158, 163
Aelfthryth, 197
Aethelbald, king of Mercia, 11, 91, 94, 134, 136
Aethelburh, 56, 114
Aethelflaed, lady of the Mercians, 144, 216
Aethelfrith, king of Northumbria, 23
Aethelgar, archbishop of Canterbury, 203
Aethelm, 192
Aethelmaer, bishop of Elmham, 152
Aethelthryth, St, queen of East Anglia,
    133, 218
Aethelwalh, king of Sussex, 75, 92
Aethelweard, 158, 194-5, 196-7, 215, 216
African administration, 175

Agilbert, bishop of Wessex, 25 n 89, 55,
    58, 60, 65
Aidan, 14, 17, 18, 23, 26, 29-30, 40, 52,
    60, 61, 62, 76, 96, 109, 111, 138, 217
Albinus, 102
Alcluith, 100, 101, 102, 116
Alcuin, 98, 163
Aldborough, 106
Aldfrith, king of Northumbria, 15, 20, 21,
    67, 94, 136
Aldhelm, St, 2, 52, 59, 62, 67, 84
Alexander, bishop of Lincoln, 211
Alfred (Elfridus), king of Wessex, 107, 129,
    144, 155, 163, 175, 180, 195, 197
–, laws of, 113n, 131, 138
Alfred the Atheling, 192, 193
Amand, Saint, 57, 58, 64
ambassadors, *see* diplomacy
Ambrosius Aurelianus, 124
Amesbury, 122n
Andelys, monastery at, 56
Angevin government, 167-8
Angli, connotation of, 224
Anglo-Saxon Chronicle, 114, 115 & n, 163,
    197, 211, 213, 215
Anglo-Saxons, origins of, 70, 86n; *see also*
    Administration, Anglo-Saxon
Anna, king of East Anglia, 145, 218
Annals of St Neot's, 153
Annemundus, archbishop of Lyons, 55
Aquinas, 98
arms and armour, 66, 92-6, 138, 200;
    see also swords
Arngrim, sons of, 192
Arnoul I, count of Flanders, 192
Arnoul II, count of Flanders, 198
Arnoul, count of Flanders, 204
Arthur, supposed king, emperor, etc,
    121, 124
Asser, 162, 163, 195, 216
Assessment systems, *see* Burghal Hidage;
    County Hidage; Dalriada; hides;
    taxation; Tribal Hidage
Athanasius, 5
Athelstan, 142
Athelstan, king, 160, 169, 197
Attila, 124

Lightning Source UK Ltd.
Milton Keynes UK
08 March 2010

151098UK00001B/130/P

9 780907 628330